# Unsettling Agribusiness

Indigenous Protests and
Land Conflict in Brazil

LaSHANDRA SULLIVAN

University of Nebraska Press    Lincoln

The University of Nebraska Press is part of a land-grant institution with campuses and programs on the past, present, and future homelands of the Pawnee, Ponca, Otoe-Missouria, Omaha, Dakota, Lakota, Kaw, Cheyenne, and Arapaho Peoples, as well as those of the relocated Ho-Chunk, Sac and Fox, and Iowa Peoples.

∞

Library of Congress Cataloging-in-Publication Data
Names: Sullivan, LaShandra, author.
Title: Unsettling agribusiness: Indigenous protests and land conflict in Brazil / LaShandra Sullivan.
Description: Lincoln: University of Nebraska Press, [2023] | Includes bibliographical references and index.
Identifiers: LCCN 2022045775
ISBN 9781496208385 (hardback)
ISBN 9781496236012 (epub)
ISBN 9781496236029 (pdf)
Subjects: LCSH: Agricultural industries—Social aspects—Brazil—Dourados. | Land use—Brazil—Dourados. | Guarani Indians—Land tenure—Brazil—Dourados. | Guarani Indians—Political activity—Brazil—Dourados. | Guarani Indians—Government relations. | Protest movements—Brazil—Dourados. | Dourados (Brazil)—Economic conditions. | Dourados (Brazil)—Social conditions. | BISAC: BUSINESS & ECONOMICS / Industries / Agribusiness | SOCIAL SCIENCE / Indigenous Studies
Classification: LCC HD9014.B83 S855 2023 |
DDC 338.10981/71—dc23/eng/20230207
LC record available at https://lccn.loc.gov/2022045775

Designed and set in Minion Pro by L. Welch.

For my mother and father,
Robbie H. Sullivan and
Charles Sullivan

# Contents

# Illustrations

# Acknowledgments

Foremost, I am deeply indebted to the people protesting for land demarcation in Mato Grosso do Sul who made this work possible. This book is a manifestation of my collaboration with them. I hope that this work contributes to the realization of their long-overdue land restitution, in addition to their broader revindications and calls for justice. I am also grateful for the work of the many activists, artists, academics, and allies directly involved in the struggle for land and redress for displacements and dispossession in Dourados, Mato Grosso do Sul, and beyond, especially those opposing the forms of genocide against Indigenous and Black people ongoing there. They do so in the face of harrowing circumstances. I hope that this work may be a contribution to theirs.

Additionally, other friends and colleagues in Brazil have been fundamental to this research. They have guided me and shared camaraderie and loyalty at different moments in Dourados, Campinas, São Paulo, and Rio de Janeiro. Particularly, at the Universidade Federal de Grande Dourados (UFGD) and Universidade Estadual de Campinas (UNICAMP) I found institutional homes and intellectual community. I especially acknowledge Levi Marques Pereira and Eva Marie Roessler for their sometimes-heroic efforts of support for me in Brazil. They believed in my project, sacrificed time and energy, and mustered resources to ensure that it went forward. In addition, José Szwako, Lucia Castro, Sandra Fioravanti, Cris Barbanti, Daniele Reiter, Liliana Sanjurjo, Célia Silvestre, Diógenes Cariaga, Aline Lutti, Lauriene Seraguza, Juliana Mota, Marcos Homero Ferriera Lima, Lia Aparecida Mendes de Oliveira, Flavia Medeiros, Pammela Pereira, Ludmila Veloso, Laura Santonieri, Clifford Welsh, Bernardo Mançano Fernandes, and Enrique Ortega were great friends and colleagues in this regard. I am grateful to Ana Perla for her assistance with translating parts of the speech of a protest leader in chapter 6 from Guaraní to Portuguese. She additionally helped with translating Guaraní from interviews during my fieldwork.

My work has benefited greatly from scholarships, grants, and support from multiple institutions and organizations, including Reed College, the University of Chicago, Williams College, Purdue University, and the United States Fulbright Program. The University of Chicago Social Sciences Division Diversity Fellowship, several grants from the Center for Latin American Studies Center, and a grant from the Center for the Study of Race, Culture, and Politics were critical to the early stages of research development. I received numerous years of support from the Foreign Language and Area Studies fellowship program of the United States Department of Education. I conducted ethnographic fieldwork with support from a Fulbright fellowship, as well as with a grant from the Land Development Politics Initiative consortium. I also received three years of support as a state of Illinois' Diversifying Faculty in Illinois fellow. Likewise, I am grateful for a postdoctoral fellowship from Williams College that also supported the early stages of writing this book.

Over the years I have greatly benefitted from critical feedback, conversations, comments, edits, and suggestions from friends, colleagues, teachers, students, and coparticipants in conference panels, writing groups, and workshops. They include Abigail George, Alex Gomez-Lacayo, Anand Vaidya, Anneleissa Coen, Asale Angel-Ajani, Benjamin Junge, Bernard Dubbeld, Betsey Brada, Brian Horne, Charlene Makley, Charles Klein, China Scherz, Dain Borges, Elayne Oliphant, Eli Thorkelson, Elina Hartikainen, Falina Enriquez, Felipe Calvão, Gregory Duff Morton, Gregory Mitchell, Jan Hoffman French, Jay Sosa, Jean Comaroff, João Felipe Gonçalves, John Collins, John Comaroff, Joseph Masco, Karma Frierson, Katherine Miller, Kathleen MacDougall, Kaya Williams, Keisha-Khan Perry, Laura Zanotti, Lee Cabatingan, Meghan Morris, Merle Bowen, Paul Silverstein, Sarah Luna, Sean Mitchell, Tatiana Chudakova, Tracey Rosen, and Wendy Wolford. Likewise, I am grateful to the editor and reviewers of this book, as well as versions of two chapters of this work that were previously published in journals. Finally, a special thank you to Anne Ch'ien, for her tremendous work at the University of Chicago.

Finally, my family and friends have been foundational for me. I thank my mother and father, Robbie and Charles Sullivan, for their many visits, hugs, phone calls, moral and material support, and a lifetime of love. The spirit of my aunt Clara Square continues to nourish and sustain me. My family includes siblings, aunts, uncles, and cousins who have always been and continue to be a critical part of my foundation. I am heartily thankful to my chosen family—that is, my close friends with whom I share fantastically deep bonds of connection and many years of friendship. They have endlessly poured love and inspiration into me, as well as kept me balanced, fortified, and well-rounded through laughter and tears, through the many highs and lows of researching and preparing this book. Finally, my partner Rosa Yadira Ortiz and our children, Emmett and Robbie Sullivan, deserve their own book-length expression of my gratitude. Without their comfort, reassurance, trust, patience, and love, I could not have done this work. I am forever grateful.

# Unsettling Agribusiness

# Introduction

Doing fieldwork in Dourados between 2007 and 2018 offered me prolonged, if only partial, glimpses of the place as a frontier of agribusiness in central-west Brazil.[1] A town of roughly 225,000 inhabitants, Dourados, Mato Grosso do Sul, borders the most populous Indigenous reservation in the country.[2] The city and the reservation are adjacent to one another, a juxtaposition of a settler-colony-turned-municipality abutting a reserved space for Indians.[3]

In 2007 I made my first trip to Dourados to learn about the lived effects of the expansion of sugarcane and soy plantations for biofuels production. At the time, Brazil was one of the world's leading producers. My work necessarily entailed paying attention to land use and the related land conflict embroiling the region. Such issues required making sense of an ongoing history of violent land expropriations in Brazil, in addition to the larger phenomenon of land-grabbing by large landowners.[4] Agribusiness complexes, though, merely continued a much longer history of settler colonial land occupation and development policies in the region. These processes, at different moments and in different ways, have relied on and operated through ethnoracial ideologies of whitening, displacement, and labor exploitation.

Since the 1980s, autonomous groups of Indigenous activists in Dourados have mobilized to "occupy" plantations to gain state demarcation of formerly Indigenous territory—that is, *terras indígenas* (Indigenous lands).[5] Though one may reasonably ask who is "occupying" whom in this relatively recently colonized area of Brazil. Indigenous protesters have met often violent opposition by large landholders (*fazendeiros*) and their private security forces, including beatings, kidnappings, and dozens of assassinations (UN Human Rights Council 2009).[6] Decades of displacements from the countryside have caused overcrowding on reservations, intermittently high rates of malnutrition, and an elevated number of physical assaults, particularly related to the drug trafficking.

Modeling their encampments on the tactics of the more famous Brazilian MST (Movimento dos Trabalhadores sem Terra, or Landless Workers Movement), Indigenous protesters (primarily Guarani and Terena) in the Dourados region set out from reservations to retake lands from which they were displaced. Guarani protesters reclaim land as their *tekoha*, a term for territory. The term refers to the *bom modo de ser*, the good way to be, that is the traditional Kaiowá way of life. Tekoha is the land necessary for survival of the ways of being Guaraní.[7]

The activists with whom I worked longed for land titling as a respite from the relentless entrenchment of settler colonial domination. The state plays a curious role in the conflict, with agencies sometimes at odds with each other as it concerns Indians' welfare. Over the history of settlement of Mato Grosso do Sul, state agencies, under varying rationales, acted to "protect" Indians through upholding land rights, while other agencies facilitated settler encroachments that opened up frontier lands for seizures and developmental exploitation.

Before the country's democratization in 1988, Brazil's military dictatorship (1964–85) used explicit authoritarian violence to limit the terms for political and economic organization. In alliance with large landholders, the government favored a capital-intensive agro-industrial model in the countryside, which some called "conservative modernization" (Forman 1975), that displaced millions of rural inhabitants (including Indians) in favor of export-oriented agricultural and livestock production. The accompanying political organization reconfigured the integration of the countryside into the national and global economy to encourage the influx of more distant capital flows and facilitate more integrated chains of management and governance.

Rearrangements of land for agribusiness in Mato Grosso do Sul further entailed reconfigurations of labor relations. The production of soy, beef, and especially sugarcane drove massive proletarianization, urbanization, and dislocations onto reservations. At the same time, the dictatorship expanded a welfare-state model to extend health care, schools, and corporatist union rights to rural workers through state bureaucracy. By the 1980s former peasants (Indian and non-Indian alike) and subsequent generations had returned to rural areas as day laborers, commuting back and forth from city peripheries and Indigenous reservations to work for the agro-industrial firms that now dominate the countryside.

Toward the end of the dictatorship's most violent period of torture and kidnappings, protest camping arose across Brazil as a political tactic to gain state recognition of land rights of the previously displaced. From 2007 to 2018 the protest camps I worked with (which included one non-Indian protest camp) consisted of people who had moved out of, or circulated between, reservations, peripheral urban dwellings, and rural work sites. At the time of my fieldwork, Indigenous people made up the majority of sugarcane cutters in southern Mato Grosso do Sul. Thus, in this book I focus on the intersections of rural-urban political economy (relations of land and labor) with Indigenous activists' deployment of protest camps to regain landed territory.

I worked with activists to support their efforts for land restitution and document their criticisms of their forced displacement from their previous territories. I discovered in my encounters with non-Indian townspeople that those activists faced an atmosphere of quotidian disgust and routine outrage over their protests. I was not surprised. In Dourados, public antipathy to their plight is pervasive, with practical impunity bestowed on those inflicting the aforementioned violence. *Branco* (white or non-Indian) townspeople openly express anti-Indian sentiments in both casual conversation and public forums on the conflict. Living in the city during fieldwork, I witnessed how the very fabric of daily life, its ideological underpinnings in ethnicity, race, and nation, as well as material bases of agribusiness production, consisted of elements that were both longstanding and uniquely contemporary in regard to disdain for Indigenous land restitution.

Displacement of Indians began long before the advent of agribusiness, which began in earnest in the region in the 1970s. Significant colonization also took place in the 1940s with the federal Westward March program, policies explicitly designed to install *colonias agricolas* (agricultural colonies). Prior still, settlers had arrived in multiple waves dating back to the late nineteenth century.

Guaraní presence in the region persists in ways not conforming to colonial or national boundaries. Kaiowá-Guaraní also live in Paraguay and Bolivia, as well as in the neighboring Brazilian states of Mato Grosso, São Paulo, and Paraná. Situated in the southern cone of Mato Grosso do Sul, the Dourados municipality is just a two-hour drive from the border with Paraguay.

Movement, mobility, and mobilization recurred as central themes during both my fieldwork experiences and my subsequent musings as I came to terms with what I had encountered. The stark contrasts between the willful movement of the people in the protest camps and their structurally induced and forced dislocations stood out to me in this regard. Their impetus to mobilize and relocate to the sites of their lost territory arose from a larger condition of deracination and unmooring engendered by the aforementioned sequences of colonization. Willful movement and forced transience under structural shifts in relations of land and labor framed these logics of circulations of people across the region.

When I began my research in Mato Grosso do Sul, I regularly took buses from town to town, particularly the Expresso Queiroz passenger buses between Dourados and nearby towns like Ponta Porã and Naviraí. My travels to the region originated from a starting point of Campinas, São Paulo, having arrived in the city of São Paulo as my port of entry into Brazil from the United States. The bus trips from São Paulo lasted twenty hours, with the bus stopping at many small towns along the way. Around the halfway point of the voyage, I crossed the state border into Mato Grosso do Sul by traversing the massive width of the Paraná River. From there, the halts and flows shifted. Fewer small towns dotted the countryside, and longer stretches of plantations appeared and expanded outward from the road toward the horizon.

Along the region's single-lane highways, I bypassed enclosed pastures of cattle, sugarcane, and soy in endless repetition. Agricultural laborers moved back and forth from city to countryside, embarking and debarking from buses that agribusinesses chartered for casual laborers, amassed at intermittent depots on inconspicuous and unmarked roadside spots.

**Fig 1.** Agribusiness bus traversing Dourados, coated with the red dirt typical of the southern region of Mato Grosso do Sul. Photograph by LaShandra Sullivan.

In my treks, after crossing the state line into Mato Grosso do Sul, I prepared myself for the invariable stops at police checkpoints. In this frontier region, the police randomly set up road checkpoints and required that random bus passengers show identification documents. Police also searched the baggage area underneath the carriage. Dogs sniffed luggage, presumably for signs of illegal drugs. I learned to always ready my passport and research visa for inspection at the beginning of the checkpoint stops. I remained ready because I was always asked to show ID. As Keisha-Khan Perry (2013), for example, describes in her brilliant ethnography set in Salvador, Bahia, such a quotidian predicament was familiar to both me, as a Black woman ethnographer, and Brazilians who are ethnoracially marked as Black. My standpoint allowed me insights into the ethnoracial distinctions structuring how one moves through Mato Grosso do Sul. Though supposedly random, the searches never failed to single me out for criminal suspicion. My Basquiat-like dreadlocks further presumably made me irresistible to police surveillance. One of my research advisors had pointed out that the prejudicial racist myth of the Black drug dealer extended deep into even the most seemingly remote areas of Brazil, no matter how out of the way the place. None of this surveillance stopped the flow of drugs over the border. A friend of mine from the town of Ponta Porã, which sits on the border with Paraguay, pointed out the mansions in her neighborhood owned by those enriched by the trade. Such homes are rare, though stand out, hidden in plain sight. Nevertheless, regional newspaper pages show the police's prize catches of kilos of cocaine and cash stacks, fruits of their surveillance operations.

Over the course of years of fieldwork, I got to know several Indigenous protestors who fell victim to these halts and flows—that is, police searches and arrests—or who were run over by buses and trucks as they commuted by foot or bicycle to and from the protest camps along the roadsides. They were especially vulnerable to such ill fate while commuting at night.

When I travelled in Mato Grosso do Sul, I always noted this combination of free flows and halted precautions. Cheaper commodities make up a notable part of that flow. The higher taxes on consumer goods in Brazil, particularly electronics like computers and televisions, mean that Brazilians regularly take advantage of crossing the border to shop for imported goods. The border between Paraguay and Brazil intersects the cities of Ponta Porã and Pedro Juan Caballero. The latter features Shopping China, a big box store that advertises its relatively cheap wares on billboards dotting the highways. Along those highways, Indigenous protest camps intermittently appear, a reminder for anyone passing by of prior histories and ongoing contestations of land and belonging.

### Ways of Life and Anthropological Knowledge Production

My approach in this book both complements and critiques the existing literature on Indigenous land demarcation in Mato Grosso do Sul, which defends Indigenous land claims on the grounds of cultural preservation. I build on some of the prominent scholarship on the Guaraní of this region (Brand and Colman 2008; Meliá 1981), which relates to how the advent of Guaraní's displacement onto reservations in the 1920s and 1930s marked the beginning of stresses on their way of life. Focus on such effects supports what I call *cultural-preservation-oriented arguments* for land demarcation. As the argument goes, land restitution aids in safeguarding characteristics of Guaraní-ness, critical for the continuity of their well-being. The state requires that anthropologists demonstrate such cultural ties to land as a precondition for demarcation. Anthropologists must thereby document evidence showing those ties to a given landscape as it fulfills that requirement for demarcation.

*Guaranílogos*[8] in Mato Grosso do Sul straddle the divide in Brazilian anthropology between structuralist accounts that focus on the cultural alterity lent by the different ontologies—for example, in perspectivist (Viveiros de Castro 1998) and new animism (Descola 1996) literature this focuses on elements like cosmologies—and those focusing on interethnic friction, as Pacheco de Oliveira (2018) explains the distinction. Regarding those utilizing the interethnic friction approach, he writes, "Rather than analytically treating Indigenous societies as closed totalities, explicable solely in their own terms, researchers in this area emphasize the need to study the institutions and dynamics of interethnic contact." Whereas I discuss elsewhere (Sullivan 2019) some of the political considerations of such divergences in these different approaches as it concerns the land conflict in Dourados, here I will simply underline that the culture concept factors into the claims-making underway in protest campers' efforts and in anthropological studies analyzing their claims. I return to this point in chapter 6.

In the years leading up to the ratification of Brazil's 1988 constitution, coalitions of anthropologists, Indigenous activists, and their allies fought hard to earn cultural preservationist terms for evaluating land claims. Anthropologist Carlos Fausto, for example, explains that we should view those efforts as a necessary political move in a context where the 1988 constitution allowed for Indigenous people "who had supposedly become 'extinct' to resurge and claim their collective rights" (Fausto 2017, 414). The focus on Indians' cultural alterity "implies not only having a culture but also a world (which includes the way they choose to change it). Instead of treating a people as subalterns (and subaltern-ing them even more), our choice has been to highlight their richness, and what it says about our poorness" (Fausto 2017, 414).

These debates matter for the people with whom I worked in the protest camps, despite the difficulties in conforming with the prescribed demonstration of cultural ties to a given parcel of land. Moreover, the idea of adhering to and preserving a discrete culture sometimes ran counter to the heterogeneity of Indigenous lived experiences and long-running internal debates within these communities regarding identification processes and cultural change. The rates of conversion to Pentecostalism among the land activists with whom I worked served as but one example of the unease of strict conformity with some ethnographic monographs' presentations of Guaraní traditions. Cultural-preservationist arguments as the ground for legal criteria for land restitution coincide with the lived realities and even diverse formulations of cosmologies. Walking the cultural-preservationist line allows taking advantage of hard-earned means for gaining land restitution. At the same time, cultural-preservationist approaches demonstrate the difficulty of expanding the grounds for demarcation of Indigenous territory under the terms delimited by the state.

In this book I ethnographically describe the activists' dual dilemmas of navigating the restricted cultural grounds for legitimizing land claims while also staring down the firearms of fazendeiros' security forces who seek to dislodge them. The extralegal violence has accumulated over many decades of forced dislocation from their lands. Cultural-preservationist approaches seek to provide a shield against such violence. They may also inadvertently, as Bessire (2014) points out in the context of the Chaco of Paraguay, further entrench the primitivist logics underpinning misreading of Indigenous cultural differences pervasive among non-Indians in Dourados. A too narrow focus on cultural distinctions risks disallowing us to understand why and how land activists are on the side of the road defying and resisting fazendeiro violence in the first place—that is, the ethnoracial logics of settler dispossession. Moreover, we must make sense of how those fazendeiros, their security forces, and their non-Indian sympathizers who make up the majority of townspeople in places like Dourados perpetually re-enact the violent displacements of Indians.

The structural determinants of such predicaments, including the components of culture, are central preoccupations in this book. I seek to chart a course beyond the seeming opposition of, on one hand, cosmological reification and, on the other hand, the denial of cultural difference between Indians and non-Indians in Brazil. Rich cultural differences and shared historical determinacies percolated through the biographies of displaced people (both Indian and non-Indian), giving credence to cultural-preservationist arguments and underscoring the importance of ethnographically detailed accounting for the circumstances and contexts situating their claims-making.

Along these lines, in this book I often use Juliana Bueno Mota's (2015) term to refer to Guaraní protest camps in Mato Grosso do Sul: *camps-tekohas*. Bueno Mota utilizes it to capture how the Guarani campers continually pursue means to recover ways of dwelling enacted prior to confinement on reservations, which prominently feature cosmogonic relations with the landscape. They pursue such reenactments as part of their confrontation with the historical and ongoing legacies with the state.

One of the overriding concerns of the Indians was the difficulties imposed by meeting the requirements prescribed by Indigenous land law. Indeed, the activists with whom I worked faced ongoing machinations by opponents of Indigenous land titling to shift the legal codes, which would further entrench the domination and displacements to buttress ruralist interests. How activists fought back while mobilizing to gain land demarcation within the cultural terms prescribed by land law reveals as much about the workings of agribusiness domination in Dourados as it does about contemporary debates regarding Guaraní culture. The heterogeneity of activists' experiences, motivations, backgrounds, and enmeshment in larger sets of relations in the region constitutes a key task in this work. Thus, this book focuses primarily on the tensions between agribusiness logics and their proponents and Indigenous land activists who seek to halt the repetitions of colonial history through their decolonial practices of protest camping.

## Land, State, and Nation

To reach an understanding of land and the conflicts in Dourados, this book explores what Indigenous protest camps suggest about some of the challenges to liberal democracy in Brazil. The hallmark of liberal democracy, political equality, has never really fit in a colonial settler context like Brazil, even during previous iterations of Brazilian democracy. As James Holston (2008) describes, despite an ideal of political inclusion in which elites at least rhetorically opened the franchise to all regardless of race and ethnicity, de facto exclusion and uneven distribution of property has prevailed throughout the country's history and remains stubbornly the case today. Contemporary Brazilian liberal democracy aspires to resolve essential questions of land use and land occupation through the guarantee of access to land via a market and protection of landed property. Where Indigenous lands are demarcated, the state compensates landholders at market-level prices of the seized land.

This book addresses the literature on landless movements in Brazil that focus on the attempts to realize the democratic potential lent by the legal framework established in 1988 by the return to a liberal constitution. For example, French (2009) puts forth a theoretical approach that she calls "legalizing identities" to understand the emergence of ethnoracial politics for land reform. Working in the Brazilian Northeast, French views pertinent laws as part of a mutually constitutive relationship of identity formation in enactment of legislation related to ethnic rights. Such enactments involve processes of governmentality in which citizen-subjects are empowered to police themselves, as French puts it, in accordance with networks of national and international institutions and actors through which the state takes shape and operates. French views this as positive, in that the revision of self-identification results from the promulgation and taking up of the law as something meaningful for those in social movements, in that they gain access to resources.

In a similarly hopeful though no less critical vein, Holston (2008) argues that we may understand social movements for land as arising from the regimes of land, labor, and differentiated or unequal citizenship in Brazil. He argues that in forms of "insurgency" (protests) for land in the peripheries of São Paulo in the later twentieth century, working poor people engage in a form of autoconstruction (construction of a self), thereby defying structural conditions of material inequality. Invoking Hegel, Holston continues with the idea of recognition through property as a basis for citizenship and equality, reinforcing the powerful potential lent by the country's liberal democratic framework. He describes how those on the urban peripheries use protest to concurrently work inside and outside of that framework and toward achieving social justice. In so doing, they seek landed property as a basis for formation of themselves as citizens.

The people with whom I worked in the land protests in Mato Grosso do Sul diverge from such views on property and citizenship, in part, because of how ethnoracialized markings of Indigenous people and landscapes eschew the terms by which such relations could be reimagined. Guaraní protesters denounce non-Indian or branco incursions into the region and refusals to return lands.

With respect to the expropriation of Indigenous lands in the state of Mato Grosso do Sul, notable historical studies in Brazil indicate that since the last decade of the nineteenth century Guaraní communities have been gradually expropriated from lands that, until that time, they had occupied exclusively and had lived in in accordance with their customary uses and traditions. The historian and Catholic cleric Antonio Brand (1997, 2004) was the first to describe this process in depth, grounding his analysis in archival documents and oral narratives. After Brand's work, a number of studies dedicated to this theme emerged, including those of Ferreira (2001), Rodrigues Pacheco (2009), and Castilho Crespe Lutti (2009). Anthropological studies like Spency Pimental's (2006) thesis, Levi Marques Pereira's (2010) report on the identification and delimitation of Takuara Indigenous lands (situated in the Juti municipality), and a book on the results of analysis of Terra Indígena Ñandeva Ru Marangatu (Eremites de Oliveira and Marques Pereira 2009) describe how the expropriation of Indigenous lands was more intense during certain periods. For example, during the 1930s and 1940s, the privatization and titling of much of Mato Grosso do Sul's rural land caused an uptick in expropriation. Likewise, the years between 1960 and 1980 brought the effective occupation of most of this land by agropastoral activities.

Demarcation studies have observed that the process of the loss of territorial control leads to the gradual loss of political autonomy for many communities. Displaced from their territorial base, the Guaraní became constrained to eight small reservations demarcated by the Indian Protection Service (Serviço de Proteção aos Índios, or SPI) between the years 1915 and 1928. In the following decades, these reservations were destinations for placing communities that had lost their traditional lands. Antonio Brand coined the term territorial "confinement" (Brand 1997) for this phenomenon. In the beginning, agro-pastoral expansion frequently dispersed Indigenous families from their communities to work in different *fazendas* (plantations). That Guaraní-led camps-tekohas today "occupy" some of these plantations reference their displacement in the name of ethnic being and cosmological belonging. Ironically, the landowners and their allies defend their own holdings by pleading for the state to defend what they consider the most basic element of freedom and democracy: the sacredness of property rights.

Of course, the terms for the conflicts do not spring sui generis from the historical events of the displacements. Rather, the protesters' claims to ethnic Indigenous land titles also take place in a broader context of such turns to ethnic identity as a basis of citizenship in Latin America (Hale 2005; Jackson and Warren 2005). Ethnic Indigenous territory is a category enshrined in the postdictatorship 1988 constitution, which established a return to liberal democracy in Brazil following decades of authoritarian rule. In the lead-up to the 1988 constitution, activists and other members of civil society, including anthropologists, led the charge for hard-won rights of land titling.[9]

Indigenous land law put in place a process for evaluating land claims utilizing anthropologists' expertise to conduct studies. Marques Pereira (2010) describes that such studies seek to demonstrate interdependency between three variables for the identification and demarcation of Indigenous lands. The first variable regards establishing evidence of the expulsion of the specified group of Indigenous land claimants from the contested area—that is, to establish whether the claimants were displaced to make room for the expansion of agropastoral activities. Anthropologists are required to procure testimonies and evidence establishing this basis of a group's claim. The second element addresses the impact of territorial expropriation on the group's social organization. This element focuses on the erosion of the political structure of communities by the dispersal of their populations over various locations (reservations), which thereby weakened their political organization. The third and last element refers to various leaders' initiatives to regroup their communities, via protest camping, toward the reoccupation of parts of territories lost to agropastoral expansion.

Land studies faced aggressive pushback against Indigenous rights by the governments of Brazilian presidents of Michel Temer and Jair Bolsonaro, who were successively in power during the time that I penned this book. Particularly, the Bolsonaro government's extreme antagonism to Indigenous land restitution casts light on the neocolonial aspects of the land struggle, particularly in light of the ongoing legacies of violent displacement that have taken place in Brazil.

This focus on decolonial aspects of the protest camps may appear as wrong-headed and beside the point, given that they occur in a national context that already legally recognizes Indians as rights-bearing subjects-citizens, entitled to cultural difference and integrity, regardless of the relative lack of fulfillment of those rights under Bolsonaro's government. According to this logic, the colonial question is settled. Instead, the Indian question regarding land demarcation turns around how to uphold and enforce their rights in the face of their recurrent degradation by national (federal, state, and municipal) politics.

Yet, the protest camps as autonomous uprisings draw our attention in situ to the very much unsettled matter of land and belonging. The demands for enforcement of Indigenous land law, particularly in the adoption of protest-camp tactics, indicate larger stakes beyond the fate of a given parcel of land. The fear animating anti-Indigenous violence in Mato Grosso do Sul stems precisely from this unsettling of taken-for-granted logics of land distribution.

My concern with larger stakes of (de)colonialism, and relatedly national integrity, refers to the at times paranoid ruralist opposition to land demarcation as much as to the contestations made by Guaraní activists. I say *paranoid* because ruralists' expressed fears are hyperbolic. During my fieldwork, protesters were demanding demarcation of only a small fraction of land in Mato Grosso do Sul. And yet, the noxious antipathy, the assaults, kidnappings, and murders of Indigenous land protesters that took place with impunity, signified something palpable at stake: that colonial settlement is an unsettled matter. The unsettling (for non-Indians) prospect of overturning the distribution of land established by the colonial past recurs as an underlying and animating affective dimension to encounters that I witnessed during my fieldwork. This affect manifests in legislative wrangling, such as the push for the *marco temporal*,[10] and echoes in the fears expressed in public forums on the land conflict that I attended in Dourados and neighboring towns in Mato Grosso do Sul.

This book ponders these unsettling effects of Guaraní activists' efforts to reclaim land vis-a-vis protest camping. They organize with larger networks of activists, both Indian and non-Indian, to carry out the work of sustaining the protests in the roadside encampments, put together consciousness-raising public forums, and carry out direct-action protests in person across the country, via websites and in court cases. Such was the multisited dimensions of the fight against the onslaught by agribusiness complexes, ruralist opponents, and proruralist allies. Debates about inclusion in the national society take place within Guaraní communities as the people go about living through and contesting the social structures, which also remain unsettled.

I make three overarching points in this book. First, we can better understand Indigenous protest camps if we come to terms with the gendered, ethnoracial dimensions of the land conflict. Non-Indian descendants of settlers expressed fears sympathetic to fazendeiros and share ethnoracial disdain of Indians. Here, my work ventures outside the explanations given on the ground in Dourados for the conflict. This is due to complicated distinctions made between treatments of ethnicity (or Indigenism) and race in Brazil. Often, speakers will utilize the concept of ethnicity to discuss Indians and the concept of race to discuss Black people. Moreover, the particularities of race and racial ideology in Brazil mitigate renunciations of anti-Indian land rights as racist. Due to notions of miscegenation as a quintessential element of the Brazilian national subject, for example, most Douradenses would not necessarily articulate a racial difference between Indians and non-Indians. Indeed, the category of non-Indian–branco includes those who may not be always marked as white, per se, as I explain in more detail in chapter 1. The stark separations from Indians, such as in terms of blood or kinship, simply do not exist in discourses and understandings of ethnicity and race in Dourados. Instead, an embrace of the Brazilian racial ideology of the mixture of three races (Indian, Black, and white) as the quintessence of Brazilian-ness prevails. Likewise, gender factors in these formulations. Aforementioned references to miscegenation operate through gender tropes. For example, as Guzmàn notes, non-Indian testimonies of Indian ancestry often reference the figure of a mythical great grandmother who supposedly coupled with a Euro-descendant forefather (Guzmàn 2013, 133). At the same time, Douradenses openly hold antipathy toward Indians as backward and a threat to productivity.

The roles of ethnicity, race, and gender, especially concerning the regional variations in Brazilian racial ideology in Mato Grosso do Sul, are critical to the workings of land conflict in the region. They likewise manifest hierarchically in indexes like income, education, and health. Such inequities transpire through effects of fear and disgust, in addition to an imagining of temporal retrocession and the Indian retrograde that gives rise to the ongoing violent opposition to Indigenous land demarcation. This, as much as any crude formulations of economic self-interest, is critical to capturing the conflict. For non-Indians, Indian-ness signifies that which is unproductive, a primordial past supposedly already overcome, or sublimated, through settler colonization of the region. In this imaginary, Indian land protesters signify the languid, dangerously off-the-reservation, and out-of-place (as in anachronistic) figures in the countryside.

Second, we should view the Guaraní protests through the rubric of what I have described as the unsettling of agribusiness, an ongoing effort of countering the ongoing aftermath of colonialism. Protesters unsettle the region in direct and often explicit dialogue with the terms expressed in ruralist opposition to Indigenous land demarcation. Protest camps brazenly call attention to the overlapping of space, of past and future land holdings, of place-making vis-à-vis dwelling, and of material and spiritual presences of an alternative to an agribusiness order.

A camp is, by definition, emblematic of the transient and temporary. As such, its temporariness highlights the precariousness of the supposedly permanent—the settler dispossession of Indians. The Guaraní protest camps presented such an alternative by their persistence on the plantations. The protest camps intimated that Indigenous people belonged there, that the plantations were actually out of place.

The so-called BBB political coalition—the vested interests of the beef (i.e., the cattle industry, a metonym for *ruralists* more broadly), bullets (right-wing advocates of reactionary violence, of which Bolsonaro's signature gun gesturing is emblematic), and Bible (politically active evangelicals) bloc—push against the intimations of Indigenous encampments. The land protesters torment them with the prospect of upending agrarian settler domination of this region, a supposed menace for economic progress. And yet, as Pompeia (2020) demonstrates, we should view agribusiness hegemony and those firms' self-asserted place as the lynchpin of Brazilian economic development, as a desperate ruse, a strategic public relations campaign. Agribusiness's place in the national politics is buoyed by its public posturing and strategic knowledge production (i.e., studies and reports) to corroborate its importance to Brazil's fortunes. Such efforts buttress public perception of their supposed unassailable preeminence.

An Indigenous protest camp unsettles the ruse. The protesters provoke feelings that colonial matters are far from settled, and that is one of the salient points underlying what I encountered in Dourados, in addition to one of the central tenets of this book. It's not that such unsettling was deliberate by the protesters—far from it. The activists sought to gain demarcation of land for reasons both cultural and pragmatic, particular to their specific biographies and inseparable from the larger historical socioeconomic conditions producing their predicaments. However, they sought merely a small portion of the land that Indigenous people have previously occupied in Mato Grosso do Sul and to which they are entitled by law. The rankling of ruralists and their proponents, however, was an effect of the protests, which, in turn, provoked an overwhelming and disproportionate counterforce of violence from plantation owners and the larger Douradense society. We should view the reaction as arising from the camps' effects of destabilizing an imagining of colonially established order of labor and land relations, both of which were ethnoracially delineated.

Third, I show the truth of the activists' claims-making, though that truth fits uneasily into the framework presented by Indigenous land law and the dictates of non-Indians. Their claims combine the historical political, economic, and social structural transformations of the region with the cultural specificities (for example, cosmogonic relations with the landscape) in ways that attend to the exigencies of land law but are not reducible to mere instrumentalism. The ethnographic evidence that I present throughout the book avers that the ways of living these activists engage in cut across both political-economic and cultural domains. They represented elements of their culture to me as a multiple-positioned anthropologist—Black woman, American, working class—whose intersections were points of interlocution. Perhaps this lent me what anthropologist Faye Harrison calls *multiple consciousness*, a play on W. E. B. Du Bois concept of double consciousness (Harrison 1991, 89). Those activists were as self-consciously aware of my positions as I was of theirs, and such awareness is inseparable from the testimony and cultural differences articulated. I characterize these elements of awareness and relationality as different planes to the encounters that I describe throughout the book. All of that added up to demonstrations of cultural ties to the land and self-conscious crafting of representations of those ties in order to contend with the forces of land and labor exploitation.

This book's focus on ethnoracialization of space concerns how we should view the cultural, political, and economic components of the conflict relative to the social order and its rearrangements over time. Here, agribusiness logics signify a realm of political and economic processes that enact the colonial and ethnoracial logics that preceded them and that they continually perpetuate. The land protesters sought to remake and transform those circumstances by reordering the hierarchical social relations bound up in land distribution and land-use practices. Moreover, as I describe in chapter 6, such a critique of established ethnoracial delineations also pertains to critiques, though in ways distinct from non-Indian Brazilian ideologies of race and distinct from my analysis of these issues. My analysis corroborates the claims that I witnessed in the camps-tekohas, however.

## Methodology

The bulk of my fieldwork from 2007 to 2018 took place between 2007 and 2011, with the most intense period of fieldwork occurring during a stretch of seven months in 2011. I returned to Dourados in 2018. While living primarily there, I regularly visited three protest camps of Guaraní (primarily Kaiowá-Guaraní) land activists. I additionally visited two communities of Indigenous activists that were no longer protesting, having achieved provisory recognition of their claims. Finally, I also conducted fieldwork in a protest camp of a non-Indian organization in the region, the Federation of Family Agriculture (Federação da Agricultura Familiar, or FAF).

Brazilian social scientists based in Dourados, introduced to me by mutual friends, facilitated my work. They, in turn, introduced me to people with whom they had already long-established relationships in universities, Indigenous organizations, nongovernmental organizations (NGOs), and state agencies.

My appearance and provenance (gringo accent, for example) caused me to stand out as I navigated the Dourados and its surroundings. I only somewhat looked the part of the stereotypical ethnographer in that part of Brazil, moving about as a Black American woman with short, spiky dreadlocks and wearing my preferred attire of masculine clothes and shoes. Although a steady and significant number of anthropologists have been working in the region for many decades, I have not met in Mato Grosso do Sul any fellow American anthropologists nor anyone not conforming to gender codes—that is, dress and mannerisms. These elements factored into how my research unfolded, the encounters besetting my studies along the way, such as during the aforementioned police checkpoints. I sensed that I also presented something of a curious novelty as an interlocutor. I made explicit my support and solidarity with the activists' cause. My contacts, both Indian and non-Indian, welcomed me into the fold, introducing me to other activists, who in turn also generously embraced my work.

Although I initially planned to focus my studies on changes to Guaraní lifeways brought about by agribusiness political economy, in the early days of my fieldwork I decided to shift the central focus of my work from that to the relations between the city and the countryside, which more broadly encompassed non-Indians, Indians, and a range of social actors that included those Indians referred to as spirit beings. The town of Dourados and the relationships that constitute its transformations, within and surrounding the town, countryside, and neighboring reservations, immediately gnawed at my sensibilities and bestowed a heaviness. The moroseness of the anti-Indigenous violence, both mundane and harrowing, moved more centrally to my research concerns. The banality of my daily life in the town, with routines of grocery shopping and sitting on sidewalks having iced Coca-Colas, intermingled with equally routine encounters with, and mentions by townspeople of, the land conflict. These scenes showed that they had metabolized the spectacular violence of the conflict as just another element of daily life. This felt to me important to understand.

The founding of the Dourados reservation, curiously enough, predates the town by several decades. The reservation was founded in 1917, and the town incorporated in 1935. Dourados, an agribusiness boomtown at the time of my research, impressed me as emblematic of the exigencies of capitalist production and accumulation that propelled so much of what transpired. The entanglement of production in the countryside (particularly of sugarcane, soy, and beef) and urban life struck me as central to the struggles of the Guaraní activists. Examining these relations thusly emerged as the more appropriate object of my research, one pursued collaboratively with land activists and academics in the region.

My fieldwork took the form of interviews and participant observation in the protest camps in the outskirts of Dourados. I lived in the city; importantly, I did not live nor conduct research on reservations. Living in the city allowed me to establish relationships and participate in and observe the workings of the town in its integration with the surrounding region. I noted the comings and goings across these spaces, discourses regarding belonging, and trajectories of those traversing and settling in town and periphery.

Restricting my fieldwork to the town and the protest camps very much prohibited discussion of life on the reservation in this book. I am careful to foreground these limits of my research and the kinds of knowledge that I can claim. Language also presented limits to my research, as I worked using the Portuguese language. My lack of knowledge of the Guaraní language prevented understanding of anything spoken in that tongue by the activists, all of whom spoke both Portuguese and Guaraní. Accordingly, translation and related types of mediation factored into my research as well, as I will discuss in chapter 6.

Through contacts at the Universidade Federal de Grande Dourados (University of Greater Dourados, UFGD) and the Universidade Estadual de Campinas (State University of Campinas, Unicamp), I also conducted fieldwork at multiple agribusiness installations in the interior of the neighboring state of São Paulo, including sugarcane plantations and ethanol fuel distilleries. In addition, I conducted bibliographic and archival research at the library and archives at UFGD.

I regularly attended public forums organized by actors on all sides of the land conflict, including state agencies, ruralist organizations, and Indian activists and their allies in nongovernmental organizations. For example, a public forum organized by Guaraní allies took place in São Paulo in 2008 at the Pontifica Universidade Católica (PUC). The event sought to publicize the beginning of a trial in São Paulo of those accused of the murder of Marcos Veron, a Guaraní activist assassinated in a land conflict in 2003. The event featured speakers from different Guaraní groups from Mato Grosso do Sul, in addition to a Myba-Guaraní leader from the São Paulo littoral. Likewise, I attended multiple forums organized by those sympathetic to large landholders, which took place in various cities of the states of Mato Grosso do Sul and São Paulo.

I interviewed members, and participated in the activities, of NGOs like CIMI (Conselho Indigenista Missionário or Indigenous Missionary Council), an important advocate for Indigenous people in Brazil. I talked to municipal authorities, members of MST Dourados, members of FUNAI (Fundação Nacional do Índio, a federal agency overseeing Indigenous affairs), as well as ruralist entities like the local agribusiness association, FAMASUL (Federação de Agricultura e Pecuária Mato Grosso Do Sul).

Variations across the three Indian protest camps my work centered on gave me a sense of the particularities of their histories and inner workings. Their proximity to the city, the multiple reservations, and the myriad other protest camps in the region—including other Indian

**Fig 2.** Example of a roadside protest camp in the Dourados region. Photograph by Lashandra Sullivan.

protest camps and the camps of non-Indian land-activist organizations like the FAF—facilitated a close-up view of the entanglements, comings and goings, and intimate relationships of lovers and kin across these sites. Gradually getting to know these people and their relationships over the years of fieldwork gave me a sense of the importance of my visiting, interviewing, and building relationships across these multiple sites in the region.

I collected three primary forms of data: recordings of interviews, daily field notes, and archival materials. I worked exclusively in Portuguese, though I hired translators proficient in the Guaraní language for translations and transcriptions as well. Finally, my archival research focused on such data as land registry, newspaper articles, and maps collected at the UFGD.

## Overview of the Book

The book's first chapter, "Ethnoracial Politics of Agribusiness in Dourados," explores how the land-demarcation processes invokes a universal yet multicultural Brazilian citizen-subject, while relying on ethnic boundaries between self-identified Indians (*Índios*) and non-Indians (*não-Índios*) that become articulated as territorial. The expansion of capital-intensive, industrial agricultural production and a model of large-scale plantations takes place through forms of rural nostalgia in which colonial settler tropes of both racial hierarchies and national progress feature centrally. Furthermore, both Índio and não-Índio landless movements that "occupy" rural roadsides via protest camps utilize rhetoric that appeals to "prior ways of life" that nevertheless acknowledge the entrenchment of agro-industrial hegemony. Thus, the chapter queries the prospects for both land reform and the Brazilian model of multiculturalism—which ironically embraces notions of ethnoracial mixture as quintessentially Brazilian—given the political and economic model of economic development embraced by the state.

The second chapter, "Floating Labor in a Bind," analyzes the land conflict between plantation owners and Indigenous activists in Dourados by ethnographically tracing the role of state-issued identification and work documents in the subjugation of Indigenous laborers. Some state agencies contradictorily attempt to protect rural workers via the proliferation of such documents. In practice, this only invisibly binds Indigenous workers to networks of local strongmen, who effectively operate as their overseers. As such, work documents facilitate new but familiar forms of exploitation of racialized labor. These circumstances are part of the impetus and logic of Indigenous land protesters' "occupation" of agribusiness plantations. Activists seek to reclaim land as a counter to historical and ongoing conditions of displacement and coercion.

Chapter 3, "The Protest Camp as a Political Form," explains the particularities of Indigenous protest camps in Mato Grosso do Sul as they arise from a larger history of agrarian change in Brazil. The chapter describes how the condition of floating labor has, at least in part, given rise to the logic of such camps in Mato Grosso do Sul. On one hand, activists mobilize due to histories of forced displacement and ongoing cultural relationships to and through the land. On the other hand, in the mobilizations we see political and economic conditions of dislocation shared by non-Indigenous rural workers, some of whom have also deployed the protest-camp tactic to agitate for land reform. The chapter contextualizes the Guaraní adoption and adaptation of this tactic in southern Mato Grosso do Sul, demonstrating the particularities and continuities to manifestations of land protest camps elsewhere in Brazil.

Chapter 4, "Agribusiness Rearrangements of Space," focuses on what I call *agribusiness space* and its role in the economic-development schemes in this region of Brazil. The economic and political transformations prompted by macroeconomic fiscal and monetary policies arose in part from the adjustment of public accounts and restrictions of public-sector expenses to encourage private investment and development. This chapter looks at the effects of changes in the countryside that have accompanied the reduction in the supply of state-subsidized agricultural credit in that era. Relations between the state, firms, and farmers produced rural space that excludes dwelling. Such relations operate through conceptions of the countryside as de facto devoid of occupants and available for large-scale maximized production and return. The chapter explains the resulting production of agribusiness space as it occurred in Mato Grosso do Sul, its historical unfolding, and lived effects. Protest camping, as a practice, is both embedded within, and a response to, the transformation of rural space into agribusiness space, which relegated residential dwelling for rural laborers to the city peripheries and reservations, a condition called floating labor (as described in chapter 2). I contend that protest camping arose as a product of a larger predicament of rootlessness initiated by this state-mediated spatial order. The displacement of Indigenous people and subsequent perpetual mobility as floating labor produces the logic inciting the camp protests, a condition that I call *permanent transience.*

The fifth chapter, "Mobilizing against Forced Transience," addresses the disjuncture caused by historical dislocations of colonization of the region, subsequent installation of agro-industry, federal administration of reservations, and municipal politics in Dourados. Amid such dislocations, the histories of factions and violence on the Dourados reservation spurred adoption of protest-camp tactics. I ethnographically describe my efforts to collect and decipher oral histories of these events while observing and participating in the day-to-day maintenance of life in the camps-tekohas.

The sixth chapter, "The Space to Be" explains the particularities of the concept of culture as it regards Indigenous land demarcation in Brazil. The culture concept presents a double bind in which questions of authenticity frame both popular antagonism to land titling and efforts by coalitions of Indigenous activists and advocates to stake out a defense of Indigenous rights. I describe the protest camps' efforts to maneuver through these binds. I consider how debates regarding the Indian question in Brazil—which play out in stakes of control over material resources (e.g., land and landscape resources, intellectual-property disputes)—continue to reverberate through questions of cultural alterity. For Guaraní protestors, this involves both self-conscious efforts at transformations or overturning of colonial subjugation through ontological, epistemological, and moral differences in ways both inside systemic (e.g., juridical) logics and radically unamenable to the prescriptions for cultural difference dictated by dominant settler society.

# Ethnoracial Politics of Agribusiness in Dourados    **1**

When I first arrived in Dourados in 2007, I occasionally saw a bumper sticker that read, "O MS É Nosso" (Mato Grosso do Sul is ours). The stickers were part of a statewide campaign by a syndicate of plantation owners (*ruralistas*). The *ours* in the slogan purports to unify the state's Brazilian, non-Indian inhabitants against the Indians who call for state recognition and demarcation of *terras indígenas* (Indigenous land). The syndicate conducted its campaign against the backdrop of two contrasting processes. First, around the time of my fieldwork, Brazil's federal agency overseeing Indian affairs commissioned studies to demarcate historical-cultural Indigenous lands in the state; second, expanding agro-industrial production had put upward pressure on land values and increased competition over land use.

The land in the southern cone of Mato Grosso do Sul is among the more expensive agricultural land in Brazil. While an agribusiness boom since the early 2000s sent land prices soaring, an influx of investment capital translated into ever-higher yields of export products like soy and sugarcane-based ethanol. The agribusiness boom of previous decades added to a long history of reorganization of the region's countryside in the last century, which featured the displacement of rural inhabitants to cities, as well as their incorporation as manual, casualized labor in agro-industrial installations. This incorporation was especially momentous for Indigenous people who constituted the majority of cane cutters in the state. The ensuing shifts in land occupations, land-use practices, and social movements for land rights must be understood in the context of the global land grab.

This chapter offers an analysis of the land grab in Brazil to focus on the political stakes of conceiving ethnic identity as constructed. In turn, this opens a perspective on the ethnoracial politics driving the land conflict. The land grab taking place at the time of my research hobbled land-reform movements, particularly Indigenous social movements. And with a high rate of violence against Indians, Mato Grosso do Sul was notable in this regard.

As described in the introduction, participants in Guaraní land protests put in place roadside camps that border plantations, and sometimes cross property lines, in their attempt to gain state recognition of their land claims. Their tactics provoked confrontations and often-violent clashes with third-party security forces. These attacks, murders, assaults, and kidnappings took place primarily at protest camps. During my multiple stints of fieldwork from 2007 to 2018, I felt the resulting tensions in the camps-tekohas (*aldeias* or villages, as the activists called them), listened to grotesque stories of protest settlements burned by third-party security forces, photographed gunshot wounds, and experienced myself the paranoia induced by the suspected surveillance carried out by those same security forces.

## The Indian–Non-Indian Distinction

Although Dourados is the second-largest city in the state with almost 225,000 inhabitants, it is a rather slow-paced municipality. Horse-drawn carts sometimes traverse roads in between cars, city buses, and a plethora of mopeds and motorcycles. Dourados flourished from the agribusiness boom, growing rapidly in the first decades of the twenty-first century. The soil in the region, with its distinctive orange and red hues, covers the town in dust (called *terra vermelha*, or red earth) and also makes this one of the more productive agricultural regions in Brazil, especially for sugarcane for ethanol fuel production.

Not only do non-Indigenous land-reform organizations, such as Movimento dos Trabalhadores sem Terra (Landless Workers Movement), get little public sympathy, but also public opinion overwhelmingly opposes recognition of Indigenous land claims. The lines of conflict over land

**Fig 3.** A side street in Dourados. Photograph by LaShandra Sullivan.

are both ethnoracial and national. Outside of designated reservations, a non-Indian, yet universal, Brazilian citizen-subject gets mapped onto a supposedly integrated national territory. Although this is sometimes taken for granted by vying stakeholders, at other times it becomes the explicit context for legal, juridical, and physical confrontations. Identities—ethnic, racial, and national—operate as markers for differing understandings of land-use practices, both narratives of the past and visions of the future. In this context, land-use practices are indexed both by ethnicity and by codes of productivity and thus have consequences for a perceived national trajectory of progress.

The struggle for land, then, is in part a struggle over perceived land-use practices. On one hand, the signifiers *non-Indian*, *white*, and *Brazilian* index[1] the high-yield, large landholder model of production, though not always explicitly as such. Agribusiness practices may go unmarked but are always understood as non-Indian–branco. This model of ethnoracial ideology underpins the rural-development policies facilitating the land grab. At the same time, the model and its role in the production of the category of non-Indian–branco are also produced by the land grab. As land concentrates into fewer and fewer hands in accordance with a large landholder model and the the capital-intensive agro-industry, the reinforcement and political weight behind this model of production factors into diminished prospects for land reform. The struggle for land, then, is a struggle over land-use practices both marked (Indian) and unmarked (non-Indian) as ethnic.

Brazil's postdictatorship 1988 constitution championed rights for Indigenous groups within Brazil under terms that were part of a shift to multiculturalism in politics. Previously troubled regimes of racial ideology sought national unity through the sublimation of ethnoracial difference via miscegenation or depicted Indians as the quintessential and original Brazilians (Garfield 2001, 36–37). As an extension of this logic, the state-initiated acculturation programs to "civilize" the Indians who were supposedly in a primitive state of development.

At least in law, such policies have given way to redress past wrongs through affirmative action programs and land demarcation for Indigenous and *quilombo* (descended from escaped African slave communities) people. The difference can be illustrated by contrasting a positivist slogan for Brazil from the early twentieth century, "Order and Progress" (brandished along with the national flag), with President Lula's slogan during that time, "Brazil: A Country for Everybody." According to Sean Mitchell, the former describes an "imaginary of future transcendence of current reality and the latter a mere imaginary of co-existence and identity" (Mitchell 2017, 30–31). Mitchell rightly notes, however, that the latter's version of multiculturalism (like its homogenizing predecessor) presents the nation as a panoply of races and ethnicities while offering scant detail on the arrangement of relations between them in the application of newly defined rights. This, of course, is the problem that advocates for robust enforcement of those rights are at pains to resolve.

The multiculturalist model seeks to resolve ethnoracial injustices against Indigenous people through the spatial accommodation of a cordoned-off reservation of land. This logic points to an aporia in the multiculturalist liberal nation-state project in the Brazilian context, regarding the supposed integrated space of the nation and the universal national citizen-subject. In their brazen presence on the roadside, hugging the borders of the plantations that they threaten to breach, Indigenous protest camps interrupt both the internal coherence of space ordered by the nation-state's bureaucratic structure and the sense of shared belonging as abstract national citizen-subjects that supposedly accommodates ethnoracially marked difference. As settlements, camps at once breach the law and call upon unenforced rights. Like their counterpart in non-Indian land reform movements, Indigenous camps openly face vulnerability to state or third-party violence in their affront to the spatial order of city, reservation, and countryside.

The era of agribusiness dominance and land grabs operates through hierarchical categories of race and ethnicity that are not necessarily resolved by ethnic land demarcation and communal titling. The priority given to the prevailing form of production—high yield, agro-industry, monocrop—complicates the notion that multiculturalist redress of dispossession through land demarcation would resolve the tensions embedded in the construction of Índio versus não-Índio categories.

However, in Mato Grosso do Sul, to assert that ethnicity is constructed puts one squarely in the middle of debates over how references to cultural difference recur regarding land titling. Opponents of land demarcation openly question the authenticity of Indigeneity, given so-called modernization and historical transformations of the region. They argue that Guaraní land protestors are not real Indians like those who are isolated in the Amazon. They assert that the Guaraní drive mopeds and use cell phones like any other Brazilian and are therefore not entitled to land. We can view such sentiments as vestiges of acculturation logics of integration of Indians into national society, by which they would gradually disappear as Indians, becoming non-Indian–branco. Ironically, such opponents of Indigenous rights simultaneously disparage the value of Indigenous land demarcation as a "waste" of land, arguing that Indians would use the land for antiquated and quintessentially Indian (i.e., unproductive) horticultural practices, thus hamstringing regional and national economic vitality.

In Mato Grosso do Sul, conceptions of land-use practices are in some ways foundational to the production of non-Indian–branco political subjectivity and its mapping onto land. Historical narratives of a non-Indian, branco, Brazilian political subject are coextensive with an imagined integrated national territory. Assertions of that subject's historical grounding in a colonial settler state, in addition to his or her forward trajectory through the nation's future progress, make conceptions of land-use practices both ethnoracial and central to the production and maintenance of spatial and ethnic boundaries defining Indian and non-Indian.

I approach these issues with two objectives in this chapter. First, I focus on the substantial role played by the shifting terms of land ownership in the contemporary coproduction of ethnicity and territory. Although the prevailing ethnoracial categories of Indian (Índio) versus non-Indian (não-Índio) are constitutive of an ongoing legacy of colonialism, their contemporary construction is part of national policies and programs for development.

Supporters of Indigenous land demarcation find themselves in the curious position of rallying for the preservation of culture and environmental conservation through forms of impact studies of economic development. Such studies use an insistence on cultural integrity and continuity to underpin efforts to redress historical and ongoing illegal displacement, marginalization, and exploitation of Indigenous people. This approach is founded on legal frameworks and traditions shaped, in part, by the efforts of academics and activists. On one hand, laws establish rights and recognition of Indigenous subjects in terms of self-identification, but, on the other hand, they also point to larger cosmological and socioenvironmental relations to land qua nature.

Land, in this way, is cast as necessary for the survival of Indigenes as Indians. For both defendants and opponents of land demarcation, then, identity and territory turn on presuppositions about land-use practices as indexes of ethnic being and territorial belonging. This sets the stage for a nest of contradictions and recriminations over the very comprehensibility of Indigeneity in contemporary Mato Grosso do Sul, as well as the terms in who can define and fight for land rights amid rural development policies.

Second, in this chapter I'm also focusing more acutely on how identity is constructed for non-Indigenous people, especially how whiteness as a produced ethnoracial category gets overlooked as such and instead operates as an unmarked universal. The aforementioned terms for political engagement around land demarcation obscure the fact that development narratives are embedded in the production of racial categories. Land-use practices are often explicitly invoked in the defining and conceptualization of Indigeneity, but rarely so when it comes to branco or non-Indian identity. For example, socioenvironmental tenets such as harmony with nature and environmental sustainability are features of Indigeneity as expressed in law and popular parlance. However, when it comes to non-Indigenous people, land-use practices constitutive of whiteness (read "development" and "progress") are insidiously unmarked as white.

A narrative of progress through high-yield, capital-intensive production practices operates via a prevailing model of land use promoted by state agencies and political and economic elites of the society. Shifting signifiers around family farming, landholding across generations, descent from pioneering forefathers, and other tropes of race, nation, and family mingle with developmentalist endorsements of agro-industry and agribusiness. The implicit indexing of whiteness through its association with modern land-use practices facilitates the land grab underway in Mato Grosso do Sul. Yet its positioning as historically evolved or advanced from nostalgic idylls of family farming and settler colonial practices of yore, sanction it as belonging to a non-Indian Brazilian-ness.

This line of inquiry raises questions about the prospects for the multiculturalist project, given the terms of rural and national economic development. Multiculturalism is in part designed or premised on some sort of legal redress for the shortcomings of prior racial democracy or acculturation models. In supposedly breaking with that past, multiculturalism today invokes a panoply of identities coming together to constitute Brazilian-ness—distinct identities brought together as Brazilians. In law this entails acknowledgement of past wrongs done to historically oppressed groups like Afro-Brazilians and Indians. Under the 1988 constitution, for example, multiculturalism signals reconciliation through establishment and enforcement of land rights.

## The Role of the Land Grab

Even during the economic slowdown in the global North in the early 2000s, Brazil received massive foreign direct investment (Lyons 2011). Some economists believe the resultant spectacular growth was simply a speculative bubble, arguing that the agricultural sector provided one of the country's few real increases in productivity (Brasil de Fato 2011). Indeed, the state of Mato Grosso do Sul saw significant growth in yields of soy, livestock, and, above all, sugarcane for ethanol fuel production, which increased more than 60 percent from 2010 to 2011 (Matos 2011). The influx of international investment capital, particularly for the purchase of land, put upward pressure on land value. Mato Grosso do Sul is one of the leading states in Brazil in terms of foreign ownership of land, with primary use allotted to agribusiness (Sauer and Pereira Leite 2011, 17).

In this section I briefly examine how different models have implicated various political alliances and conflicts. The point is to draw clear lines of distinction regarding the configuration of political and economic order facilitating the land grab. Opponents of land reform in the state argue that the government should safeguard the rises in land value, windfall in agribusiness profits, and the subsequent economic boom to the region and nation over land reform. Although agricultural policies in Brazil have long favored large landholders, numerous types of large landholder models exist, as well as political terms to defend and contest them.

Over the course of the twentieth century in the Brazilian countryside, seigneurial relations between landowners and peasants gave way to a process of proletarianization. There was also a tremendous accumulation of land and displacement of smallholders. Although with much regional variation and historical specificity, this in turn gave rise to social move-ments for land reform. Many rural inhabitants moved to cities; others continued agrarian work for subsistence. In both cases, work was carried out under a variety of labor relations; some were salaried or affiliated with a union, but most worked as day laborers with third-party labor contractors as the middlemen between them and the plantation or firm (Pereira 1997).

Since the colonial era, Brazil has famously supplied world markets with significant sums of agricultural exports like sugar and coffee. However, this overgeneralizes nuanced shifts in the agriculture sector's partici-pation in international capital flows and exchanges. As I will discuss in more detail in chapters 3 and 4, the transformation in the structuring of agricultural credit supply played a significant role in the land ownership and land use over this history, particularly as it concerned central-west Brazil. In the years prior to the foreign debt crisis of the 1970s, Brazil had followed an import-substitution industrialization policy. Exports in manufactured goods and cheap loans met the country's foreign exchange needs. Agricultural output primarily remained within a domestic market. At that time, the Banco do Brasil supplied agricultural credit and operated on reserves from Brazil's Central Bank. The latter automatically supplied resources to the Banco do Brasil for subsidized credit for commercial agriculture. However, when the foreign debt crisis hit, the exorbitantly high inflation that ensued made this unsustainable. Thus, this prior transfer mechanism was replaced by the restrictive monetary policy deployed to counter inflation and meet International Monetary Fund demands for reform of the agricultural credit system.

In response, the government replaced the agricultural credit system with a minimum price policy to push the production of agricultural exports. This policy prioritized safeguarding foreign reserves as a response to the debt crisis of the 1970s. Mueller (2004, 5), explained that by the 1980s agricultural credit "had become a major source of income transfer in favor of those which had access to the rural credit system—mostly large, commercial farmers." As a result, Brazilian agriculture shifted significantly toward substantial growth in exports. A key and significant component of this was a focus on increases in yields and a major expansion of "modern agriculture" in the *cerrado* (savannah) of central-west Brazil, where Mato Grosso do Sul is located. The expanded role of agribusiness and the associated production of export-oriented crops—particularly sugarcane and soybeans—continues (Mueller 2004, 6).

International investors and financial institutions purchase land and install international agro-industrial firms like Adecoagro. Based in Buenos Aires, this corporation owns hundreds of thousands of hectares in Uruguay, Argentina, and Brazil; in Mato Grosso do Sul, it specializes in the production of sugar and sugarcane-based ethanol fuel (Adecoagro 2010). Such investors raise land prices and bring added complications to processes of land reform as taken up by postauthoritarian governments—that is, land redistribution through the purchase of land from private owners. When land was cheap, the government could more easily procure land for redistribution. With ever-increasing land prices, the politics of agricultural and rural development necessarily encounter constraints of both state resources and political will for land reform. Just as important, the cast of actors involved in the process has been transformed.

Overall, ruralistas have come a long way in the last fifty years. At the time of the 1964 coup d'état in Brazil, they were more of a planter class, oriented toward a mix of coffee and sugar for the international market and foodstuffs and commodities for the domestic market. The "professionalization" of this class brought in an array of other actors, including financiers, state development agents, insurers, land speculators, development NGOs, and international institutions like the World Bank. Mueller (2004, 7) writes,

> The traditional farmer that prevailed in the past, mostly interested in reaping capital gains from land ownership or in milking the favors and subsidies provided by state agricultural policies gave way to a new breed of professional farmers. Most of those have their origin in parts of the south of Brazil and in the state of São Paulo, where they acquired experience in effectively managing their establishments. Many were able to sell their usually small farms in the south and to purchase much larger establishments in the frontier regions [like Mato Grosso do Sul]. The new breed of farmers has been extremely receptive to advances in agricultural practices, having markedly intensified and modernized their operations. Their main concern is with profits from their agricultural operations.

This certainly describes the dominant model of ruralistas in Mato Grosso do Sul. However, testimonies in public forums and presentations on the land conflict exceed mere instrumentalist managerial reasoning. Ruralistas and their supporters often present themselves as frontiersmen, cowboys, and patriots who "settled" the region during the colonial era to advance the nation. These narratives and self-presentations are intrinsically linked with understandings of land as commensurate with forms of value entailed in finance capital and land-use practices elicited in high-yield, agro-industrial production.

## Land Politics and Ethnoracial Antipathy

"Do you like Indians?" I was asked by a Douradense as he lounged stone-faced in a hammock on my front porch. A friend of my roommates, he was passing through for a brief visit. We all drank *tereré* and chatted. He is a second generation *sul-matogrossense*, his parents having migrated to Mato Grosso do Sul from Rio Grande do Sul. I had just explained to him that I was in Dourados doing fieldwork with roadside protest camps of Guaraní.

"What?" I replied. I was not surprised by his question: I had heard it often during my time in Mato Grosso do Sul.

"Indians. Do you like Indians?" ("Indios. Você gosta de Índios?").

I paused. Then I attempted to turn his question back to him in his own terms: "Do you like them?"

"No," he stated matter-of-factly, and continued without pause, "Do they have Indians where you live in the United States? You [Americans] killed all of your Indians, why don't you let us kill ours?" I never quite got used to such questions, though I heard them all too frequently during my periods of fieldwork in the region.

In addition to the multiple self-identified Guaraní camps-tekohas where I conducted interviews and participant observation, I also worked with a non-Indigenous protest camp of the FAF. Whereas non-Indigenous land reform organizations seek land in general—and not necessarily in the area where they conduct their protests—Guaraní camps-tekohas border or cross into specific plantations from which they claim they were forcibly displaced and that are part of their traditional ethnic territory. Moreover, as Levi Marques Pereira (2003, 143–44) describes, Guaraní activists do not have a central organization coordinating their protests. By contrast, the FAF has a central organizing body located in Dourados (Dourados Prefeitura).

The Guaraní land claims invoke land rights outlined in Brazil's 1988 constitution, the UN Declaration on the Rights of Indigenous Peoples, and the International Labor Organization's Indigenous and Tribal Peoples Convention, as well as the landmark 2009 Brazilian Supreme Court ruling in favor of continuous land demarcation at Raposa Serra do Sul. In 2008 FUNAI, Brazil's federal agency for Indian affairs, commissioned studies to demarcate historical-cultural Indigenous lands in Mato Grosso do Sul. However, the deployment of the resources and personnel for these studies provoked hostility and opposition from plantation owners, who organized a public relations and legal battle to persistently delay (if not permanently derail) the studies. They used public forums, publicity campaigns (bumper stickers, billboards, favorable media coverage), as well as private security firms and police confrontations with those in the camps-tekohas, as part of their tactics. Additionally, they waged a juridical battle to preemptively block the studies or challenge their possible findings.

Such was the tense backdrop to my fieldwork. Though I primarily worked among activists and opponents of land demarcation, I also got to know an assortment of townspeople who could be described as "uninvolved" but with strong opinions on the issues. Whereas self-identified Guaraní often expressed a yearning for "the space to be themselves," or to be Guaraní, it became clear to me that non-Indians–brancos as well felt a stake of identity. Guaranís complained that existing reservations provide insufficient space to carry out so-called traditional Guaraní activities, including prior modes of economic production. Non-Indian–branco townspeople also complained about constraints on their capacities to realize their way of life. In short, for them, Indians posed such constraints. They were fleshly embodiments of the frontier history that the townspeople invoked as perpetual antagonists.

I likewise observed other Douradense-perceived constraints percolating in their complaints over casual conversations and media (television, blogs, and print media) narratives: frustration with municipal, state, and federal government corruption and with inadequacy of respect for hard work by fellow townspeople, particularly the poor.

Both Índio and não-Índio rural Brazilians have faced displacement. Over the course of the twentieth century, Brazil's population shifted from roughly 80 percent agrarian to 80 percent urban.[2] Both push and pull factors were at play: People were attracted to industrializing urban areas by the prospects of work, education, and services. Simultaneously, they were pushed off the land by droughts in the Northeast, massive deforestation (Dean 1995), and public works like hydroelectric projects (Bloemer 2000). Changes in the regulation of land and labor also displaced millions of people in favor of large fazendeiros and agro-industry.[3]

However, this history is represented differently in different social movements and in treatments in the academic literature in Brazil. In other words, the politics of historiography differs for Indian versus non-Indian land struggles and for knowledge-making practices in the Brazilian academy. Some Brazilian researchers have tended to analyze non-Indian people in terms of their transition from peasants to wage laborers, focusing on proletarianization (Conceição d'Incão 1984; Aparecida de Moraes 1999; Stolcke 1988). By contrast, many specialists on the Guaraní concentrate on the continuities of Indigenous culture along lines of kinship and ethnicity (Ferreira Thomas de Almeida 2001; Brand 1997, 2004).[4] Presenting a narrative of cultural loss and recuperation, this literature pleads for land restitution to protect and preserve Guaraní culture. This approach presents an impact study of land loss in which the goal is to advocate moral redress for victims of colonization and dispossession by demonstrating the cultural loss.[5] In these analyses, restitution of land would allow greater autonomy to live in accordance with prior ways of life and ameliorate problems like high rates of starvation, crime, and suicide.[6]

This type of literature on the Guaraní (for example, Ferreira Thomas de Almeida 2001; Brand 2004; Marques Pereira 2004a), often aligns with Frederick Barth's (1969) analysis of ethnicity as determined by the boundaries recognized between groups. For Barth, the positive definitions or characteristics delimiting a group are not the basis for the discreteness of the group's ethnic category. Although such positive definitions contain contradictions and inconsistencies, the groups still recognize themselves and are recognized in relational opposition to other groups. Indeed, it is this relational opposition, mediated by ethnic boundaries, that distinguish groups and is the basis for the ethnic category itself. In the case of Mato Grosso do Sul's category of Índio, the ethnic boundary arises in contradistinction to the não-Índio or branco, broadly defined. Such ethnicization is further complicated by the invisibilization of Black people in the region, which I describe in more detail elsewhere (Sullivan 2017).

Political and economic contexts of different scales and extensions are also a factor in the emergence or endurance of ethnic boundaries. By *different scales* and *extensions*, I mean the national and international processes that produce structures of authority and the networks of production and exchange of ideas and commodities. For example, in the 1980s the World Bank and the Inter-American Development Bank exerted considerable influence on Brazil's military dictatorship by linking financing for development projects in Indigenous areas to assurances of studies for demarcation of Indigenous territory and the impact on these populations (Carneiro da Cunha 1987, 132–33). Such conditions mandate an articulation of ethnicity as a basis for dialogue with the state and transnational institutions. They rely on an established legal framework for state recognition of ethnic subjects, such as the 1988 constitution and legal precedents previously described.[7]

Recognition by states and institutions links identity and its mapping onto land to stakes of material survival—survival through acquisition of landed property via ethnic communal land titling. Such stakes reshape the operations of the concept of territory with what we might call identity-through-property. In this conception of territory, a subject gains recognition via being an ethnicity as facilitated through territorial claims. Essentially, the conditions lent by the contemporary juridical-economic order creates a context mode of survival lent by being a particular ethnicity. This mode of survival presents identification with a particular ethnic category as both the terms for the group's historical socioeconomic marginalization and, ironically, a basis to counter that marginalization through demands for material resources like land. Transnational financial institutions, international organizations, and different Brazilian state agencies may facilitate access to the means of survival for such ethnoracial subjects in their operations at different economic and political scales. However, I witnessed both a refusal to participate in such politics of recognition (Simpson 2014) and a strategic embrace of their possibilities. Here, the fact of alterity coincides with the self-conscious navigation of structurally imposed constraints for regaining territory.

The politics of territorial recognition, ostensibly centered on the category of Índio, likewise concerns the dialectical production of the category of não-Índio. Insofar as the land conflict implicates ethnoracial Índio "being," it centrally involves questions of belonging, recognition, and recognizability of the não-Índio via the settler colonial claim to landed property. The defining of place is interwoven into the land contest. Concepts of territory extend beyond economic survival, subsistence, and thriving; national identity and ethnicity register narratives of time and place, trajectories of where one comes from and where one is going. Neither necessarily aligns with the terms of contemporary economic production nor its historical transformation. Rather, like the emergence of cowboy narratives through twentieth-century country music in the United States, notions of rural selfhood linked to prior modes of production on the land—always shifting and contingent—become idealized at the moment in which those former relations of production have been utterly transformed. Such narratives emerge in urban contexts in folk remembrances of a romanticized past, achieved through reference to a sense of place to which one belongs.

In Mato Grosso do Sul, invocations of a romanticized rural idyll in the expressions of ethnic identity—cowboy culture[8] for brancos, for example—contrast with the contemporary agro-industrial context. In narratives of place, in which Mato Grosso do Sul operates as a site of "traditional" Guaraní way of life, or, alternatively, as a frontier of pioneer cowboys, social actors perform a sense of self. Brancos experience identity and self-fashioning through moments of nostalgia. Indians, like those engaging in protest camps, in contradistinction, insist on an ongoing relation to and through the landscape, despite brancos. The coconstructedness of ethnic categories is overlooked when land is said to belong to an ethnic people, like brancos. Regarding the Guaraní, such constructedness does not diminish their distinct conception in which they do not maintain that the land belongs to them, per se. Instead, for the Guaraní, the people belong to the land (Mura 2006, for example).[9]

In the ethnoracial land claim, land is the material anchor to a way of life that calls on the past as a means of producing one's future. In other words, Guaraní invoke a primordial tradition that opens a solution to present crises. This invocation emerges from precarious material conditions as a means of envisioning possible futures.

I have foregrounded land as a point of analysis to be accounted for in relation to its position as a means of survival through its anchoring of claims on the state and as an object to which one's relation serves as a point of longing. Land serves as a point of struggle both in one's material reproduction and in competing maps in narratives of belonging, subjectivity, and citizenship. It is interesting to contrast the specificity of content of the category of Indian as required by law, presented by Indian informants and analyzed in social science literature, to the content of the non-Indian–branco ethnic category, to which I will return subsequently.

Guaraní proponents of demarcation express a longing for the "space to be themselves" in at least two senses. First, during their interviews, Guaraní informants, including sugarcane cutters and schoolteachers, complained of not having the space to enact traditional social organization. Second, some Guaraní informants discussed land restitution as a means of returning to previous forms of economic production and spiritual relationship with land and forests. I will analyze each of these in turn.

Most Guaraní people rely on remunerated work in order to live. Buses for manual laborers depart the reservations before dawn, carrying workers to plantations and ethanol distilleries. The enmeshment in larger national and international networks of production and exchange presents a juxtaposition between contemporary means of social reproduction and understandings of its predecessor and hoped-for successor—a self-contained community within a Guaraní way of life. Some Guaraní object to having to live in close proximity with groups outside their extended kin on reservations. They complain that such proximity, even with other Guaraní, causes unease and creates conflicts, jealousies, and accusations of witchcraft.

Having the proper amount of space would relieve those tensions by allowing a return to living in extended family groups on large swaths of land, spread far apart. According to this logic, the history of crowding onto reservations contributes to the urgency of needing to reclaim dispossessed space—expanding the availability of land for Guaraní. In these claims, self-identified Guaraní invoke a past social harmony wrought by a former, larger territory that allowed them to *be* Guaraní.[10]

Brazilian law and state agencies charge anthropologists with documenting and outlining the terms of Indigenes' previous social and spatial organization, with its stated territorial social harmony, that is often referred to both in the testimonies of informants and in much of the literature cited in this book on the Guaraní in Mato Grosso do Sul.[11] In the work of documenting contemporary narratives of the past, anthropologists simultaneously make the past intelligible and render that past commensurate with the stakes of state recognition.

For example, early on in my fieldwork with two Guaraní camps-tekohas, the leaders brought to my attention burial markings on plantations as evidence for their land claim. They pointed to these ancestral cemeteries as evidence of the cultural imperative to return to live near those sites. Use of burial grounds as evidence of ethnocultural belonging is consistent with legal imperatives for establishing "cultural" land claim in Brazil. However, in the case of the Guaraní, such grounds are complicated; according to Schaden (1962), the Guaraní refrained from living near such burial sites at the time of his research.

In terms of the second sense of the call for space "to be themselves," some Guaraní argue that land restitution would allow them to return to a past way of life, namely through a return to forests. Brazilian laws connect ethnicity to land rights through socioenvironmental claims on the relation of traditional modes or types of production to environmental factors. Here, Indigeneity is tied to foraging, horticultural activities, or both. Traditional ways of life rely on the sustainability of forests that house both spirits and species of flora of religious and cosmological significance. Land-demarcation proponents demonstrate that Guaraní continue to carry on these practices, to the extent possible, using the few remaining forested areas on public environmental reserves and private plantations (Eremites de Oliveira and Marques Pereira 2009, 75, 85–86).[12] Socioenvironmental arguments favoring land restitution take seriously the very different relations to land and nature involved in Guaraní cosmology and economic activities, as opposed to the agro-industrial logic of the exploitation of nature (Munn 1996).

It was a challenge for my informants to imagine how previous modes of production would allow access to commodity goods, the acquisition of which they agreed would continue to be a priority. For example, a thirty-two-year-old Guaraní informant, who had been a full-time cane cutter since the age of thirteen, complained of the diminishing availability of work due to mechanization. When I asked him to suggest an ideal solution, he stated that he wanted more work (remunerated labor). More land would offer him greater security, but the land would not provide what he needed to buy materials for building a house or furnishing it. Although this particular informant did not mention a reverence for, and relations with, spirit protectors (of forests, for example) in and of the landscape, other Guaraní with whom I worked did. They also expressed desires for more work on plantations and satisfaction with remunerated work. The conundrum of needing more work while also desiring more land for traditional ways of living presented them with complexities to navigate. Whereas these seeming contradictions emerged during our conversations, my informants did not remark about them and did not seem troubled or irked by them. I am not suggesting they should be troubled but rather pointing out the kind of heterogenous logics through which ethnic categories operate.

## Whiteness and Land

At a 2008 public forum in the town of Naviraí, hosted by the plantation owners' syndicate of Mato Grosso do Sul, dozens of local municipal functionaries, members of nongovernmental organizations, and diverse local inhabitants filled the auditorium. Land demarcation was an issue of great concern in the town. Local media, including television and radio stations and newspapers, covered the event. Two radio stations interviewed me after learning I was conducting research on the issue in the region.

A tone of subdued outrage and explicit panic permeated the forum, in both the formal presentations of the organizers and in audience testimonies and interventions. One fazendeiro joked about the shooting of an Indigenous protester on his land. Another complained that the Índios are not really that desperate for land since some of the protestors that showed up at his plantation were using cell phones. The cognitive dissonance provoked by seeing an Índio with a piece of modern technology apparently offended either his sense of what it meant to be a real Indigene or really indigent, or both.

Syndicate representatives gave PowerPoint presentations and speeches criticizing the roles of law-transgressing Indians, anthropologists, left-wing clergy and foreign-funded NGOs in the land struggle, accusing them of undermining the well-being of Mato Grosso do Sul with the threat of land seizure. One syndicate representative complained that his ancestors had come to Mato Grosso do Sul to clear the forests and make the region productive. "We whites" (brancos), he proclaimed, were Brazilians who fought to establish the area as a frontier to advance the country. Accompanied by the vocal approbation of many in the audience, he lamented that the state wants to seize their land to give it to "*Índios quem não produzem nada"* (Indians who do not produce anything). Invoking a shared identity for descendants of the region's não-Índio pioneers, the syndicate representative set up an opposition between these descendants as Brazilians, a category distinguished by their productivity, and unproductive Índios. In a different context in Brazil, the syndicate representative might not have identified himself, nor have been perceived, as branco. Rather, he might have been identified as Negro (Black).[13] Such is the complexity of race in Brazil and the particularity of the context of Mato Grosso do Sul in the production of ethnic boundaries.[14]

Even self-identified não-Índios who defend Indigenous land claims sometimes do so in accordance with the very developmentalist logic that produces ethnic Índio versus não-Índio categories. Referring to the FUNAI study to demarcate Indigenous land underway in the state at the time of my research, a Partido dos Trabalhadores member of Mato Grosso do Sul's state congress explained, "The Indians will not derail the development of the state. Mato Grosso do Sul is not in financial difficulty."[15] Indeed, he said, the lack of demarcation generates legal uncertainty for the state's potential investors. They fear buying more land to augment production since they do not know if that land will one day be designated Indigenous territory. "If we do not demarcate the land now, the insecurity will remain for the rest of our lives," he predicted (Chileno 2009).[16] Presumably, such a hindrance to the inflow of investment capital would constitute an unnecessary brake on the state's development. These public discourses distinguish between Índios who will inhibit advancement by carrying out their traditional ways of life and não-Índios identified with agro-industrial productivity, progress, and finance capital.

However, unlike the legal definitions of Indigeneity, such as its socio-environmental framing, no set of social practices is presumed to define agrocapitalism as a way of life. The lack of specificity is a function of its privileged status as the unmarked universal—hence the absence of requirements for a recognizable continuity of contemporary social practices with the historical narratives of frontiersman invoked. In addition, the expansion of the agribusiness model into the central-west region, along with its concomitant capital-intensive techniques and materials of production (e.g., herbicides, modified seeds, machinery), while pushed by the state, collided with some small-scale farmers and land protesters.

In Indigenous land rights, the socioenvironmental linking of ethnicity to land use recognizes an Indigenous land claim as a legitimate alternative to a capitalist way of production. Embedded in that recognition, however, are the assumptions of fundamental differences in the relation of Indians to nature vis-à-vis non-Indians' relations to nature. In this imaginary scenario, the viability of the expansion of Indigenous lands comes into conflict with the question of whether Indigenes should be put ahead of, or allowed to obstruct, development. In short, in law and political discourses that reference essentialist notions of nature-bound Indians, the Indian has no place, at least in developmentalist narratives of Brazil's history and future.

Beyond the somewhat banal point that identity is constructed, I underline how its construction can be at once acknowledged and obscured in political contests over land ownership, land occupation, and land-use policies. Specifically, anthropologists are the target of ire and suspicion by opponents of land reform. Yet the state calls upon and requires social science expertise in the establishment and attestation of the legitimacy of claims for Indigenous territory.

The Guaraní with whom I worked welcomed my presence and fieldwork both as part of a long line of anthropologists visiting their aldeias for similar reasons and for the prospect that my work could lend legitimacy to their land claims. On one hand, these groups, their opponents, and state bureaucrats acknowledge that anthropological knowledge-making practices translate ethnicity and territorial belonging into social outcomes, such as land demarcation. On the other hand (as discussed in chapter 6), an explicit acknowledgement of ethnicity as constructed, as relying on such studies for legitimacy, endangers Indigenous land claims, a fact frequently deployed in the public relations arsenal of ruralistas, who challenge Indigenous land claimants' authenticity. At the same time, these ruralistas insist upon the supposedly primordial retrograde characteristics of Indigeneity in their opposition to land demarcation and championing of non-Indian–branco land-use practices.

In this chapter, I have tried to show how, in the context of Mato Grosso do Sul, ethnicity can be both constructed and understood as such, yet deeply taken for granted as primordial in land politics and state policies due to the pervasiveness and perniciousness of ethnoracial categories.[17]

Much of what I describe here resonates with Ramos's (2001) analysis of the larger context of what she calls "indigenism" in Brazil. She describes how Brazilians talk about Indigenous people as embedded in nature. They are exoticized despite their so-called proximity. At the same time, Indians may take up their own essentialization in a performance of authenticity as a strategy or pathway to political-economic claims. Ethnicity emerges as a political instrument to overcome material deprivation (for example, starvation) and exploitation (for example, as poverty-wage cane cutters) that have accompanied the agribusiness era. Despite its drawbacks, such Indigenist politics present a positive possibility for knowledge production and the realization of land rights.

Such possibilities are not recent. For example, in Brazil's Amazonian regions, for many decades Indians have engaged in activities like video production to self-consciously and strategically deploy their images to navigate public relations and other politically fraught domains of interlocution with national society (Conklin 1997, Graham 2002, and Turner 2002). Video productions continue in Mato Grosso do Sul through events like the "Video Índio Brasil" event, which featured the work of organizations like Video na Aldeia (Video in the Village) (Lobo Digital 2008).

In Mato Grosso do Sul, an ethnic self—Índio versus não-Índio—is constructed through a relation to land and understandings of its contemporary, past, and future forms. Champions of the development policies driving the land grab present the familiar characterization of agro-industrial, capital-intensive production as logical and essential to regional and national progress, whereas other types of production are alternatively Índio or Guaraní. The presentation of the former as nonracial or nonethnic effaces the fact that industrial, capital-intensive production is already understood as branco–non-Indian in its recurrent opposition to the Indian way of life.

Ethnographic subjects present these oppositions in ethnoracial terms without always explicitly talking about them as such. As an object of ongoing articulations of ethnic boundaries, in accordance with socially produced categories and within the legal stipulations for recognition of land titles, such ethnoracial terms remain open-ended and ever determined by both practices and self-conscious critiques—as do the claims to the land itself.

This chapter has taken contests over understandings of the past and visions of the future, both across and within the categories of Indian and non-Indian, as an analytical focal point because of the centrality of these categories to the production of a sense of space and belonging. Land in Mato Grosso do Sul represents a key contradiction in the struggle between how ethnicity and territory factor into an understanding of the past, future, and contemporary terms for material survival. Land conflicts are centered on the outcomes for economic productivity and distribution of resources associated with Brazilian citizenship and ethnic categories. The expansion of global capital and land-grab pressures are part of a historical shift in land appropriation and responses to it. Contested land claims take place in a context in which the influx of international capital and concomitant transformations of the organization of production have rendered rural inhabitants increasingly marginal, regardless of ethnic identification.

# Floating Labor in a Bind 2

One day during fieldwork in Mato Grosso do Sul, I found myself on the side of a highway pondering what to make of an unusual request. When Diego[1] asked me for a ride to the town of Amambai to pick up his *carteira de trabalho* (worker identification document), along with other documents, my initial reaction was to ask why the papers were not with him in Dourados. We stood on the side of the highway amid the ramshackle dwellings that composed the Indigenous protest camp where I was conducting fieldwork.

Diego and his fellow activists are Indigenous Guaraní people who are "occupying" a sugarcane plantation to gain state recognition of the land as their traditional ethnic territory. We may reasonably ask, though, who is occupying whom in this relatively recently colonized region of Brazil. Protesters demand demarcation of land for restitution. In so doing, they push back against the material hardships wrought with settler colonial takeover of the region and its abstractions of land as empty and ever available for capital investment and accumulation. The protesters refer to the area they are reclaiming as their aldeia.

Being as he was on the rural outskirts of Dourados, about a two-hour drive to Amambai, Diego, dirt poor and without transportation, would have had an interesting explanation of how and why his documents ended up in Amambai. (See figure 4.) I immediately found the situation curious. Diego's initial story made no sense to me. His subsequent versions, after I asked him to explain again and again, further made no sense. Only

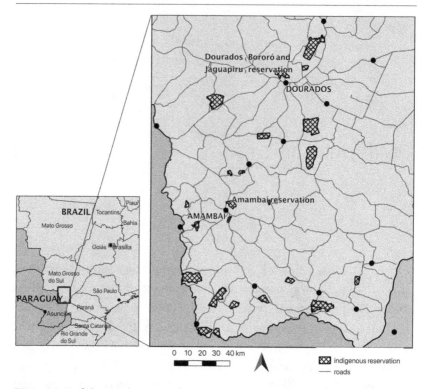

**Fig 4.** Map of the southern cone of Mato Grosso do Sul, Brazil. Dourados and Amambai, with their respectively adjacent reservations, are indicated, as are outlines of the small islands of Indigenous reservations in the region. Map by Abigail George.

after traveling with him to Amambai, revisiting different stops along the way, would the pieces of the story begin to come together coherently. Encountering the various strange characters, mostly among networks of local strongmen (middlemen between the state, agribusiness firms, and workers) with whom Diego had "lost" the documents—or rather with whom the documents (and therefore Diego) were being held hostage—helped me to understand.

Diego's ordeal demonstrates how such documents effectively serve as a form of racial tethering. Dispossessed of land and inculcated by dire material conditions on reservations, Indigenous workers are bound to networks of strongmen intermediaries, the third-party labor contractors for agribusiness firms. Workers are thus overseen in ways resonant with how plantation labor has historically required overseers. Diego's ordeal makes plain the shortcomings of state agencies, those would-be enforcers of labor rights, for whom Indigenous workers' struggles go unseen. Land restitution lends to activists the hope of gaining greater means to lessen and sidestep such bondage.

As I discovered during fieldwork conducted between 2007 and 2011, the unusual checkpoints and degrees of illegality that Diego had to traverse in order to work presented complicated interconnections with parallel degrees of obfuscation by all involved (including Diego). Presenting that story here requires laying out how relations between land, labor, agribusiness firms, state and nongovernmental actors intersect and operate. Likewise, we must delve into how the historical reorganization of land and labor in Brazil's countryside created Diego's predicament.

Diego's case demonstrates how ethnoracial othering and exploitation occur through and in spite of the social inclusion that documents like the carteira de trabalho are supposed to convey. As they are ethnoracially marked as Índios, laborers experience their subjugation to such networks as being ignored by the larger branco–non-Indian society in the region, which generally views Indigenous people with disdain. I am uniquely positioned in this work as a Black American woman working in solidarity with Indigenous people in a context of decidedly anti-Black and anti-Indigenous sentiment (Sullivan 2017). Douradense townspeople regularly spoke to me about their antipathy toward Índios when discussing my fieldwork. Such ethnoracial remarking occurred as neither out of the ordinary nor purely incidental. Such were the terms and stakes of the land conflict preoccupying non-Indians–brancos in the region.

The prevailing agribusiness order of land use and land occupation operates through racialized hierarchies that reenact longstanding modes of social hierarchies and control. I argue that protests of fazendas (plantations) call upon the state to rectify the injustices of past dispossession of Indigenous people and ongoing delimitations of their freedom. Such struggles were even more striking in the context of the heightened national hostility to Indigenous activists following the 2019 inauguration of President Jair Bolsonaro. Land demarcation offers Indigenous people greater control over their own labor by recognizing and securing ties to land as an alternative to being tethered to networks that oversee their coerced labor.

### Work Documents Versus Land Titles

Protest camps consist of people who have moved out of, or circulate between, periurban[2] dwellings and rural work sites. The protestors sustain their lives through a combination of government welfare programs and remunerated work for agribusiness firms. Work and welfare documents attach rural laborers to larger networks of local strongmen, who essentially refix these workers to land, in ironic contradistinction to the floating, casualized nature of their employment with agribusiness firms.

Diego's life of transience as a manual laborer, as well as his quest to recover his documents, exemplify long-standing conditions of unmooring, originating with settler colonial displacement of Indigenous people in Mato Grosso do Sul. Such conditions date back to the nineteenth century, though they have undergone important transformations in the interim. Diego's case shows how such documents mediate relations of land and labor in ways that echo prior systems of peonage in Brazil and elsewhere in Latin America.[3] Their effects replicate ethnoracial hierarchies between Indians and non-Indians in Mato Grosso do Sul, as well as plantation logics of racialized labor.

The people with whom I work are not using tools like Indigenous land law to protect against territorial incursions, as is the case elsewhere in South America. Examples include struggles against the intrusions of miners, ranchers, and oil companies in the Andes (e.g., Cadena 2010) and the Amazon basin (Cepek 2011; Sawyer 2005; Turner 1995). Likewise, Indigenous politics among the Guaraní of lowland Bolivia (Postero 2017; Fabricant and Postero 2015) see them fending off the encroachment of state highway-construction projects. Those groups seek to defend their already existing and enduring territorial holdings from further invasion. Instead, Indigenous activists in Mato Grosso do Sul seek to retake lands that were stolen long ago, from which they were displaced, and that had been subsequently reinscribed as non-Indian and merely agribusiness space. Their protests, thusly, present a unique decolonizing practice that opens up prospects for viewing multiculturalist tools as a means to unsettle land, with all of the accompanying connotations of re-presenting the colonial past as unfinished and unsettled.

The protesters' demand for land counters the perpetual displacement endured by Indigenous laborers. It is this aspect of the land protests, particularly the ethnic terms for titling, that presents a counterpoint to the condition of coerced labor underpinning Diego's quest to recover his documents.[4]

While state agencies like FUNAI facilitate access to welfare and advocate for land reform, there is often a remarkable lack of state intervention, silences, and seeming procrastination in countering high degrees of exploitation and marginalization of the poorest of Indigenous rural workers. Therefore, Indigenous bondage goes unseen. Indeed, the very government documents that support their subsistence may facilitate their subjugation to local strongmen and agribusiness firms. These circumstances are part of the impetus of the protest-camp mobilizations.

Given the critical role played by documents, it is not surprising to see current efforts by the state to confer more documents, more widely, to Indigenous people. For example, in June 2011, the government distributed "civil and Indigenous" documents to more than eleven thousand people on the Bororó and Jaguapirú aldeias on the outskirts of Dourados. Nearly 6,700 people received birth certificates for the first time. At that time, 90 percent of Indigenous Brazilians possessed only an identity card for the Registro Administrativo Nacional do Índio (National Administrative Registration of Indians, or RANI), issued by Fundação Nacional do Índio (National Indian Foundation, or FUNAI).

Such programs are taking place elsewhere around the globe. For example, in 2011, a *New Yorker* article described, "Indian billionaire Nandan Nilekani intended to create a national biometric database ten times larger than the world's next-largest biometric database. The aim is to help reduce the extraordinary economic distances between those who have benefitted from India's boom of the past two decades and those who have not. The effort has been called 'the biggest social project on the planet'" (Parker 2011).

In Mato Grosso do Sul, the identification-document event took place as part of the "Programa Cidadania, Direito de Todos" (Citizenship: everyone's right program) of the Conselho Nacional de Justiça (National

Justice Council, CNJ), in partnership with another program. The Comitê Estadual Para Erradicação do Sub-Registro Civil de Nascimento e Ampliação ao Acesso à Documentação Basica (State Committee for Broad Access to Basic Documents and the Elimination of the Under Registration of Birth Certificates, or CEESRAD-MS) offers civil documents like birth certificates, identity cards, and documents required for commercial and financial transactions (Souza 2011).[5] The government also launched public-awareness campaigns to draw television and newspaper attention to registration drives. Typical coverage shows photographs and videos of lines of Indigenous people at tables signing up for their documents and contractors from notarial agencies explaining to Indigenous people the details and importance of government documents.

According to the CNJ, the program aims to grant thousands of Brazilian citizens access to fundamental rights like health care, education, and inclusion in the labor market (Bandeira 2011). In 2011 Daniel Issler, project coordinator of the program, publicly announced, "These documents will permit the Indigenous people to study and work, and enable them to receive benefits like the family welfare, pensions, and social security. Without these indispensable documents, the Indians who live in urban regions are pushed into the informal labor market. Both the birth certificate and the work document will register their ethnicity and name of their village, a form of preserving Indigenous tradition" (Bandeira 2011).

Yet this proclamation contrasts with the ethnographic account introduced at the start of this article, to which I return now. I arranged transportation to reunite Diego with his documents. He said that it was impossible for him to work for any of the agribusiness firms in the region without his *carteira de trabalho*. He had previously lived on the reservation in Amambai, where he worked for an ethanol distillery cutting sugarcane. I was already planning a trip to Amambai, as a professor friend at the Amambai campus of the State University of Mato Grosso do Sul (Universidade Estadual de Mato Grosso do Sul, UEMS) had asked me to give a guest lecture. So, as quite a few professors at the Amambai campus commute from Dourados, I arranged for Diego and myself to ride with a carpool.

I was under the impression that recovering the documents would be relatively straightforward. However, the morning of our trip, shortly after picking Diego up, it was clear that it would not be so simple. Diego explained that a man who owned a supermarket refused to return the documents to him. So, he thought it best that I pretend to be his American lawyer when we arrived. He explained that if the market owner thought that I was Diego's lawyer from the United States, then he would be intimidated into returning the documents. This surprised me, obviously. He had not previously indicated the utility of such a ruse. However, by this point, it was obvious that his relationship to this merchant was not aboveboard. I worried that he was asking me to play the role of intimidator, with only my gringo accent to protect me, and that I would be vulnerable to a person who, minimally, holds others' documents against their wishes.

Clearly, Diego was attempting a sort of scaling up in power, essentially attempting to leapfrog local bosses by linking his demands to the assortment of international actors who had entered the region in recent decades. Also, Diego did not go to the police or FUNAI to solve his problem, nor did he ask that I pretend to be an American journalist, for example. The conflicts over land, transpiring at the protest camps and sometimes involving violent confrontation with plantation owners, parallel juridical battles and court proceedings sorting through land disputes. So asking for a lawyer in this case, so to speak, and an American one at that, is not merely a coincidence.

The merchant's store was a small market with four or five shallow aisles of convenience and grocery commodities. Despite being located relatively far from the Amambai reservation, most of the clientele were Indigenous. The storeowner was a Brazilian branco. He had several colleagues who looked on attentively, some of them keeping a slight distance, lingering. One of these associates was aggressive, seemingly in a drug-induced hyperintensity, as he approached me and the UEMS professors. He drifted over, arriving uncomfortably close to my face, staring into my eyes. The whole exchange seemed surreal in its very strange mix of people and odd behaviors.

The merchant told Diego that he did not have his documents; they were with a third person. This person was an Indigenous gato ("cat," a colloquial term for a third-party contractor of manual laborers) who had facilitated Diego's connection to the store owner and to the sugarcane plantation and ethanol fuel distillery.[6] Gatos are called such because they are thought to mirror cats' stealthiness, slickness, and quickness. The gato holds the workers' documents while they labor for agribusiness firms. He distributes the workers' pay and mediates their relationship to local merchants. The workers shop at the merchants' stores exclusively, their purchases deducted from their salary and state food allowances (welfare benefits). This merchant proceeded to reveal how and why Diego had really lost the documents, accusing him of stealing from the store. He said that he had it all on videotape. Diego owed him money, he said.

Later, the gato repeated the accusation that Diego also owed him money when we confronted him on the Amambai reservation, located just outside the city, similar to the city-reservation spatial arrangement in Dourados. Diego's ordeal began when he was living on the Amambai reservation before moving to the camp-tekoha. One day the gato showed up at his house asking if he wanted to work. The relationship ended with Diego owing hundreds of Brazilian reais (Brazil's currency) and being accused of stealing from the company merchant, with his work documents held for ransom.

These types of relationships are the norm on the reservations. In their role as mediators with firms or plantations, gatos maintain power. They enforce their authority over the workers by withholding their documents, requiring them to continue to work for them. Not having his documents in his possession and control prohibits the worker from simply moving on to work for a different gato and firm or to shop at different stores. In essence, control over the documents fixes the worker to a specific network of gato, firm, merchant, and mode of exploitation. The relationship is premised on the worker's labor and accumulated debt. The debt accumulates structurally, as the goods available in the store are sold at prices above market rate. The worker's consumption therefore exceeds his salaries and benefits. When this occurs, he is tethered to a gato-firm-merchant network by debt, not contractual remuneration.

From the store we went to the local office of FUNAI, a much smaller building than FUNAI's Dourados office. A feeling of futility permeated the whole encounter. We wanted to inform FUNAI of the situation and to seek its input; after all, it was the state agency with jurisdiction over the reservation. The representative from FUNAI, a low-level functionary, said that he could not assist us at that moment for lack of available agency vehicles. He then proceeded to write down the report on the back of a random, used piece of scrap paper on his desk. He said that someone would follow up with the issue in the coming week, which no one did. It was curious to me how anyone could follow up since the functionary did not write down a telephone number or any contact information for Diego.

Years later, while perusing a newspaper archive, I discovered that that FUNAI office had been subject to controversy as recently as a few years before my visit there. An October 6, 2005, article in the *Correio do Estado* (a newspaper in the state capital Campo Grande) reported a protest staged by Guaraní people outside of the Amambai FUNAI office. Guaraní overtook the building on September 22, 2005, demanding the firing of the then regional administrator of FUNAI, William Rodrigues. The protestors demanded that Dilson Duarte Riquelme, the president of the Association of Indigenous Kaiowá-Guaraní Captains of Mato Grosso do Sul, be named as the new regional administrator. They accused the sitting FUNAI administrator of trafficking in drugs, firearms, and alcohol on the Amambai reservation.

On the day of our quest to recover Diego's documents, we were left to wonder where the state was in all of this. Presumably Diego, the professors, and I were trying to rectify a violation of the law, of Diego's rights. I was told repeatedly, including by various members of state agencies, that Diego's problem was a common occurrence. In that they describe Diego's predicament as commonplace, I wondered how this had become an open norm.

### Law Arrives in the Hinterlands?

One afternoon in 2008, during a conversation with an anthropologist who worked for a federal law enforcement agency, he explained to me that Mato Grosso do Sul has long been famous for its lawlessness. That reputation dates back to its origins as part of the state of Mato Grosso. "In the North [of the state], there is a region that is named from one of your [American] cowboy westerns" he laughed. "You know, from the Wild West." He described Sonora, a region far in the hinterland, a no-man's-land for outlaws. The anthropologist explained that the mayor named that region of southern Mato Grosso Sonora because it reminded him of the lawless Wild West depicted by Hollywood. At the time, Sonora's location near the Pantanal, along the present-day border between Mato Grosso and Mato Grosso do Sul, was remote from any populous settlements. Its equidistance from Cuiabá (the capital of the state of Mato Grosso) and Campo Grande (later state capital of Mato Grosso do Sul) made it exemplary of the larger region's remoteness from the reach of the law. My colleague referenced a sentiment that I heard often in the central-west region from people spanning a variety of backgrounds and sectors: Mato Grosso do Sul was a state without law. There, it was said, problems are resolved with bullets.

However, many have said that things are better now than they had ever been. The arrival of more federal agencies was a major factor in this. An office of the Ministerio Publico Federal (federal attorney general) arrived in Dourados in the late 1990s.[7] Likewise, Dourados, received a regional FUNAI office around the same time. Previously, these agencies' regional jurisdictions were overseen out of Campo Grande and Amambai, respectively. Undoubtedly, the degree of political violence—exemplified by land disputes—calls for a greater federal presence. The scores of murders and kidnappings related to Indigenous land protests had garnered negative attention from international organizations, including the United Nations (UN Human Rights Council 2009) and World Bank (2011). In August 2010 President Luiz Ignacio Lula de Silva (a.k.a. just "Lula") visited the region and took photographs with Indigenous leaders to show support.

The early 2011 trial of the suspected murderers of Guaraní leader Marcos Veron sparked renewed hopes of justice. For example, "Por fim a lei chega ao MS (Finally, the law arrives in Mato Grosso do Sul)," wrote a university student on a Facebook status update on the opening day of the trial. Although three men were convicted of kidnapping and torture in the death of Veron, public reactions were mixed as the jury acquitted the men of both murder and attempted homicide. While local news coverage in the state lamented the ruling as unfair to the defendants, advocates of the Indigenous land movement decried the lack of murder convictions (Heck 2011). The effects of the precedent remain unclear, however, because additional kidnappings and a murder recurred in November 2011 near Amambai. A local newspaper headline concerning the latter heinous acts depicted typical popular sentiment among nonactivists: "After Killing, Town Reacts as Though Nothing Happened" (Maciulevicius 2011).[8] Still, the president of the Organization for Brazilian Lawyers (Organização de Avogados Brasileiros) threatened to take the case to the Organization of American States (OAS) on the grounds that there could not be a just investigation by local law enforcement (MS Noticias 2011). A federal intervention then began.

The expansion of the reach of the state and the enlistment of more people for government documents to ensure access to the rights of citizenship would seem to fit into this narrative of law arriving in Mato Grosso do Sul. However, the story of my personal pursuit to assist Diego recover such documents complicates this narrative.

Mato Grosso do Sul has taken part in larger trends in Brazil. Over the course of the twentieth century, Brazil's population dramatically shifted from roughly 80 percent agrarian to 80 percent urban.[9] In Mato Grosso do Sul, I would characterize the reorganization of land occupation and use in the state as taking place over three phases during the history of the twentieth century. In the first phase, the federal government gave away monopoly land concessions, for example an *erva mate* concession to the company Matte Larangeira. Those concessionaires coexisted with Indigenous people already in place in the region, missionaries, and in-migrating small holder "pioneers," for example. That period gave way to the mid-twentieth-century influx of cattle ranchers and plantation owners from the states of São Paulo and Rio Grande do Sul. Additionally, assorted colonists from these states and the Northeast arrived with the federal government's Westward March colonization program. This second phase lasted until the 1970s, when a third form of land occupation and use came to the fore: corporate colonization. This third phase more heavily involves the influx of international finance capital toward using machinery, pesticides, and genetically modified seeds. Examples include investments in plantations that were previously owned and operated solely by Brazilian families and outright land purchases for agro-industrial installations, particularly for sugarcane-ethanol production.[10]

Over the course of this history, some rural inhabitants remained dispersed throughout the region. In the latter half of the twentieth century, the more complete enclosure of lands into the hands of private plantation owners and corporations began. In the aforementioned second phase of economic production, harmony sometimes existed between fazendeiros and others residing in rural areas. The large landholder might allow a family to live on a parcel of land in exchange for clearing forests and providing primary labor to set up the plantation. Such families raised their own food and sold any surplus for money. Over time, after they cleared the land and established a portion of the plantation, the fazendeiro could displace them to another parcel of his land to repeat the process. In many cases, fazendeiros clashed with rural small land holders. Fazendeiros won such fights violently, juridically, or both. Fazendeiros expanded or maintained their holdings with the means available to them by attempting to empty areas.

Guillen (1999) presents the history of land politics in the region of Mato Grosso do Sul as far from harmonious. She disputes the idea that the land in the southern region of Matos Grosso was mostly empty and unpopulated during the period of the late 1880s and first half of the twentieth century. Colonization by Brazilians featured land contests between Guaraní *changa-y (remunerated labor)*, gauchos (non-Indian settlers from the southern region of Brazil), and concessionaires like the Matte Larangeira company. While Matte Larangeira's private security forces clashed with *posseiros* (land occupiers), Guaraní changa-y resisted the company through selling contraband erva mate in Paraguay and other forms of banditry. Matte Larangeira also fought land rivals in court and used its considerable influence with state politicians to maintain its monopoly on land.

As Guillen presents it, this battle over land was fierce, with shifting sets of alliances among local elites and members of the federal government. The concessionaire maintained close ties with local oligarchic families, whose power derived from wealth accumulated through land grants during the colonial days or after the war with Paraguay, and later from commercial interests. Frank (2001) points out that such oligarchies maintained internal rivalries that sometimes culminated in violence and assassinations.[11]

Regarding the second phase's transformation of the federal state by the Getúlio Vargas government (called *Estado Novo* or new state), Frank (2001, 71) describes that political power in Mato Grosso during this period lay in the hands of "transitional oligarchies." Those oligarchs resembled the types of blood-letting, ruthless, *coroneis* (local political bosses called colonels) depicted in the literature (Leal 1977). They depended on the state for wealth and authority. However, with the end of the old republic and the rise of Vargas, there was a shift away from older local *coronel* political violence and assassinations toward control over state apparatus by bureaucrats. The intervention of federal forces with the railroads of Ferro Noroeste, constructed in the 1920s, shifted more population and political power to the south of Matos Grosso (Agostinho 2009a), later Mato Grosso do Sul. The tracks ran through Campo Grande and Corumbá. Along this route, the railroad line spurred the formation of plantations and population centers and led to an increase in trade in regional commodities to extended networks.[12] These transformations to the economic organization contributed to the already existing separatism of the southern part of the state (previously in place due to tensions over the Matte Larangeira concession). Federal intervention with the designation of Ponta Porã as a federal protectorate zone (in 1943) and the launch of the Colônia Agrícola Nacional de Dourados (in 1943) furthered these trends.

Maybury-Lewis (1994) argues that as the struggle for land between elites and rural inhabitants unfolded during this period, a tacit agreement existed between the Estado Novo government and landed elites. Rural and urban elites coalesced behind Vargas's dictatorship in his support for a vigorous import-substitution program that buttressed their production of traditional agricultural products, which would be used by the state to finance such a program. In exchange for this support, the Estado Novo prohibited legal recognition of rural labor unions. Despite this, peasant organizers like Francisco Julião in the Northeast of Brazil created the category of the liga (a mutual-aid society subject to the civil code). Registering ligas gave "legal recognition to labor organizations that were not formally corporatist sindicatos" (Maybury-Lewis 1994, 6). Similarly, the Brazilian Communist Party organized networks of associations in Rio de Janeiro, São Paulo, and southern Bahia, many of which were involved in armed struggles with elite interests over land. Maybury-Lewis (1994, 7) notes that rural dwellers "had violent disputes with fazendeiros, public and private companies and real estate concerns all over rural Brazil, but particularly in central western states," such as Mato Grosso.

Changes after Vargas had a profound impact on relations between state and society relative to the land struggle. President João Goulart passed the Rural Worker Statute in 1963 to divert rural discontent and the growing influence of the Brazilian Communist Party by removing bureaucratic blocks to union recognition, thus incorporating them into the corporatist state. The law guaranteed salaried workers such things as minimum salary, a weekly paid day off, paid vacations, maternity leave, indemnification in case of dismissal, job security after ten years of service, and employer obligation to sign each worker's work documents. The rights won in the Rural Worker Statute of 1963 and later legislation under the military government put in place much of the terms for the relations between state agencies and rural workers as well as creating, perhaps inadvertently, the context for local strongmen (gatos) to exploit these relations.

During the military dictatorship, two initiatives played an important role in promoting the growth of the "rural union apparatus and, to a lesser extent (and of course indirectly), the development of progressive labor politics" (Pereira 1997, 39). The initiatives were part of the military regime's new rural social policy that it implemented between 1967 and 1971 in which the government offered health care, disability, and retirement benefits to rural workers for the first time. It offered those that founded and managed rural labor unions the chance to control the distribution of government resources allotted for providing the afore-mentioned benefits.[13] Yet the program had significant deficiencies. The National Institute of Social Welfare (INPS), which typically administered health benefits, was mostly located in urban areas distant from rural workers. According to Maybury-Lewis, moreover, many rural work-ers had difficulty accessing the benefits because they lacked an official, employer-signed *carteira de trabalho assinada* (signed work document).[14] Welfare politics arguably directed the unions' energies toward admin-istering health programs and away from combating "the political and economic circumstances of developmentalism that was marginalizing various categories of rural workers" (Pereira 1997, 42).

Still, the shift to state-incorporated rural patronage politics does not account for the increased precariousness in the countryside, with greater land concentration in the hands of plantation owners. Instead, as I stated at the beginning of this chapter, one must explain the exploitation and alienation that takes place in the control of the movement and labor of rural workers, which sometimes plays out through the very work documents and union politics designed to ensure their welfare.[15]

The aforementioned push to expand distribution of government work and identification documents to Indigenous workers in the state exemplifies the expansion of the federal government. Much as in earlier variations of the state governance, though, the Workers' Party's governments of Lula and later Dilma Rousseff likewise integrated such relations into the expansion of agro-industrial production and land concentration. This, despite best intentions, along with its accompanying agribusiness exploitation and marginalization, included policies maintaining the priority of increased agro-industrial productivity, safeguarding of land speculation, and upward pressure on land values.

As Diego's story shows, networks of local strongmen, merchants, and employers at agribusiness firms utilize the existing system of state-issued documents to control a supply of laborers, in addition to the flow of their earnings and welfare benefits. The supposed safeguards of the system, the very documents that presumably confer rights and protections by the state, delimit movements and pathways for material survival. Thus, the state continues its central role in mediating relations of land and labor in the region at municipal, state, and federal levels, as well as in the organization of production and exchange. As the history and contemporary setting described in this chapter show, however, this state consists of agencies and actors often at odds with each other, working toward differing ends. Someone like Diego may find himself ensnared by such machinations of governance. Diego's participation in protest camps, an effort to insist upon an alternative outcome, resembles an "insurgent" (Holston 2008) mobilization that seeks to reshape the political and economic order. His protest counters an otherwise business-as-usual form of politics that the government's documents distribution program (CEESRAD-MS) exemplifies through calling for land restitution.

The model of agribusiness expansion and land politics underlying Diego's circumstances, which is an essential part of the agricultural boom, relies on cheap labor and readily available agrarian real estate. Such structural conditions offer scant hope of the type of heroic enforcement of rights and justice promised by the state documents. Such are the perceptions of some land protesters as well, Indian and non-Indian alike.

For example, I recall commentary from Alberto, a non-Indian FAF protest camper, about his thoughts on the prospects of the Instituto Nacional de Colonização e Reforma Agrária (National Institute for Colonization and Land Reform, or INCRA) designating land for members of the FAF camp soon. Alberto asserted,

> There are many hectares available near Ponta Porã. However, INCRA is in crisis, and things are not as easy as they were before. They no longer deliver *cestas basicas* to everyone, whether you're living in the camp or not. You have to actually be present there at the camp to get a *cesta basica* when they are distributed. It wasn't like that before. Also, the politics of the governor and Dilma seem to be against agrarian reform and for increasing production. They want to keep down inflation, specifically gas prices. With the government selling gas in Bolivia for 1 real [$1.30 at the time], but selling it for 3 reais[16] in Brazil, Dilma wants to prioritize dealing with this gas problem. Dilma wants people to be able to buy telephones and televisions. Her priority is this. For this, you have to increase production. The priority is not the small producers, not agrarian reform (May 22, 2011).

The state acts as intermediary between agricultural and agribusiness interests and the shifting assortment of land-reform proponents (social movements, advocate organizations, academics, and international institutions like United Nations). The rhetoric of an empty countryside, so central to agribusiness investment and talk of production expansion, runs up against the contradictory closed frontier of land colonization in the cerrado, where previously displaced people wage battles over land-distribution and land-use practices.

With Lula and Dilma, land-reform rhetoric and land-reform action involved a Janus-faced orientation of the state to agribusiness complexes on one hand and land-reform proponents on the other. Both yielded to the priority of agricultural development in macroeconomic policies to fortify the role of agribusiness production in the country's economy. Support for modernization programs designed to attract international investment in land and influx of capital for agribusiness expansion continued at the time of my research. Although Lula and later Dilma did not engage in the sort of criminalization of land-protest tactics to which Fernando Henrique Cardoso (a predecessor of Lula) took recourse in his second term, the Partido dos Trabalhadores (PT) governments abetted the foot-dragging and delays that haunted the land-demarcation process.

Moreover, the PT government conceived of agrarian reform in terms of monetary compensation to land holders instead of land seizures for redistribution, which could have been a vehicle for historical injustices of displacements of rural inhabitants. Market-led reform failed to fully resolve the agrarian issue that protests camps of groups like the MST, Guaraní, FAF, and others pressed. For these protestors, land reform was not fully taken up anew in the PT governments despite promises made during Lula's initial campaigns for the presidency.

During my fieldwork, demarcation for the activists with whom I worked remained perpetually delayed by the priority of a national capital intensive, conservative modernization. The foreign reserves and revenues generated by the agribusiness sector ironically helped to fund the massive welfare programs, like the basic food basket (*cesta basica*), that were among the hallmarks of the PT governments. These food allotments sought to address the problems of starvation and immiseration that were outcomes of rural displacement and landlessness. Agribusiness-generated reserves and revenues likewise helped to fund major infrastructure projects, like hydroelectric dams and stadia for global spectacles such as the Olympics and World Cup, which took place in Brazil in 2016 and 2018, respectively.

### Racial Tethers and the Contradictions of Citizenship

When I say that Diego's work documents were racial tethers, reified handles that facilitated control over Diego by gatos, I speak about the ethnoracial subjugation of Indian manual labor. These are not the terms people use to speak of race and racism; instead, it is commonplace to put forth notions of racial democracy. In this formulation, an open antipathy for Indians and Black people coexists with an ideology of primordial mixture with Indians and Afro-descendant people, who, along with Europeans, constitute the so-called three races foundational to the Brazilian nation. Such mythology negates awareness of anti-Indian and anti-Black sentiments, even though such feelings are openly expressed. This is a local variation of what Costa Vargas (2004) describes as an essential feature of Brazilian racial and national ideology: the hyperconsciousness of race and its negation.

Brazil's version of racial ideology famously operates through a combination of colorism and professed color blindness, though one that nevertheless presupposes racial binaries and hierarchies. Costa Vargas (2004, 449) writes, "There would be no color multiplicity if it were not for the awareness of the polarities of the races that generated them. . . . An underlying color spectrum is a clear understanding of a white/non-white binary system that determines social privileges based on race." I would add that such binaries further include those of Indian and non-Indian, though non-Indian–branco Douradenses typically deny the existence of such binaries and hierarchies. Such are the workings of a racial ideology in which color blindness coexists with open disdain and anti-Indigenous violence with practical impunity.[17]

Garfield (2001, 36–37) describes that early-twentieth-century regimes of racial ideology sought national unity through the sublimation of ethnoracial difference via miscegenation and depicted Indians as the quintessential and original Brazilians. The state conducted acculturation policies to "civilize" the Indians, who were supposedly in a primitive state of development. At least in law, such policies have supposedly given way to a multiculturalist embrace of difference. However, prior acculturationist justifications for demarcated exceptional spaces of nature preserves and reservations for nature-bound Indians continue to underlie public discourses that pit land demarcation against national development and so-called progress. Recall that agribusiness land-occupation and land-use practices go unmarked as branco–non-Indian.

Guzmàn (2013) argues that under prior eras' acculturationist policies, Indians were considered to be moving away from Indian-ness toward whiteness, enacted by stripping away Indian culture. Under contemporary multiculturalism, she avers, state agencies pursue policies aimed at inclusion and redress of this history. My sense is that this includes attending to prior displacements of Indian people through designations of still merely exceptional spaces, such as reservations, which are state administered. However, such recognition does not and cannot fully extend to other landed property due to the imperatives of capital accumulation and national progress, which are necessarily non-Indian–branco, though unmarked as such. Ethnic land titling provides exceptions to the rule of the logic of landholding, where even those pushing for exceptional space in the form of Indigenous reservations and quilombo land claims face a hostile and often violent opposition. What is transpiring in Mato Grosso do Sul—a context of intense land-grabbing and agribusiness development—is an instance of this larger history and context of a racial ideology that finds its most crystallized expression in land.

In Mato Grosso do Sul, protests take place not in terms of labor rights but in terms of land (*terra*).[18] We could view their retaking of land—called *retomadas*, a legal distinction for Indigenous versus non-Indigenous forms of land-protest camps like those of the MST—as nevertheless very much attuned to the entwined histories of colonial dispossession and labor exploitation as described. In Diego's case, we see the importance of ongoing attention to reconfigurations of labor, particularly its ethnoracialization.

Amid all this, entrenched ethnoracial hierarchies reproduced through local histories and ongoing practices of displacement and exploitation persist. This, of course, is the problem that Indigenous land activists are at pains to resolve. By retaking plantations, protesters at once rebuke the failure to enforce their rights to Indigenous land titling and draw our attention to a longer history of colonial displacement.

When I say that Diego's case highlights how Indigenous workers are "overseen," I refer to how neocolonial forms of ethnoracial subjugation in this part of the world are so brazen and mundane as to garner little attention as anything outside the norm. The series of manipulations of Diego as described, though commonplace, occur at odds with the aims of document-distribution programs, though they operate in plain sight. Racial markings of Indigenous people, and their concomitant logics, play out in practices of obscuring ethnoracial exploitation amid the hypervigilance of ethnoracialized labor.

I recall a visit to my neighborhood grocery store shortly after arriving in Dourados for fieldwork in 2011. In the middle of the city, a small truck sat parked in front of the supermarket. In the store, a white man stood by the checkout counter with a clipboard tracking the purchases of a line of Indigenous people checking out. The Indigenous shoppers filed onto the truck after making their purchases. The store was running a similar operation to that encountered at the market in Amambai with Diego. The gato-merchant-agribusiness network of Indigenous exploitation in Dourados is not restricted to the reservation itself or to a single neighborhood in the city.

Racial ideology explains how such ethnographic moments are possible. Through racial ideology, Indigenous workers' condition of being controlled by local bosses goes unseen by the larger society and state. Such oversights are central motifs to the workings of agribusiness capital. Famously, part of the dynamism of capital is how it operates through older forms of hierarchy, uniquely and differently insinuated within and across locales.

The land conflict between protesters like Diego and agribusiness interests brings into concrete confrontation the admittedly abstract dialectics that I have been exploring regarding seeing (i.e., epistemology, or understanding or knowing) and ethnoracialized being (ontology).[19] Diego's case underscores a dialectic of the unseen and overseen internal to the workings of race and capital. We see the difficulties imposed on Indigenous workers' mobility and their ability to materially survive as they are ethnoracially subjected to hypersurveillance by the local strongman. Indigenous workers are overseen and unseen.[20]

Here I am engaged in a deliberate play on words between perceiving and the connotative references to conditions of slavery. The conditions of being overseen and the role of the overseer in the context of Brazilian plantation economies conjures a strange feeling of déjà vu. After all, there is something familiar about coerced Indigenous labor carried over from colonialism and challenged via protests, underscoring land struggle as a decolonial practice. Again, Indigenous workers draw our attention to who exactly is occupying whom given the larger colonial history. In Diego's case, we see how this colonial past of racialized subjugation is not past and how it comes into being again in this moment—the same, but different.

The state actors involved in programs like CEESRAD-MS, seemingly well meaning, are aware of the abuses yet are convinced that doubling down on document dispersal will facilitate the realization of the protections of the law. It is a strange myopia—an almost irrational optimism through which the structures of labor exploitation continue unabated. And yet the prevailing model of agribusiness expansion and land politics relies on access to cheap labor and the readily available agrarian real estate underlying Diego's circumstances. Such structural conditions offer scant hope of the type of heroic enforcement of rights and justice promised by the state documents.

In the abstractions of land and labor configured in agribusiness, Indigenous workers circulate, but only within certain prefigured circuits. They are free to go, but only insofar as the preexisting networks of intermediaries extend. This echoes long-standing historical modes of labor exploitation and neocolonial reworkings of settler-colonial racial hierarchies. Networks of local strongmen, merchants, and employers at agribusiness firms utilize the existing system of state-issued documents to control a supply of laborers as well as the flow of their earnings and welfare benefits. The supposed safeguards of the system, the very documents that presumably confer rights and protections by the state, delimit movements and pathways for material survival. Thus, Diego's participation in land protests amounts to something like an "insurgent" mobilization (Holston 2008) to counter the otherwise business-as-usual form of politics of the government's documents-distribution program (CEESRAD-MS).[21]

As the aforementioned history of the region makes plain, the movement for land is not a product of a shift from freedom to bondage, nor even toward a greater degree of bondage, for rural workers bound to gato networks. Rather, it is a reconfiguration of forms of subjugation in relations of land and labor in the region that have a much longer history. State agencies attempt to more widely issue documents to improve their capacity as guarantors of rights. They claim these documents make people more visible, enabling the state to safeguard supposed universal rights of citizenship. However, Diego's story shows how this purported visibility nevertheless facilitates some rural workers' manipulation by shadow actors and extralegal networks of power. Although Diego chose to initially join the gato as a worker, his choice was delimited by the structural conditions in which the gatos operate and in which the state-issued work documents play a crucial role. The influx of agribusiness interests and land purchases from increasingly remote actors (e.g., financial investors, real estate speculators, and insurance agents) relies on such local networks of labor contractors for profitability. Contrary to state programs alleging the invisibility of Indigenous people as culpable for their conditions of exploitation, the organization of agricultural production and exchange in Mato Grosso do Sul takes place through widely known exploitative networks. In this context, programs for greater distribution of state identification documents seem hardly sufficient to achieve their stated aims.

Some Indigenous protestors in the camp mobilizations, like Diego, imagine land as a means to greater security in multiple senses of the term: food security, avoidance of high rates of violent crime on the reservation, respite from attacks by plantation owners, and escape from the constraints on movements imposed by gatos. Additionally, land reclamations are important for cosmogonic relations to and through the landscapes in areas from which they were displaced, which I discuss in more detail in chapter 6 and elsewhere (Sullivan 2019).

Land is a counterpoint to state-issued documents. The inaction and seeming lack of political will by state agencies for the enforcement of labor and land rights arises from sets of constraints that elude accountability. For example, when discussing the process of land-reform and labor-rights enforcement, none of my informants understood the legal processes or means of recourse available to them. They spoke of the opaqueness of the bureaucratic functioning of the state. None of the members of the camps-tekohas, nor any of the state agents with whom I spoke, moreover, expressed faith in the eventual enforcement of such rights. Relations between networks of gatos-merchants-firms are ignored by local powerful figures and everyday townspeople alike. The mix of apathy and paralysis by these social actors makes the mobilizations of the protest campers that much more remarkable. Still, protest camps, like the gato-merchant-firm networks, are viewed in seemingly contradictory ways, as both exceptional *and* routine. The camps have been around for some time, but few people express any sense of an endpoint to solving the agrarian question. Yet, the camps are a means of insisting on land restitution as a form of insurgency that signals a break from the all-too-normal violation of rights.

In this chapter we have seen the conflicting trajectories and perceptions of the role of the state (at federal and local levels) in the transformed

**Fig 5.** Photograph of roadside sign reading "Indigenous Population" one kilometer away. Photograph by Lashandra Sullivan.

relations of land to labor in rural Brazil. Some state agencies put forth earnest efforts to improve the safeguarding of the rights and well-being of those displaced by rural development in Mato Grosso do Sul's countryside. However, these efforts butt against agribusiness interests, actors, and organizations with greater material well-being and political power. Diego's story shows the convergence of contests for land occupation and those seeking gains as rural workers. His story, and the shared predicaments of many Guaraní workers, challenge triumphalist historical narratives of a linear arc of improvement in state governance.

Diego has lived without roots, a legacy of colonial displacement. Diego's life has been marked by a decided lack of fixity; he has wandered to more than a few locations to live and work. His story is quite common among the rural laborers in the region. Floating labor has been a fixture in rural Brazil with the mass displacement of rural people, both Indigenous and non-Indigenous, in the last century. Diego's participation in the camp is to lay claim to a particular parcel of land, to securely remain in the place from which he was so ruthlessly displaced.

# The Protest Camp as a Political Form                                      **3**

Protest campers revendicate rural land and reclaim the countryside as a site of dwelling. They do so while carrying out relations to and through the landscape that contradict developmentalist discourses that view rural areas as empty and displaced rural residents as eminently disposable. This is the case despite earnest political rhetoric to the contrary, as exemplified in former President Dilma Rousseff's speech during a visit to a dairy cooperative of the Landless Workers Movement (MST) in Paraná in February 2013. Dilma proclaimed, "Nós queremos criar uma classe média no campo, uma classe média de pequenos produtores, uma classe média de cooperativados" (We want to create a middle class in the countryside, a middle class of small producers, a middle class of cooperatives) (Reuters 2013). It is important that, in this gesture, the state directed 115 billion reiais to large producers in its 2012–13 agricultural plan and only 18 billion reiais to small producers (Valor 2013). Land redistribution remains perpetually intractable despite, as geographer Wendy Wolford (2010, 211) points out, a relative consensus emerging in the 1990s regarding the need for land reform.

Although depictions of rural areas as empty hinterlands are not without precedent, this is of a different order than previous regimes of emptiness in settler colonial history. For example, earlier forms of colonialism routinely moved residents into perceived empty areas to reproduce a way of life enacted in already-colonized areas. Multiple programs existed to move rural inhabitants westward from the eastern littoral of Brazil. Among these programs was President Getúlio Vargas's Marcha Para Oeste (Westward March) colonization program for the central-west and Amazon. Hecht and Cockburn (1989, 57) describe how such schemes "echoed earlier imperial compulsions" that led to the subsequent assertion of sovereignty over vast forest tracts.

Since the 1970s agro-industry in Brazil expanded into areas previously unavailable for mechanized production due to the hilliness of the terrain or inaccessible due to the lack of connections to central transportation networks. Multiple scales of international capital inflows facilitated this farther reach. For example, in 2010 the World Bank provided the state of Mato Grosso do Sul with a loan of $200 million to expand and improve the state's rural roadways for agricultural development. Significantly, the study for the loan described the countryside as relatively devoid of inhabitants (World Bank 2010).

Such discourses and practices produce and reproduce the countryside as de facto empty through the effects of increasing land value (through speculation) and expanding capital-intensive methods (e.g., use of heavy machinery), which displace small land holders. They render small holders (who have less capital) unable to compete and thus make it impossible for them to maintain their holdings. Of course, these outcomes directly result from state policies that often work at odds with programs designed to support smallholders or attend to their concerns and demands.

The displacement of formerly rural people onto Indigenous reservations and cities, in addition to subsequently channeling them back to the countryside as agricultural workers, recasts them as labor. As a result, the circular movement from rural to urban areas creates transience for these individuals, even as their residence on reservations and in urban peripheries becomes tenuous under development pressures similar to those in the countryside.[1]

Protest camping as both a strategy and tactic makes sense because of the transient nature of settlement prefigured for rural workers in urban peripheries and in reservations in Dourados. Such transience is a feature of the patterns of resettlement, a hallmark of conservative modernization and development in Brazil.[2] A camp, in its impermanence, juxtaposes contemporary marginality and tenuous settlement. As the precariousness of urban settlements makes clear, permanence itself is both contingent and liminal, depending on (and at the mercy of) the larger forces that initiated prior unmooring from the countryside. Thus, the activists' camps are both an outcome of and response to the terms of what Lefebvre ([1974] 1991) calls the production of space.

The camps disrupt space and rupture the relation between city and country, which is reconfigured by the historical political and economic transformations previously described. In so doing, the camps call into question a Brazilian political model that, on one hand, favors liberal, capital-growth-driven policies that maintain unequal accumulation for elites and, on the other hand, under the Partido dos Trabalhadores (in power from 2003 to 2016), provided welfare-state redistribution with expanded proletarianization at the bottom.

In their confrontation with the violence of state and extralegal private security forces, land protesters take part in a sort of life-or-death political theater.[3] They operate within a form of protest that acknowledges the state's authority (i.e., appeals for state demarcation), while simultaneously offending the viability of the economic and political model that the state maintains. However, more than a mere instance of bottom-up resistance, the camps are a product of larger scales of national and international networks of actors that compose the conservative modernization of Brazil begun by the dictatorship (in power from 1964 to 1984) and continued under subsequent liberal democratic governments. The camps both reproduce and challenge narratives of citizenship and national belonging by questioning the terms for the presumed post-authoritarian social contract.

Importantly, the Guaraní-led protest camps that I discuss in this book both appear to breach politics-as-usual and conform to a form of politics in which "insurgency" operates within the frame for mainstream political action (Holston 2008). They roundly criticize the state and call for its attention to the injustices of their historical dislocations. The protest camps rely on the support of state welfare programs and assistance, as well as nongovernmental organizations (NGOs) and missionary groups, like Conselho Indigenista Missionário (Indigenist Missionary Council, or CIMI), that advocate for Indigenous people.

There is a mismatch, though, between the historical transformations I am describing and the terms through which non-Indian–branco people in Mato Grosso do Sul make sense of them. As I observed daily life in Dourados, sul-matogrossenses rely on forms of nostalgia through which people explain the past and envision ways forward. Ironically, the axiom about Brazil as "um pais do futuro" and Dourados as a frontier (edge of the future) constantly referencing the past (settler colonial legacies) is the modus operandi. And these sentiments are not merely subtly expressed but also brazenly voiced. Many non-Indians in the region view the camps as an offensive, potentially mortal threat to the political and economic order.

Of course, this is not new. Historian Seth Garfield (2004), for example, describes the role of geographers and depictions of western and Amazonian areas as frontier sites for whitening and incorporation into the nation. At the same time, over the course of the nineteenth and twentieth centuries, politicians, scientists, and elites wary of industrialized urbanization looked to frontier regions as sites of both intervention and preservation. As such, the Indigenous people that were the "biocultural primogenitors" of Brazilian-ness resided in these imagined areas of pristine and untouched land, flora, and fauna. And according to a nationalist developmentalist state, these areas and the people inhabiting them were both subjects to be civilized and land to be integrated (Garfield 2004, 159).

Thus, Brazilian myths of progress underpinned Brazil's versions of Occidentalism, as Coronil (1997) describes—that is, a forward trajectory of progress through history understood vis-à-vis the relationship to colonized peoples. In Brazil's case, the colonized are Indians, though settlers further considered them part of larger ethnoracial categories to be incorporated via ideologies of whitening, or *embranquecimento* (Skidmore 1993). The important unique features of Brazilian ethnoracial ideology carry over this imagined onward march through history, still spatialized in terms of center-periphery (center and frontier) within the nation and an international order of nations (e.g., global South versus North). Such is the temporalization of space and spatialization of time ongoing in its Brazilian variation (Coronil 1997).

## The Spatializing State and Protest Camps as Counterpoint

Although I am focusing on Guaraní protest camps and land protestors, I am primarily concerned with the fundamental contradictions around which the land conflicts in Mato Grosso do Sul transpire and the impediments to fulfilling Indigenous rights. Land, in this formulation, retains multiple meanings and effects not reducible to instrumentalist ends of capital accumulation, nor to the triumphalist pride and rhetoric undergirding discourses of Brazilian-ness. In Dourados, understandings of the constitution of the nation—what and who is inside and outside of it and its territorial integrity, history, and future—revolve around land demarcation, land-use practices, and land occupation.

Conservative modernization under the dictatorship entailed both a continuation of and departure from a longer history of mobility in the Brazilian countryside. In the nineteenth century, free laborers and large landholders maintained any number of labor and land-occupancy arrangements, including sharecropping and other forms of tenancy (Forman 1975; Holloway 1980). Additionally, free people in the countryside occupied lands of the frontier. In São Paulo and its western frontier (which formerly included Mato Grosso do Sul), especially, the migration of so-called pioneers into the hinterland allowed the expansion of agricultural (particularly coffee) production.

Changes in land law, land tenure, and land-use practices happened incrementally. The Lei de Terras (Land Law) of 1850 ended the former colonial-era land-grant system by which grantees held swaths of land as given by the king of Portugal. Postindependence governments allowed land occupancy through purchase, effectively instituting a regularized system of strictly private property. Those people already squatting on land could receive a property title if they resided and produced on the land. With respect to land distribution in the early twentieth century, this law proved important for the settlement of the interior of São Paulo and lands west. Between 1890 and 1930 the government offered 40 percent of lands for colonization via auction of public lots, which were in turn resold to small- and medium-scale farmers.

The social primacy given to the concept of the hetero-patriarchal conjugal family featured centrally in what unfolded. In 1946 a new constitution attributed a new function to land, one that would complete the social function of a means for Brazilians to sustain and reproduce their families and thus the nation while simultaneously integrating the nation's frontier regions. However, this pre-1964 era featured a seemingly open-ended hinterland with access to land for transferring the subsistence farming mode of life farther into the Brazilian interior. Post-1964 modernization spelled the closure of the frontier and increased claims and competition over land. Additionally, the technology required for exploitation of the land (such as machines), expanded transportation networks, and communications systems increased the value of the land. This, in turn, intensified competition between small and large landholders.

Communities became more tightly integrated into techniques of production and governance. In the prior era of the subsistence economy, rural communities, which Durham (1973) calls *segments*, lived in relative isolation. According to Durham, it was as if trade and communication between the rural dweller and those outside of the community took place between two different universes, the inner world and the outer world, the *universo caboclo* versus the *universo exterior*. Family units were linked to one another through extended *parentesco* (kinship relations), like marriage, *compadrio* (a system of parenting between the parents and godparents), and *vizinhança* (shared beliefs regarding neighborly obligations). Durham describes these as networks of interdependency hierarchically structured according to seniority, political power, and access to land. The latter created hierarchies within and across families. These segments depended on the outside world for trade farming supplies and consumer goods, for which they would sell their agricultural surplus through a mediator. Large landholders increasingly played the role of mediator, fomenting debt relations that contributed to the further integration of these communities into the monetized economy (Queiroz 2006).

The post-1964 conservative modernization of the rural economy meant state and private-sector policies that increased the value of lands previously occupied by peasants. State investment included infrastructure like highways and telephone lines into remote areas. Additionally, land speculation surged as the land market became a means to hedge money against the era's famously high inflation. These prices enticed peasants to sell their land when they encountered difficulties in selling their crop surpluses in the newly structured market (Forman 1975). Middlemen who worked as buyers of agricultural products from small landholders changed their preferences to high-volume purchases and preferred to buy in larger quantities to meet consumer demands and maximize value to the rapidly growing cities. This put smaller peasant farmers at a disadvantage in meeting their own consumer needs. As these small holders became further integrated into a consumer-oriented economy, the combination of rising land value and the changes in the middle market for selling goods forced many to choose to sell their land. Absentee owners of peasant-occupied land also reappeared or land investors claimed rights over *posseiro*-occupied lands by buying titles from former absentee owners.[4] In these cases, large land owners sometimes hired privately contracted security agents to remove posseiros through threat or outright violence.

Additionally, fazendeiro manipulation of laws, like the Rural Labor Statute (Estatuto do Trabalho Rural) and the Land Statute (Estatuto da Terra), helped to forcibly displace many peasants through hired muscle. In the favorable political landscape immediately preceding the 1964 coup, lawmakers conceived the statute for the benefit of agricultural laborers and land reform. Following the ousting of President João Goulart, however, the law became an instrument of manipulation to assist in the displacement of posseiros. The Rural Labor Law required a standard for wages and benefits comparable to the gains made by industrial organized labor for permanent agricultural laborers. However, fazendeiros used the loophole of "permanent" workers to hire only temporary laborers through labor contractors and thus avoid the expense of living wages or benefits.

With the manipulation of the law in favor of increasing the flexibility of labor and avoiding the increased costs and responsibilities of permanent, directly contracted laborers, fazendas continue to hire labor gangs through the *empreteiro* middlemen, colloquially called gatos (cats). As explained in chapter 2, the name derives in part from their perceived qualities of being stealthy and loyal to no one in particular (Stolcke 1988). In sum, this context created a system for *volantes* (floating labor), available for maximum exploitation because the workers were poorly educated, landless, and without contracts. These workers were vulnerable in that they were newly installed as residents in cities without the accustomed access to land or its concomitant social networks for subsistence. They had to float from city to country and back, from fazenda to fazenda, forced to take whatever they could get (Conceição d'Incão 1984).

Although many former rural residents relocated to larger cities, like São Paulo, Rio de Janeiro, and Belo Horizonte, others moved to smaller cities that dotted the countryside and continued to work in the agricultural economy. They were in turn transported by truck or bus to work in the fazendas. Although these so-called *cidades-dormitórios*, or bedroom communities, are relatively small, they are still classified officially as urban areas (Falconi da Hora Bernadelli 2006). The aforementioned spatial reordering of the countryside challenges the status of the distinctly rural in Brazil, given the more complex relationship with the surrounding countryside and intimate entanglement of policies and institutions governing these spaces. This complex has led some scholars to refer to the Brazilian countryside as *rurbano* (a portmanteau of rural and urban) when describing this state of entanglement (Graziano da Silva, Del Grossi, and Campanhola 2002, 38).

Much of the literature on these changes in Mato Grosso do Sul treats Indigenous people separately. The Guaranís[5] in the central-west region of Brazil eluded missionization and slave raiders in the colonial era by "hiding in the forests" (Meliá, Grünberg, and Grünberg 1976, 175–77) until late-nineteenth-century legal precedents and settler expansion altered these relations.[6] In this period, the government initially leased the land area as a concession to an erva matte[7] company, Matte Larangeira. Matte Larangeira then lost monopoly control over the exploitation of the region with the early twentieth century influx of fazendeiros for agriculture and animal husbandry. They violently dislocated the Guaranís onto reservations or restricted them to "protected" areas under the direction of the Serviço de Proteção aos Índios (SPI or Indian Protection Service).[8] Displacement sometimes occurred due to missionary encouragement or diminishment of resources resulting from deforestation (Brand 1997, 123–33). Although creeping settler encroachment onto demarcated reservations significantly reduced SPI-protected land from the beginning, displacement reached epochal proportions with the aforementioned Westward March program. The aggressive colonization program under the Vargas government encouraged deforestation for agricultural development and land appropriation for fazendeiros (with exceptions to attract small producers from São Paulo and the Northeast).

Two opposing roles for the state were in play: to somehow ensure forward progress (read, development) of an integrated national territory and to maintain demarcated spaces for continuation of ethnic Indigenous ways of life. The latter are defined as outside of the advances mandated in the former. The idea of national progress, of a forward trajectory through time, despite its fundamental contradictions, messiness, and incoherence in Brazil, nevertheless looms as recurrently celebrated both discursively and in practical activity through forms of land use practices and occupation.

Importantly, social movements for land that seek a return to a prior way of life, as described previously regarding historical forms of family subsistence agriculture or ethnic Indigenous horticulture and foraging, clash with the historical structural reorganization of the countryside (i.e., agribusiness space) that rendered said ways of life no longer possible.[9] The state has mandated implementation of market-led land reform via state agencies like the federal Instituto Nacional de Colonização e Reforma Agrária (INCRA, National Institute for Colonization and Land Reform) for non-Indians and land demarcation studies by FUNAI for Indigenous people. At the same time, the government relies on and encourages hyperdevelopment of agribusiness production via other levers of the state.

Because settler colonial displacements intensified with the advent of agribusiness, people are continuously deracinated and unmoored, so that the effort to survive is part of the impetus for the protest movement. None of this is to say that the protesters are not real Indians. Nor does this detract from the fact of their histories of displacement. Rather, the terms in which they must present their claims—that is, verification of cultural authenticity—do not allow foregrounding of denunciation of settler-imposed dislocations as sufficient basis for land restitution.

The displacements imposed by agribusiness expansions have denied many Indigenous people the material means to enact land-use practices consistent with their distinct modes of territorial emplacement, or *tekoha*, for the Guaraní. While the state looks favorably upon such basis for granting land, this erects a formidable barrier for many of the protest campers, which we should both question and challenge.

## The Protest Camps and Cosmo-Geographies

More than a dozen Indigenous protest camps were in Mato Grosso do Sul at the time of my fieldwork. I conducted fieldwork in three such protest camps, which were led by Guaraní people. In what follows, I use geographer Juliana Bueno Mota's term *camps-tekohas* to refer to the protest camps.[10] It captures how the Guaraní campers continually pursue means to recover ways of dwelling enacted prior to confinement on reservations, which prominently feature cosmogonic relations with the landscape. Guaraní people pursue such reenactments as part of their confrontation with the historical and ongoing legacies with the state. Moreover, I sometimes refer to the camps-tekohas as *aldeias* (villages) out of respect for what the protesters themselves called their communities.

When referencing specific camps-tekohas, I use pseudonyms to maintain anonymity of camps and campers. Thus, I call the different sites where I worked Aldeias A, B, C, and D. At the time of my research, Aldeia D had already gained some degree of state recognition and land restitution. The fifth group with which I worked extensively was a camp run by the non-Indian Federation of Family Agriculture (Federação de Agricultura Familiar, or FAF). The two camps-tekohas with which I worked most intensely, Aldeias A and B, are located within twenty kilometers of each other. Aldeia A is close enough to the city of Dourados that members of the camps-tekohas sometimes take shortcuts through the fazendas sprawled between them and the city limits proper, choosing a more direct route than that offered by roads.

Aldeia A sits across the highway from a sugarcane plantation, the target of its protest. The plantation's history is similar to that of another in the region whose ownership changed hands in 2007. A local fazendeiro sold the land to a subsidiary corporation of Grupo Bertin, a company founded in the 1980s and based in the interior of São Paulo state. The corporation's holdings range from civil infrastructure subsidiaries to hydroelectric plants and biofuel production plants. At the time of my fieldwork, the Ministerio Publico Federal (Federal Attorney General Office) was considering charging the company and its security subcontractor firm, Gaspen, for "attempted genocide" (Glass 2009) for a 2009 attack on a Guaraní protest camp. Security forces burned down the campers' dwellings, attempted to run over the campers, and shot several of them, killing the camp leader. The security firm Gaspen also faces denunciations related to its involvement in the 2004 forced dispersal of Indigenous Guaraní campers at the Fazenda Campo Belo (in the Pôrto Cambira region of Mato Grosso do Sul), the 2005 murder of thirty-nine-year-old Guaraní leader Dorvalino Rocha (in the Antonio João region, an area on the Paraguay border), and the 2007 murder of a seventy-year-old Indigenous woman, Xurete Lopes, during a forced dispersal of an Indigenous camp on the Fazenda Madama in the municipality of Amambai. A large regional player, the sugarcane-ethanol fazenda and firm Usina São Fernando (a Grupo Bertim subsidiary), had numerous trucks and buses that rumble frequently through Dourados and the surrounding area. When this book was written, its company website presented the *usina* (distillery) as a model for regional development in terms of being both environmentally responsible and sustainable, as well as a substantial generator of local jobs.[11]

Several of the aldeias were headed by women. Such leadership took place in a context in which violence against women was commonplace, including happenings that I became privy to during fieldwork. The women's status additionally stands out due to the need for women to assert leadership in overtly political spaces in this social context. Such efforts are exemplified by the occurrence of a women's *aty guasu* (formal political gathering) in the region around the time of my fieldwork. Anthropologist Lauriene Seraguza (2017) notes some of the strategies of navigating gender dynamics in political forums that she observed during her fieldwork. She noted that women's efforts in this regard sometimes included rhetorical strategies like making explicit references to women's decision-making prerogatives regarding sexual partners. In oratory at public forums, for example, such remarks underscored the gendered, and not just ethnoracial, terms of politics in the land struggle and (I add) politics in Brazil writ large.[12]

The composition of Aldeia A changed regularly in terms of its members and built structures. The location moved to different areas along the highway that stretches by the revendicated plantation, in large part due to forced removal similar to the aforementioned expulsion incidents. Outside of a core group of members of the camp-tekoha, the residents may come and go as well. The core group consists of the leader, Carmen, and her three sons. Carmen has two other children and several grandchildren who live in a separate camp, Aldeia C. Aldeia C is peculiar in that its absentee landlords (rumored to be based in São Paulo) had largely tolerated its presence via their on-site property managers (often called *peões* or peons). The campers work for a grass-and-brick-making company that uses the land, although this arrangement was changing as I was finishing fieldwork in the latter part of 2011. The peons' attitude toward the camp had shifted, and their presence was no longer welcome. As a result, one of the leaders of Aldeia C, Carmen's brother, relocated to Aldeia A with his wife and children. That was just as well, because Carmen constantly occupied herself with gaining and keeping members, a necessity to sustain the ongoing well-being (e.g., morale, safety) of the camp. The difficult material conditions in the camp, in addition to the security threats, influenced the constant effort to maintain a sufficient number of protesters.

In comparison, Aldeia B sits at the intersection of a dirt road that bypasses fazendas between it and the city of Dourados. The leader of the camp, a cacique named José, lives full time on the city's reservation. He somewhat regularly commutes to attend to his camp. José's oldest son lives in the camp full time, with his wife and small infant child, in makeshift shacks (*barracos*) distinguished from such in Aldeia A by the building materials. Whereas both camps use such materials as wooden and metal planks, thick black plastic sheets, wooden sticks, and discarded billboard materials, for example, Aldeia B's structures also utilize *sapo*, a long, bushy grass that is dried and commonly associated with precolonial traditional Guaraní-built structures. (See figure 6 for an example of such a structure from another location.)

José's son has a badly mutilated arm that he says was injured by security forces of the fazendeiro that Carmen is protesting. He described to me how they beat him and threatened to kill him on multiple occasions. He further showed me a deep scar on his inner thigh almost a foot in length where, he says, one of the security agents chopped him down with a machete. He pleaded for his life and that of his family to escape. He occupies the camp alone much of the time, though José and around a dozen others stay occasionally to tend to the small crops they maintain on the roadside. The son works for an agro-industrial firm nearby, commuting to and from the aldeia by foot.

Sometimes it was hard for me to catch up with José at the aldeia. Occasionally stopping by, I might find the camp completely devoid of people. Of course, this was no different than when I found no one at home

**Fig 6.** Juxtaposed Guaraní-constructed thatched roof structure in Dourados municipality. Photograph by LaShandra Sullivan.

during unannounced visits to friends in the city. People come and go to and from the camp-tekhoa as they need to work and otherwise attend to matters of life and living. What made these times unusual was that, in my experience, the other aldeias where I worked maintained people on site at all times to safeguard things and to strategically maintain a visible presence. José spent quite a bit of time on the reservation where he, his other children, and his wife have a plot of land that stretches over multiple homes and areas for crops. They had a horse and a buggy (*carroço*) with which they commuted from the reservation to the city and camps. Nearby on the reservation sits a corn fazenda that was owned, José said, by a branco (white man).

A fourth settlement, Aldeia D, was headed by the cacique Rubem. Located the farthest from the city, it was by far the most stable of the communities I studied. The aldeia consisted of nearly fifty people and had attained some degree of state recognition and formal demarcation as Indigenous land.

All of the aldeias that I worked with had their origins in mobilizations out of the Dourados reservation that took place in the 1980s and 1990s, which I discuss in more detail in chapter 5. Many people in the aldeias come from, and circulate between, reservations near the towns of Caraapó and Amambai.

Finally, the FAF camp consisted of a few dozen small shacks that sat parallel to one another on both sides of a stretch of highway outside of Dourados city. These campers, like the Guaranís, also worked primarily as manual laborers in the region's agribusiness firms. However, unlike the Indigenous campers, most FAF campers maintained additional residence part time in the city of Dourados. Most of the FAF shacks in the camp were uninhabited much of the time. New arrivals, furthermore, had to construct their own dwelling, schlepping wooden planks, discarded billboard rubble, and other random construction materials on their shoulders as they carefully walked along the edge of the highway median.

Despite access to multiple functioning water wells, the conditions in the FAF camp, with its location mere feet from the highway and its rudimentary nature, made for difficult living conditions. Moreover, these people have siblings, children, and grandchildren in the city with whom they maintained close relations. Most of their histories were as transplants to the region from the interior of São Paulo, with others coming from Brazil's northeast and southern regions (primarily from Paraná and Rio Grande do Sul). Such migration patterns were consistent with those found in the larger Dourados population (Gressler and Swensson 1988, 130).

It is worth reviewing some of the anthropological literature on so-called traditional Guaraní arrangements of territory given its importance in state mediations of land claims. They partially frame camps-tekohas leaders' efforts to navigate and pursue their claimants and protest activities. Besides meaning "territory" and "the Guaraní way of life," *tekoha* also means "extended family," in conventional usage.[13] In the precolonial arrangement of territory, systematic intermarriage between affinal houses created loosely bounded, endogamous local groupings of longhouses constituted by close kin and affines. The Guaranís lived in large houses (*ogajekutu*) located preferably on the border of forests or in their clearings. The villages were formed by one or several longhouses, constituting the tekoha. Each longhouse was occupied by an extended family, which developed both collectively and individually the economic agricultural activities that held them in one place. The land belonged to the entire village, with each family having its own lot. They observed the limits of neighboring tekohas, which according to Gadelha (1980) generated a stable equilibrium between them. Sometimes relatives would leave to form other longhouses, augmenting the tekoha.

Meliá, Grünberg, and Grünberg (1976) describe the land of the tekoha as a well-defined area whose size and quantity of nuclear families may vary but whose structure and function are always the same. It is headed by both a religious (*tekoharuvixa*) and political (*mboruvixa, yvyraija*) leader and has strong social cohesion. The land of the tekoha is understood as collective property and belongs to all who inhabit it, who are linked by kinship. To each family, there corresponds a parcel of land for usufruct for their own garden and the construction of a house (Schaden 1962). The tekoha is also a site for large religious ceremonies (*avati kyry* and *mitã pepy*) and decisions at the political and formal level (*aty guasu*). It is a divine institution created by the entity Ñande Ru Guasu. The religious authority is always a man, who is generally older and serves as a stand-in for the creator god, Ñane Ramõi Jusu Papa. The religious system elaborates a notion of territory in which the gods have placed people, grouped in tekoha, in their various regions to establish political relations and solidarity with other tekohas.

Meliá counters Hélène Clastres ([1975] 1995) with an emphasis on the "resistance" in Guaraní views of land territory (Meliá 1981, 16). For Meliá, the Guaranís idealize land-territory as an offshoot of their fierce resistance to colonizing missions. The category of "*espacialidad es fundamental para la cultura guaraní, ella asegura la libertad ya la posibilidad de mantener la identidad étnica*" (10).[14] He notes that in missionary texts the *modo de ser* of the Guaranís emphasizes polygamy (12) and ritual dancing. Missionization meant the loss of freedom to practice these traditions, which missionaries focused on eliminating. Meliá stresses ritual dancing as a site of Guaraní self-production. Here, resistance occurred in shamanic communication, for example, where prophecies warned of cataclysm, especially with colonial invasions (16–17). Meliá seems to take Guaraní identity to be self-evident and emphasizes the perception of freedom embodied in the Guaraní modo de ser. For Meliá, recuperation of land entails the recuperation of the freedom envisaged in the way of life of the ancestors. Meliá describes a longing for a way of life that Clastres ([1975] 1995) asserts was itself considered cumbersome within the Guaraní cosmology. He invokes the recurrent saying "sin *ha* no hay *teko*," or "without *ha* (space), there is no *teko* (way of life)" (Meliá 1981, 10).

Brand (1997, 46) analyzes the oral testimonies about the modo de ser of the ancestors as a longing for the lost freedom envisioned as territorial space to practice a past way of life. His informants emphasize the overcrowding on reservations, the diminishing subsistence afforded by family *roças* (cultivated fields), increased reliance on *changa* (remunerated labor), and breakdowns in social relations, particularly the end of traditional male initiation rituals. Brand blames these things for the high rate of suicide among young Guaraní-Kaiowá. For him, it is the need for land beyond the islands of confinement on which their survival, and the survival of their culture, depend.

Ferreira Thomas de Almeida's (2001) critique of developmental policies from the 1980s and 1990s takes up the mantle of cultural preservation of the Guaraní-Kaiowá modo de ser. For Almeida, land was necessary for aspirational social relations. These include the priority of distribution of goods within and between families and the preference for sustenance through the family's roça, or subsistence farming plot, over exchange. He argues that the continuities in the Guaraní-Kaiowá way of life, priority of family, and rejection of an accumulation and surplus demonstrate the held-over Guaraní-Kaiowá culture that belies developmentalist notions of acculturation. Guaraní-Kaiowá culture has persisted despite the changes incurred by the increase of changa in these communities. Ferreira Thomas de Almeida pleads for the return of lands to counter the social ills that have hampered realization of their modo de ser.

My visits to the aldeias would often begin or end (or sometimes both) with the camp-tekoha leader conducting a prayer. Likewise, testimonies regarding belonging to the land and conflicts with fazendeiro were interspersed with references to relations with spirits in the landscapes. Shortly thereafter, a protester exalted parts of the landscape (animals and vegetation) to be reckoned with, relatedness to things that are also relations with those things' spirit owners. These elements of the landscape included "Aguapé, Jagua Ygua, Kai Ygua, Kurusu Amba, Mboi Ygua." The latter he described as a water snake that would bite and cut down (cobra d'agua que vai picar e cortar). All belong and dwell in the Guaraní's *tekoha guasu*.[15] All of these things have spirit masters with whom the Guaraní engage in ongoing social relations, mediated through chanted prayers (*ñembo'e*). In these relations, the invocation of the dwelling of these spirits entails presences who are in emplaced in their territory or tekoha guasu, a site of Guaraní being and belonging. This counters the supposed emptiness of space insisted upon by agribusiness and não-Índio–branco spatial logics and practices.

The protester's invocation of spirit owners was interspersed with commentary and witnessing of the violence incurred from the fazendeiros. For example, on another occasion, a protester testified to me the following:

É sacrifício que estamos passando. . . . Já passamos fome. Queremos muito entrar na nossa terra. Temos muitas crianças quem choram e eu estou lutando. Não têm ninguém. . . . Foi mesmo aqui veio o fazendeiro quem matou e jogou aqui naquele tempo nossos avôs. Ele matou e jogou aqui. . . . Não vamos deixar aqui de graça pro fazendeiro, por que o fazendeiro tem dinheiro. Sim fazendeiro tem bastante dinheiro. Chega bastante dinheiro! Chega pegar dinheiro pela nossa vida. Chega pegar essa canalha. Sou como essa terra. Somos terra. Estamos vivendo sobe a demarcação de terra . . . Eu vou viver junto com meu filho e vou ficar sofrendo como indígena. Kaiowá-Guaraní em Mato Grosso do Sul parece que não tem apoio. . . . Quero só um pedacinho da terra. Essa minha criança tinha 1 ano e agora tem 3 anos e ali [o fazendeiro] matou.

(This is sacrifice that we're going through . . . Already we are starving. We want to be able to go onto our land. We have many children who are crying and we fight on. We don't have anyone . . . It was right here that the fazendeiro came and murdered and threw [poison] onto our grandmother. He killed and threw [poison] down here. We are not going to leave here for the fazendeiro because the fazendeiro has money. Yes, he has a lot of money! But enough with his money! Enough with the assaulting our lives through his money. Enough with hitting us with this vileness. I am like this land. We are this land. We are living for the demarcation of this land. I am going to live together with my child and I will keep suffering as an Indigenous person. Kaiowá-Guaraní in Mato Grosso do Sul seems to have no support. . . . I want only a little bit of land. My child was one-year-old and now has three years, and there [on the land] the fazendeiro murdered.)

—*Interview recorded May 2011*

In our conversations, protesters recurrently spoke plainly about their clearly disadvantageous asymmetrical position with brancos, viewing themselves as subjected to domination.

Though situating their testimonies in this political-economic context, I do not reduce their cosmogonic invocations to political claims-making. Proper comprehension of the Guaraní cosmological traditions entails noting how such attention to ethnic asymmetries is an internal element of the cosmology. Specifically, such accounting occurs via the Guaraní peoples' understandings of the ordering (or attempted ordering) of separate spheres and levels (*yváy*) of a shared cosmos with brancos and não-Índios.

My work with Guaraní protestors accorded with various ethnological treatments of Kaiowá-Guaraní cosmologies (Ferreira Thomas de Almeida 2001, Brand 1997, Chamorro 1995, Mura 2006, Marques Pereira 2004b), which share testimony regarding the cosmological composition of land. The earth is composed of different levels or plateaus called yváy, in which dwell spirits, souls, deities, with whom, among humans, only shamans are able to communicate bidirectionally. The yváy are vertically overlapping and hierarchical. Guaraní shamans use ñembo'e to exercise control in the world through highly esteemed oratory practices that mediate relations with the spirit owners of the worlds' different domains. Mainly from this, they build strategies, determine alliances, and execute actions that facilitate the supply of goods from their different domains, goods that are always under the control of someone (i.e., *donos* or spirit owners). All places, objects, or neutral beings can be accessed, collected, or captured by engaging with donos through acquisition techniques. All practical activity aimed at acquiring objects is subordinated to complementary ñembo'e verbal techniques whose effects are political and delimited by ethnicity.

What geographer Juliana Bueno Mota (2015, 18) calls the "cosmogeographies" of the Guaraní protest camps also contain a critique of ethnoracial subordination and ongoing effects of colonization. The protest camps as a political form underscore their confrontation with both the fazendeiros and the state. The predicament of having to mobilize for land arose from state mediation of rural economic development and its violent displacements. Moreover, the displacements from the reservation arose from state management of reservations, which I will describe in more detail in chapter 5.

### State Relations and the Politics of Protest Camping

We should look askance at the peculiarity of the Brazilian state in this state of affairs. State agencies mediate the city-reservation-countryside relation from which protest camps arise. These agencies play an important role in structuring how spatial categories get mapped out and contested. The federal government has the constitutional mandate of the *tutela* (tutelage) of Indigenous territory, which it executes through the administrative arm of the FUNAI. Indigenous lands are categorized as sites for the preservation of Indigenous ways of life.[16] As such, they are categorically different than cities or rural areas as understood in popular vernacular and codified in law.

It is helpful to understand the state's role in how Guaraní land protests have emerged with a reconfiguration of space. The concept of a spatializing state, as James Ferguson and Akhil Gupta (2002) describe it, facilitates agribusiness practices of production and capital accumulation. Hegemonic practices by state and substate actors at the level of local, national, and international bureaucratic institutions, including police and security forces, make it difficult to discern the boundaries of the state, yet effectively facilitate the reinforcement of power by institutions and actors, both public and private.

My work with the protest camps presented me with two primary interventions: the concern to offer an addendum to cultural preservationist advocacy for Indigenous land reform in Brazil, and an objective to make sense of the spatializing state of the postdictatorship agribusiness era. Protestors invoke earlier ways of life in their struggle for land through camping. Though they do so in line with codified, sanctioned terms for resistance, which ultimately reinforces the logic of that order—namely, displacement and dislocations as a means of resistance, or mobilizing camps to claim land as a means of recapturing a lost way of life. In this way they alert us to a structure of feeling in relations with the landscape (Williams 1975), which refers to how sentiments and understandings of transformations may involve a longing arising from the losses wrought with capitalist enclosures of the countryside. However, protesters revendicate land in terms that are also deeply cultural, indexing spiritual and cosmological relations that are likewise debated and reworked among Guaranís in their critical, multivocal dialogues regarding their culture and cultural difference.[17]

Protest camps disrupt the visual layout of the of the countryside. For those favoring agribusiness hegemony, the protests camps are an eyesore. The camps-tekohas stand out from the otherwise seamless flows of plantations that one views along the highways. Thus, the protests engender violence by the state or third-party security forces and thereby create moments of potential rupture of the social order. Those moments are both routinized (i.e., townspeople react indifferently, or even sympathetically to murders, kidnappings, and torture against land protestors) and a constant preoccupation, as I noted in day-to-day conversations and witnessed in public forums, like those described in chapter 1. As such, and in some contradiction, the protest camps disrupt by insisting on a break from the norm. They thereby create an opening for change by viscerally disturbing the plantation-strewn landscape. They also do so by potentially putting into motion challenges to fazendeiros' land tenure by compelling state recognized demarcation studies.

Anthropologist June Nash (2001) argues that we should view the Indigenous social movements for land as evidence of forms of resistance and expressions of alternative cosmologies. Yet, Indigenous social movements face the impossible task of both articulating alterity and doing so from positions within the very totality of social order for which they are positioned as the alternative. Nash characterized the alternative cosmologies presented by Indigenous social movements in the Americas as a contributive critique of neoliberal capitalism. For Nash, this instantiated Brazilian Darcy Ribeiro's description of Native Americans as "testimonial peoples." Along similar lines, in this book I am interested in the utterances of those testimonies as oriented toward decolonial ends, not merely as evidence of cultural difference and alterity in itself.

Given the particularities of Indigenous land titles in Brazil—in which the *União* (federal government) maintains ownership of the land, with the exclusive rights of use and usufruct granted to the recognized Indigenous group—the Guaraní campers are not so much interested in testimonies toward sovereignty as they are pushing toward a fulfillment of state-promised land rights, their "originary" rights (Kelly 2017). The fulfillment of their originary rights (at least insofar as they are also ethnoracially marked) requires a reckoning with the state's imposition of agribusiness hegemony. Such reckoning must account for its role in the production of agribusiness space, which for decades (if not centuries) has not completely fulfilled the aforementioned rights. Such is the legacy of the 1964 coup, as well as both prior and subsequent moments in the history of protests for agrarian reform in Mato Grosso do Sul, Brazil. Such is also the thorny conundrum and unrelenting continuation of ethnoracial hierarchies, violently imposed and maintained, beget by settler colonial histories and their afterlives, the resolution of which anthropologist João Costa Vargas (2012) refers to as the impossible national project of Brazil.

By reading the Guaraní protest camps as a disruption in space, we can view their strategic invocations of cultural belonging to land and historical (and biographical) removal from the land that they claim as beckoning both further demarcation of Indigenous land and a critical intervention against the domination of agribusiness. Their activism helps us to understand the regional context in which they wage their battles against the ongoing impositions of a settler-colonial-turned-national order of land occupation and land use. Protest camps, arising from the reconfigurations of land and labor induced by the growth of Dourados, demonstrate the logics of movement, circulation, and settlements. Agribusiness settlement overlays prior forms or colonization of land and people, though in ways unique to the decades of financialization and integration with a national politics of development ever reliant upon it, which I will describe in more detail in chapter 4. All of this happens amid and despite efforts at redress of inequalities through land restitution undertaken by the state. Protest camps are efforts at intervention in this regard, beckoning state action to redress and remedy displacements by rearranging the spatial order. It is to a deeper explanation of such arrangements and rearrangements that I turn in the next chapter.

# Agribusiness Rearrangements of Space          **4**

In June 2007 I chatted over lunch with a midlevel manager for a sugarcane plantation in the western region of the state of São Paulo. He informed me about the widespread availability of land for the expansion of sugarcane-based ethanol fuel in Brazil. I had just received a tour of his plantation, complete with a demonstration of the workers' pristine royal blue uniforms, safety equipment, and sparkling portable toilets at the cane-cutting sites. Worker safety and well-being are of the utmost concern, he assured me. At the entrance to the complex, I had taken a photograph of a green, red, and white sign that held a numbered flip board to indicate the count of days, referenced in all capitals: "ESTAMOS TRABALHANDO HÁ ZERO DIAS SEM ACIDENTES DO AFASTAMENTO." Below that line read, "NOSSA META É UM CLIMA DE 'ACIDENTE ZERO.' NO EMPENHO DE CADA UM, A CONQUESTA DE TODOS!" ("We're working zero days without any accidents. Our goal is a climate of zero accidents. Through the efforts of each, the success of us all!")

This chapter is not about the rhetoric of managers and how it contrasts with workers' reality. I am not interested in undermining this manager's testimony, at least not in a sort of exposé of worker exploitation, deplorable conditions, and so on. I would instead like to focus on the manager's rhetorical rendering of rural space in Brazil, which points to the production of a country-city relation that is distinct in the country's history. I refer to this as the production of agribusiness space. I visited workers in several agro-industrial complexes (plantations, distilleries, and other agricultural processing firms). I saw a variety of worker conditions and facilities, some excellent, others less so. Regardless, the people that spend their lives engaged in the most menial labor conditions in plantation work, the manual day laborers, generally lead hard lives with little remuneration and much precariousness.

I focus on recurring narratives of an open or closed frontier of land available for national expansion, improvement, and progress that characterize discussions of the countryside in development narratives. This allows us to query the social production of rural space to account for agribusiness hegemony, whereby *hegemony* refers to that which goes unquestioned and unspoken.[1] Of note are the signs and practices through which people nevertheless go about representing their societies. As such, we cannot take for granted the terms *empty* or *available* land as accurate or unproblematic descriptions. Rather, these terms carry meanings that arise from and produce the political and economic order of a given time and place.

In this chapter, I make two primary points. The first regards the concept of agribusiness space, which in Mato Grosso do Sul is a unique historical configuration. Reorganization of land-use practices, land ownership, and land tenure in the state have produced conditions of permanent transience for formerly rural people and, subsequently, protest camping as a logic and tactic for those pursuing land reform. Second, I am concerned with what Ferguson and Gupta (2002) deem "spatializing states," or the role of the state in the coming into being of the spatial order—in this case, the city-countryside-reservation distinctions in which land politics play out in Mato Grosso do Sul. Agribusiness rearrangements of space operate through categories of race and ethnicity while contending with and conjuring reconfigurations of land and labor laws, racial ideologies, and land-use practices.

To better lay out what I mean by agribusiness space in Dourados, I begin by describing the city, countryside, reservation, and Guaraní-led protest camps where I conducted fieldwork. I provide a brief, specific history of Dourados, and the protest camps at the heart of this book. I then provide a succinct history of the changes in the spatial rearrangements of the countryside as it concerns the rise of agribusiness in the region. Theorizing space as provided by James Ferguson and Akhil Gupta's concept of a "spatializing state" helps us to make sense of the rise of protest camps and the terms in which state and nonstate actors meet in the political battles over land, both between Indians and non-Indians, as well as between advocates for land reform.

### City-Reservation-Camps

The anthropology of space enables us to understand how the state mediates an imposed configuration of space as abstract and empty. We can see, as the previous chapter showed, that imagination of space as empty and available conflicts with the realities of how areas are very much inhabited, and densely so, by those ethnoracially marked as Indian, which erases their presence in the countryside. So, when one travels around the Dourados region, one experiences a configuration of space organized not only by ethnicity, race, and class but also in line with practices of production and exchange both newly emergent and reliant on longer histories of ethnoracial spatial categories.

In this section, I revisit the stark contrast between the production of space as abstractly empty with which I began this chapter and the density and texture of space as lived in the greater Dourados region.

### The City

Dourados is a city of roughly 225,000 people that has grown rapidly in the past few decades, particularly since the 1970s. In my fieldwork experience, no one explicitly called the city a space for non-Indians–brancos.[2] They did not have to; white places are unmarked. Only the presence in these places of Indians engenders marking and verbal remarking. Physical markers designating Indigenous space from city space would be superfluous and ridiculous. One knows that he or she is on the reservation, or rather approaching it, merely by looking around, like being in a different neighborhood of a sharply segregated urban area in the United States. The ethno-racial markers will have changed.

As a Black person, marked recurrently as *negra* (Black woman), I encountered a strange mix of unsolicited stares and comments from the friendly, provincial townspeople of Dourados. Randomly and regularly, I heard comments about the lack of Black people in the city. For example, in conversations, my interlocutors would remark that the city had no Black people (as described by a woman from a small town on the border of the southern states of Rio Grande do Sul and Paraná). These characterizations are wholly inaccurate.[3] Both census and anecdotal data testify to the presence of Black people in the town, as does the active quilombo and movimento Negro (Black movement) activism underway in Dourados since the early 1990s. What is important here is the way ethnic and racial discourses marking the city as white abound.[4]

I received such characterizations of the town completely unsolicited, at moments in which no one had mentioned race or ethnicity. For example, over lunch with Douradenses, one commented to me that Dourados had a lot of Indians and asked if I had ever seen so many. Dourados is full of *poeira* (red dust), mosquitos, and Índios, people would say.

Amid one such exchange, an interlocutor lamented that Dourados had so many Indians. São Paulo does not have this "problem," he said. I reminded him that there is also a large Guaraní reservation within the city limits of the city of São Paulo. He shrugged this off, insisting that Dourados had to deal with a lot more. He then asked me if my home region in the United States had "a lot of Indians like Dourados."

Such remarks are not uncommon in Dourados. There are common unabashed expressions of fantasies of genocide. For example, when one Douradense bristled at my condemnation of the violence directed at Indigenous land protesters, another Douradense interlocutor stated point blank that although "the United States killed all of its Indians," they did not want Brazil to kill its own. Thus, this Douradense complained of the perceived injustice of American hypocrisy. An archaeologist at the Federal University of Greater Dourados (Universidade Federal de Grande Dourados) published an article in a local newspaper, "On the Presence of Indigenes in the United States," in which he laments that "in Mato Grosso do Sul, one frequently observes people saying that we should do what was done in the United States with Indigenous people from there: total annihilation!" (Eremites de Oliveira 2012).[5] He counters that such extermination did not take place in the United States and that there are still vibrant Indigenous communities through the continental United States, Alaska, and Hawaii, although "everything is not roses for them." The minimal attempt to encourage education and recognition of historical struggle and survival as a counter to open musings on the annihilation of Indigenous people puts into perspective the gravity of anti-Indigenous sentiment in Mato Grosso do Sul.

Typically, highways entering and exiting cities in Mato Grosso do Sul have roundabouts marking the entry along the road. For example, in the center of one such roundabout, ten-foot-tall letters rise from the ground, spelling out the city name. Additionally, the letters have giant, colorful statues of regional wildlife, like parakeets, accompanying the letters. Yet there is no such treatment for the nearby reservation.

A state highway cuts through the reservation, connecting Dourados with the nearby northern town of Itaporã. The reservation actually consists of two agglomerated aldeias, Jaguapirú and Bororó, which are separated by the highway. Transit rumbles through at such a rate that the state installed speed bumps to prevent injury to pedestrians and cyclists that cross back and forth on the reservation.

Douradenses commonly reacted negatively to my suggestion that the reservation effectively could be considered a part of the city, as a sort of ethnic slum. I discussed with Douradenses if one should consider the reservation more as a peripheral area of the city, similar to other peripheral spaces in cities of other regions that suffer social marginalization. Indeed, Dourados has its own such peripheries internal to the city proper. For example, townspeople spoke of the neighborhood of Cachoeirinha as one such area in the city. Cachoeirinha is prominent in local newspapers and conversations for such stereotypical disparagements as crime and drug trafficking. I underline here the distinction between the talk of such areas and the realities of day-to-day life, in which people are going about their lives just as anywhere. Discourses of crime and poverty clash with the liveliness and life-affirming practices in these places. I regularly passed through and stopped in Cachoeirinha en route to the camps-tekohas where I conducted fieldwork. Members of some of the camps-tekhoas also go to convenience stores and grocery markets there. At least one camper attended an evangelical church in the neighborhood, which is bound to one side by a fazenda.

Another highway circles the city of Dourados, thus gaining the nickname the *anel* (meaning "ring"), although it was not yet completely encircling the city at the time of my fieldwork. Along the anel, one passes sugarcane plantations, a facility for drying corn kernels and other freshly harvested crops, soy plantations, and other agro-industrial installations. The city of Dourados does not have suburbs. One may leave the city in a given direction by crossing a road, finding oneself on an agribusiness plantation. The exception lies along the city's northern border, where one could leave the city and cross onto the reservation as described.

That said, I heard complaints about fazendas operating within the reservation as well. Their presence is technically illegal, although they are remarkably unhidden. Attitudes toward fazendas are mixed. I was told that some people on the reservation might informally lease land to fazendeiros. Yet others complain of fazendeiro encroachment. A camp-tekoha member who previously lived on the reservation told me that he filed formal complaints with FUNAI about the pollution from a fazenda that sits on non-Indigenous land across the road from his home on the reservation. Still another self-identified cacique[6] launched a protest camp in 2011 to protest a fazenda just northeast of the reservation. He and fellow protesters claim to have lived and to have been displaced decades ago on the land that the fazenda currently occupies.

### The Reservation

The federal Serviço de Proteção aos Índios (Indian Protection Service) created the Dourados reservation in 1917. The area contained, in its 3,539 hectares, displaced Guaraní (first Kaiowá and then Ñandeva) and later Terena. Maria Lourdes Beldi de Alcantara described that "the SPI began transferring hundreds of Terena, an Aruk tribe, to the reservation in the 1930s. Historically, the relations between the Guaraní sub-groups and the Terena have been strained at best. Considered by the Brazilian colonizers to be more 'civilized,' the Terena were transferred to the reservation with the purpose of accelerating the acculturation process of the Kaiowá and Ñandeva. Exacerbating the poor relationships between the different tribes, FUNAI treated the Terena as a 'privileged' tribe. The benefits of this elevated status have been preferential treatment for FUNAI projects and the uncontested ceding of Kaiowá lands" (Beldi de Alcantara 2010, 2). Moreover, the state sought to promote integration into Brazilian society through "agricultural and productive" work (Aylwin 2009, 49).

Many of the reservation roads, consisting of dark red dirt, become difficult to traverse when it rains, except by horseback. Most of the housing structures are sturdier than those of the roadside camps and spread out far and wide over subsistence plots on the reservation. Some houses are made of *tijolo* (brick). Residing in a brick home is a sign of having lived longer on the reservation and of having better means. The reservation also has its share of ramshackle structures that are not too different from those found in camps-tekohas.

Moving around the reservation, one encounters quite a few livestock (chickens and pigs) wandering along roads and near homes. Cattle are rarer and more confined in pastures. Stereo speakers blast music of all sorts from local radio stations. People commute in the middle of roads to and from reservation schools, moving to the side of the road to allow frequent passage of motorcycles and, less often, cars and trucks. One sees young people in baseball caps and T-shirts with images of popular hip-hop artists, like the American Tupac Shakur or the São Paulo–based Racionais MC's, scenes equal to what you see in the city. Just as commonplace, one sees buses from agribusiness firms billow wafts of red dust from the dirt roads into the air. They begin transporting cane cutters to sugarcane plantations and distilleries as early as three o'clock in the morning, returning in the night. I heard complaints of people sometimes waking with dust on their faces, which also caused lingering respiratory problems.

The reservation was crowded; it was the most densely populated of any reservation in Brazil, with 0.29 hectares per person (Beldi de Alcantara 2012). I heard Indians complain that residents and townspeople outside the reservation object to social problems like street crime, such as robberies, fights, murders, muggings, rapes, and even beheadings by youth gangs. I was warned and overheard frequent complaints that it was unsafe to travel at night. Once some interlocutors cut off a conversation with me in the city at dusk in order to get back to their homes on the reservation safely. The stated culprits behind the problems and disorder are most often drug use, drug trafficking, and heavy alcohol consumption (*pinga* and *cachaça*, types of Brazilian rum).[7] Members of camps-tekhoas complained frequently that overcrowding was one of the motivations for their mobilizations. José, a leader of one of the camps in which I researched, faulted the most recent arrivals to the reservation for the overcrowding and crime problems, by which he meant people

arriving since the 1980s. Those people were displaced by the latest significant influx of settlers into the region, which took place during that era.

As with Cachoeirinha, discourses of crime should not overshadow
the multiple forms of liveliness and flourishing occurring on the reservation. Rather, such discourses arising in the forms of complaints aims
to draw attention to the larger political and economic circumstances,
particularly forced dislocation of Indian people from their territories,
underpinning the circumstances.

I heard Guaraní frequently state that the Índio is not meant to live like
this, so crowded together, a parede (wall to wall). Instead, the traditional
Guaraní way of life, they say, is to live spread out far from your neigh-
bors in extended kin groups. More space, meaning more demarcated
Indigenous reservations, would allow for a return to a Guaraní way of
life as a solution to the contemporary crises. That protesters routinely
eschewed the notion of returning to live on the Dourados reservation
struck me forcefully, given the comparison of living conditions, which
were demonstrably worse in the camps-tekohas. Such statements coming
from people who had survived multiple violent attacks on their camps-
tekohas, and who live on the side of a highway under surveillance and
threats, indicated their level of commitment.

Reservation residents circulate regularly across the region, especially
through Dourados. However, I never heard any of the protesters raise
the possibility of living in the city proper. Some of the non-Indian FAF
campers also ruled out the city because of the expensiveness of rent and
cost of living. Even city residents regularly complained about real estate
speculation and how expensive Dourados had become. In the case of the
Guaraní campers, misery-level wages[8] for manual labor in agro-industrial
firms (for mostly men) and as domestics in the city (for some women) do
not afford "integration"—not that people desire such living. The reservation and city are de facto segregated spaces. For example, it is uncommon
for me to see Indigenous people in restaurants, shopping malls, movie
theaters, and shops, which were overwhelmingly frequented by brancos.

The agribusiness complexes that sustain the town rely on the manual
labor and primary consumption of people who live on the reservation.
More than that, businesses such as small-to-medium-sized supermar-
kets also benefit from extralegal networks of intermediaries that have

control over Indigenous laborers' work permits and welfare benefits, as I describe in more detail in chapter 2. Protest camping is, in part, a rebuke to those forms of confinement.

During my many conversations and arguments about the importance of the city-reservation distinction, townspeople, reservation residents, campers, and government officials insisted that the reservation's problems are not the city's problem. According to those interlocutors, they are problems of cultural disorder, a crisis in the Guaraní way of life.

As an example, in a conversation with a federal official in the region, who also happened to be an anthropologist, I explained that my research on the Guaraní camps was concerned with the larger socioeconomic transformation of Dourados, the expansion of the city via the transformation of its surrounding countryside, with agribusiness as a prime factor. I explained that I was increasingly seeing the demands for land by campers as a way of them envisioning a way out of social problems that emerge from processes of urbanization and rural expulsions, of which the Dourados reservation was undoubtedly a part. In this context, I explained, the distinction between the urban and rural is the product of both economic and political reorganization and ways of perceiving the historical changes therein. I shared that I struggled to understand how to think about the reservation outside its relationship to the city, in its relative material deprivation. Here, I learned an important lesson from my colleague. He explained that the reservation cannot be characterized as a part of the city for specific "sociological" reasons. He pointed out how opponents of the Indians' land claims use the idea of the Indians' supposed integration into the national society as an argument against the need for land demarcation. They say that Indian integration shows that they are not really Indians (i.e., that they are culturally modern and non-Indian, although of Indian ethnicity). So, he explained, there are political stakes in identifying the area as indeed distinct from the city, because to do otherwise would call into question the basic logic of land demarcation, as codified in law. These basics set the terms for the political context of the dispute for land and the political stakes and consequences of maintaining a fundamental distinction of this kind in analyses of the region.

Spatial demarcations are part of the terms for debates on the historical reckoning of colonialism. As one anthropologist put it, what cannot be stated explicitly in these debates is that all of Mato Grosso do Sul was once Indigenous territory. She said that those who advocate for Indians in the region see the material hardships of the Guaranís and are shocked. The fight for land demarcation is an engagement that is politically practical and not merely theoretical. Spatial categories—city, reservation, center, and periphery—are lived as sites of ethnoracial marking, legal juridical differentiation, and ongoing, unresolved confrontations with settler colonial delimitations of territorial belonging.

## Agribusiness Space and the Logic of Permanent Transience

One can glean the pervasiveness of rhetoric regarding Brazil's countryside as vast, empty, and available for expanded agro-industrial production, such as that of the plantation manager with which I began this chapter, and in the language of policy makers, investors, and economic literature. For example, a 2010 *Economist* special volume on Brazilian agribusiness reads, "Much is made of Brazil's vast supply of available frontier land—71 million hectares, according to the Ministry of Agriculture. But it may be greater efficiencies and new farming techniques that allow the country to meet the needs of its own population, while supplying growing global food demand over coming decades" (Gartlan 2010, 4). Indeed, it is a presupposition shared by politicians, financiers, business managers, and the media, who view the countryside as fundamentally available and an empty canvas for intervention and management, despite the fact that land in Brazil has been a site of confrontation and conflict, often violent, since early colonial settlement.

The low population density in the interior of the country has alternately been treated as a problem for national security, which is to be solved by colonization, or as a desired reserve of land for new settlement to safeguard large landholders against land reform. The conflict over land between small and large holders and Indigenous people, *quilombolas*, and later arriving immigrants has not ceased. The conflict has taken on different configurations that have arisen from transformations in the structures of social organization. Still, the idea of the countryside as empty and available endures. Its contradictions have been and remain central to the politics and economics of the region.

Analyzing the production of space helps explain the contrasting terms for land occupation, exploitation, and land conflict. The invocation of an empty countryside is a part of an unquestioned *doxa* that sets the parameters for land politics. The unquestioned and unquestionable limits for politics are set by the terms in which members of civil society and the state comprehend rural space. Thus, the agrarian question is not the same question that was posed decades ago, when a more radical confrontation with the state and large landholders factored in the coup d'état that ended the rule of President João Goulart.

The terms for developmentalist characterizations of "available" land clash with a contrasting conception of a closed frontier. The government of the Workers' Party (PT), which took power with the inauguration of Luiz Ignacio Lula de Silva in 2003, began as sympathetic to those favoring agrarian reform—for example, the Movimento dos Trabalhadores sem Terra (Landless Workers Movement, or MST) (Mançano Fernandes 2008, 81). Lula had a splintered task and was committed both to land reform and to the encouragement of agribusiness expansion. Brazilian land reform as "market-based" sought to divide land through government indemnification for landowners or land purchased on the real estate market.

I do not intend to present the state as a monolith. It is difficult to account for where the state begins and ends or how it often works at odds with itself. Different agencies and branches overlap and contend for jurisdiction in their policy pursuits and programs. The example of the carteiras de trabalho in chapter 2 illustrates that. At the time of my fieldwork, President Dilma Rousseff headed a government of the PT that had been supported by the MST at times. However, due to the makeup of Congress, she had to rely on the plantation-owners (*ruralista*) bloc in the Senate to pursue her legislative agenda. A 2012 showdown with environmentalists over revamping the previous 1965 forestry code exemplified the tensions. Among the many gains for agribusiness interests, the new code opened up previously restricted areas along hillsides and river basins to agribusiness and loggers. Katia Abreu, senator from the central-west state of Goiás, president of the National Agricultural Confederation, and head of the proruralist bloc in the Senate, stated, "Farmers have obtained the legal security they needed to produce. This is the end of the environmentalist hegemony regarding environmental issues" (Agence France Presse 2012).

Protest camping in Mato Grosso do Sul is the product of a reconfiguration of Brazil's spatial categories of rural, urban, and reservation. In this historical unfolding, multiscalar forces have pushed and pulled people off of the land into cities and reservations. In the circumstances that incite their movement and perpetual mobility, many in the urban-rural frontiers in which camping takes place relate to the land through a logic of permanent transience.

The practice of protest camping arises from, and is partially a response to, the reimagining of rural space that I described previously as agribusiness space. In the production of agribusiness space, the state's role is fundamental. I am both drawing upon and diverging from Ferguson and Gupta's (2002) work on "spatializing states." Ferguson and Gupta call for an anthropology of the state that pays attention to the ways that the state produces space. Like Gupta and Ferguson, I approach "spatializing states" by examining the production of space at the level of multiscalar discourses, with attention to how states spatialize their authority.

We must likewise factor in the material practices of production and movement of capital in the circulation of people through the region, since the representational thought entailed in spatial practices are not mere products of discursivity. For example, understandings of spatial distinctions like countryside, city, reservation, periphery, and nation arise with and through practices of material production and exchange. As Lefebvre ([1974] 1991) argues, space and time are not merely categories of the mind that we project onto the world of objects, but rather categories that are themselves products of engagement with the world of objects in practice. Therefore, practices of everyday life are those through which mental representations of space take shape.

What Lefebvre called representational spaces, the conceptual configurations of perceived places (e.g., the beach, the countryside), are likewise premised on representations of space produced by multiple scales of social practice. To clarify what he means, Lefebvre gave the example of tourism, which is organized, marketed, and delivered via varied industries (e.g., airlines and hotels); the organization of time between work and leisure by industry and government; and the consumption of leisure as "nature," beaches, and so on. So, the representations of space (e.g., as the scene of relaxation and as ecologically isolated) impact representational spaces (sea, sun, and mountains) as produced via people's practical activity ([1974] 1991).

I therefore think about the historical and ethnographic context presented earlier in terms of the Brazilian spatializing state and substate levels that mediate the social production of space with and through the installation and expansion of agribusiness complexes and bureaucratic apparatuses. Here, representational thought of space (Lefebvre [1974] 1991) arises out of practices of the production of space in which production entails material objects in addition to discursive arrangements.

Anthrpologist James Ferguson's (2006) concern with how global capital puts in place forms of territorialization that facilitate accumulation comes to mind. Ferguson refutes James Scott's (1998) idea that global capital works through a deterritorializing optic of eradicating difference. Although one no longer sees modernist states that put in place homogenizing spatial forms over swaths of territory toward nationalist developmentalist projects, nation-states facilitate global capital's efforts to put in place forms of territorialization. Corporations may run such territories as enclaves, a form of states within states.

In the case of Brazil, however, we see something somewhat distinct. First, note that state spatialization is homogenizing only to the degree that it puts in place shared sets of practices, necessarily predicable forms of accounting, and production of profit margins required for capital investment and agribusiness competition. To that degree, a certain amount of homogenization is associated with agribusiness, because these practices have to be in place to attract and maintain global investments and competitiveness. These transactions may take the form of use of certain machinery, genetically modified organism (GMO) seeds, herbicides, insurance, and outright land purchases for the launching of new firms or investment in preexisting agribusiness firms in Brazil.[9] Unlike Ferguson (2005), I am not talking about an extractive industry; a different type of state spatialization is produced here. There is a tremendous particularity to the location and regional specificity of and within central-west Brazil. Moreover, what counts as the state, inside or outside of it, or what it is doing at a given moment may be difficult to decipher.

Regarding the particularities of the spatial conundrums in Mato Grosso do Sul, we are confronted with having to make sense of this status of abstract space as an effort at hegemony, as part of the quotidian workings of a cross section of category interests, including agribusiness elites and the military. The region of Dourados is a militarized space—a site for military administration and jurisdictions in which the frontier has long been imagined by elites as fraught areas for national security (Foresta 1992). Likewise, civilian administrators participate in and reinforce militarized, nationalist perceptions of the region as a frontier.[10] In this configuration, the Dourados municipality and larger Dourados region operate as what Mercolis Ernandes (2009, 26) calls a "uma reserva de brasilidade" (reservoir of Brazilian-ness). As I describe in more detail in chapter 1, such a reservoir indexes a Brazilian citizen-subject understood as both universal and branco–non-Indian, despite the seeming contradiction in terms. These vagaries of the marking of space as particular—ethnoracialized—in practice occur in dialectic with the aforementioned rendering of space as abstract and empty.

Agribusiness space in Dourados is not just a problem because of its resulting unmooring of people. The abstract and empty space I describe is enacted through structural and interpersonal violence, saturating the lives of the campers at every turn. They live this sociospatial production as forms of violence that prohibit them from escaping. These are the conditions from which protest campers emerge in Dourados. Protest camps are products of, and responses to, historical violent reorganization of daily life that state and nonstate actors like agribusiness firms, private security forces, and local networks of strongmen (see chapter 2) seek to reify. Reification pretends to naturalize a condition that has come into being through historical transformations, which both Indian and non-Indian land protesters, though for different reasons and motivations, seek to upend. To this history, then, I now turn.

## The Rise of Agribusiness Hegemony

In this section, I briefly examine how different models of land use and land ownership over the course of the twentieth century have involved different political alliances and conflicts than those existing at the time of my research. These models include terms for political identifications and forms of organizing by large, medium, and small landholders and other rural inhabitants. The point is to draw clear lines of distinction regarding the agribusiness era's political and economic order. What one calls agribusiness (*agronegocio*) in Brazil is somewhat unique in this history.

While not exhaustive, this narrative captures major points of the historical shifts in land and labor relations. In the academic literature, a narrative prevails in which proletarianization of peasants arose with the end of seigniorial relations between plantation owners and peasants in the early twentieth century. With the shift to mechanization and more rational management practices, such plantation owners forced peasants off the land. These laborers then moved to cities or continued agrarian work for subsistence under any variety of labor relations (salaried or affiliated with a union) but most often as day laborers with third-party labor contractors as the middlemen with the plantation or firm.

There are nuances to the transformations, however, that are essential to the argument of this book. The beginning of commercial agriculture in Brazil dates to the period that Mueller and Mueller (2006, 2) call "horizontal" expansion around World War II. In this period, federal officials prioritized urban industrial development. They viewed agrarian production as a means to manipulate macroeconomic policy to ensure the foreign reserves necessary to pursue an import substitution industrialization (ISI) strategy, which involved the reimagining and top-down reorganization of agricultural production as a facilitator of a modernizing qua an industrially burgeoning country. From its "backward" agrarian economic base, the country would build an industrialized (so-called developed) nation. There was no structural change in agricultural policy to encourage higher yields, only more widespread agro-industrial production. For this reason, Mueller considers the growth in agricultural output during this World War II period as horizontal expansion.

The spatial metaphor of horizontal is important. For example, despite a continuation of low-yield production techniques, the creation and extension of road networks that enlarged markets for agricultural products added to the quantity of land accessible for agriculture, primarily in the Amazon and central-west regions of Brazil. Such expansion further facilitated the massive deforestation necessary to convert that land for large-scale agriculture. Much of the technology needed to make the land arable throughout the central-west region of Brazil (i.e., the cerrado, or savannah) did not previously exist. The cerrado emerged in the purview of planners and private-market actors alike as they increasingly developed arable lands near urban areas. With space nearly exhausted throughout urban areas, greater attention turned toward the central-west frontier.

It's not that any of the frontier land that had previously been viewed as available (if less than arable) was ever really empty. These lands were more often than not already occupied by an assortment of Indigenous, peasant, or quilombola people.

With the advent of the authoritarian governments of the military dictatorship era, attention turned to rendering already accessible lands more productive through technology and mechanization and putting already occupied land into "more productive" hands. Conservative modernization meant a reformulation of a state-led agricultural strategy with agencies like the Empresa Brasileira de Pesquisa Agropecuária (EMBRAPA or Brazilian Company for Farming Research) and the Comissão de Financiamento da Produção (CFP or Commission for Financing Production). The state created the CFP during World War I, but only during the dictatorship did it begin to exercise its power to reduce the volatility of agricultural prices and thus incentivize investment (agricultural credits). To this end, in the mid-1960s, the state also created the National System of Rural Credit (SNCR) to finance increasing amounts of operational credit, marketing, and investment credit. The goal was to encourage farmers to improve their production methods. Likewise, in pursuit of these ends, in Brazil's central-west region, the state put in place the Nipponese-Brazilian Cooperation Program for the Development of the Cerrado (Programa de Cooperação Nipo-Brasileiro para o Desenvolvimento do Cerrado, or PRODECER) to accommodate a windfall of Japanese capital investments (Inocêncio 2010).[11]

This period also saw the incentivizing of the expansion of agribusiness complexes.[12] Although agribusiness already existed, the government induced capacity-building in the areas of pesticides, agricultural machinery, fertilizers, and other inputs. Additionally, agribusiness expansion included industries for processing agricultural raw materials for domestic market and export. This shift was consistent with transformations taking place internationally through policies pushed in the international market for food, led notably by the United States.[13]

By the late 1980s, agribusiness complexes had become a central element in Brazil's agriculture, with agriculture related to agribusiness exhibiting substantial productivity gains (Florêncio de Almeida, Zylbersztajn, and Klein 2010). Mueller (2004, 5) describes that in state agricultural policy in the 1980s, agricultural credit "had become a major source of income transfer in favor of those which had access to the rural credit system—mostly large, commercial farmers."

In contrast to the import substitution system of the past, this favored the domestic market. Manufactured goods exports and cheap petrodollar loans met foreign-exchange needs until a severe foreign-debt crisis struck in the late 1970s. Agricultural credit had been supplied primarily by the Banco do Brasil, a bank that did not operate from its reserves. Brazil's Central Bank automatically supplied resources for subsidized credit for commercial agriculture. However, with the famously exorbitant inflation of the period reaching a head with the foreign-debt crisis, this transfer mechanism ended with the restrictive monetary policy deployed to counter inflation and meet International Monetary Fund (IMF) demands for "reform" of the agricultural credit system.

The government replaced the agricultural credit system with a minimum-price policy to push the production of agricultural exports, once again prioritizing the safeguarding of foreign reserves in the face of the debt crisis. As a result, by the end of the 1980s, Brazil experienced a substantial expansion of agricultural and agribusiness exports. A key and significant component of this was the increases in yields and major expansion of "modern agriculture" in the cerrado of central-west Brazil. The outsized role of agribusiness and production of export-oriented crops implicated in agribusiness encouraged the production of cotton, rice, oranges, wheat, and especially sugarcane and soybeans.

International investors and financial institutions have increasingly led financing for agricultural credit (Florêncio de Almeida, Zylbersztajn, and Klein 2010). Moreover, there is now a notably important role for land prices in attracting and underpinning such investors. This has complicated the land-reform issue as well, since the state insists upon market-based land reform. When land was cheap, the government could more easily procure land for redistribution. However, procuring land was arguably hardly a major priority in high-value areas close to urban centers.

The debates about the large landholder model turning around the agrarian question took place through tremendous violent repression of political activists in the countryside and the installation of a corporatist model for rural unions for workers and top-down policies favoring large landholders. State policy attempted to accommodate both the expansion of agribusiness production and resettlement of those pushing for land reform via redistribution by encouraging movement of farmers and settlers into the central-west region and the Amazon as well as through pushing techniques and materials of production that rely on capital-intensive machinery, herbicides, modified seeds, and so on.

The Brazilian state operates at multiple levels, and state actors pursue often-contradictory tasks. State actors enforce laws and policies that protect private-property owners, social-justice demands of land reformers, and national priorities of development. These tensions amount to lived effects that reinforce the logics of agribusiness space regardless of, and indeed often despite, the best intentions of many involved.

Ferguson and Gupta (2002) use the concepts of *encompassment* and *verticality* to describe how the state is imagined and operates through hierarchies. Asymmetrical power relations between people and bureaucracies (verticality) orient toward administering an imagined national territory (encompassment). Ethnographers, then, should query how people on the ground come to understand the state as above and distinct from society. Ferguson and Gupta reject the alleged distinction between a private domain and a public domain, between the state and civil society, all of which the state contains within it as the basis for society, or indeed for ethical life. Ferguson and Gupta further deploy Foucault's (1991) concept of governmentality, which argues that through its institutions, the state educates, disciplines, and regulates the functioning of everyday life. Governmentality operates through biopower (Foucault 2003), an amorphous agglomeration that exists through its articulation in disciplinary and regulatory mechanisms of state and substate actors and institutions. Ferguson and Gupta challenge that one must account for the enduring metaphors of the state as operating via top-down practices.

They question whether discourses produce our conception of resistance to the state as ground-up. Anthropologists must ethnographically explain how such processes do or do not take place.

With Ferguson and Gupta's challenge in mind, in the final section of this chapter I look more closely at the discursive practices around the state and land-reform activism that I encountered in Dourados.

## Why Space Matters

"If anything you say in England has any repercussions here, you could be sanctioned." I received this warning informally and off the cuff from a Brazilian federal bureaucrat about my participation in a conference on the "Global Land Grab" that took place at the University of Sussex in April 2011. He brought to my attention the paranoia over what happens when knowledge production goes beyond the borders of the nation-state territory, including possible repercussions for the land conflict, such as fomenting negative international publicity that could affect Brazil's standing with international financial institutions. Part of the bureaucrat's worry was the prospect of me simply presenting an embarrassing portrayal of Brazil. Activists' politics of shaming such institutions as the World Bank and the BID (Inter-American Development Bank) has led to these organizations requiring accounting for human rights— particularly impacts on Indigenous groups and the environment—in loans for development projects.

His warnings also struck me as insightful for their degree of assertion of state power over the production and dissemination of knowledge, whether text or images, of Indians. He asserted hegemony over how lines are drawn across land and over bodies. Moreover, his arguments further made clear attempts at state power over Indians across space, whether inside or outside of the reservation, what counts as Indian territory, and the extent and extension of the state's responsibility and authority over the demarcation of such lines within and as constituting Brazil's official borders.

Finally, the bureaucrat's warnings marked me in space as a foreign researcher. He fixated on how my movement and capacity to produce knowledge and disseminate it internationally spelled a double danger. I could cause negative repercussions for fazendeiros, who may in turn create a backlash of negative consequences for me. He made very explicit the possibility of the state sanctioning me as a researcher, spelling out the risks presented by my movement across borders.

Of course, as with any country, proponents of Brazilian development, particularly those in the state, have a lot at stake in presenting a positive picture. At the time of my fieldwork, a concerted and deliberate tone of triumph dominated discourses on development in a country that for so long brandished the slogan "A country of the future." In 2011, then President of the United States of America Barack Obama echoed this tone during his visit to Rio de Janeiro. He announced, "For so long, Brazil was a nation brimming with potential but held back by politics, both at home and abroad. For so long, you were called a country of the future, told to wait for a better day that was always just around the corner. *Meus amigos* [my friends], that day has finally come. And this is a country of the future no more. The people of Brazil should know that the future has arrived. It is here now. And it's time to seize it" (Obama 2011).

Such rhetoric left me feeling uneasy when I recalled the land conflict in Mato Grosso do Sul. I attended public forums in the state where plantation owners and their supporters openly grinned while discussing assassinations of Indigenous protestors. Beyond these twisted laughs, in such forums the fazendeiros and their sympathizers also railed against the FUNAI-led land-demarcation process and the threats (as they perceived it) of land seizures and losing their families' land. A government official recounted to me a meeting with fazendeiros after a protest camp that had been on the roadside for many months invaded his plantation. FUNAI hosted a meeting toward reconciliation between fazendeiros and land protesters. At that meeting, my friend relayed to me that a fazendeiro said that he and his security forces were prepared to defend the land. The fazendeiro went on to say that although he was not going to personally perpetrate any action or order any such actions in retaliation for the invasion, he could not speak for his *seguranças* (security forces). Once the seguranças have cachaça (a liquor made from sugarcane), he could not tell what they would do. They lose it a bit when they have cachaça, the fazendeiro said.

The FUNAI official recounting this story stated that such thinly veiled threats arose due to the unfortunate absence of the state in the region. By this he meant the state's failure to prosecute attacks on land protestors, which produces a general atmosphere of lawlessness and impunity. Some FUNAI and Ministerio Publico officials feel hamstrung by the lack of political will elsewhere in the state to protect Mato Grosso do Sul's land protestors. Like so many of the Brazilian anthropologists who work with the Guaranís, these state officials are in the somewhat impossible position of being both within the state *and* with little power to alter the course of political marginalization of those in the camps-tekohas. Those state agents sympathetic to land restitution and knowledgeable of protesters' just claims to land, nevertheless are bound by processes in which the state is impotent to fully meet its mandate of fulfilling Indian land rights.

There is a contrast here between state control of the monopoly of violence and state control in terms of maintaining and perpetuating the social order through the social production of space (in Lefebvre's sense of the term). The land dispute arises from the production of the countryside as an abstract, empty space for maximized agro-industrial production and the city and Indigenous reservations as sites of dwelling. Dwelling itself becomes contentious. Much like those in the more famous Movimento dos Trabalhadores sem Terra (MST) camps, Guaraní protest campers seek to reclaim rural space as a site of dwelling. The Indigenous camps of Mato Grosso do Sul, however, claim land not as "landless workers" (in which any parcel of land might do), but in terms of ethnocultural belonging to the specific parcel of land for which they are protesting.

Brazil's 1988 constitution mandated demarcation of cultural Indigenous lands within five years of the establishment of the constitution.[14] After two decades of delay, FUNAI finally assigned working groups to begin demarcation studies in Mato Grosso do Sul in 2008. While conducting fieldwork in 2011, I asked an official with the Ministerio Público Federal why the demarcation process had not yet been settled. He replied, "This is not Chicago," my place of residence in the United States at that time, meaning that I should not expect anything in Brazil to be resolved quickly. I did not bother to correct him that in my experience most people in Chicago also do not expect the state to accomplish much all that quickly.

In Brazil, particular impediments illuminate effective state and non-state actors' combined perpetuation of the land dilemma. One problem is that working groups (consisting of anthropologists) have difficulty informing property owners that their land is under investigation and that the anthropologists will need to access it. The law required such notification. Second, either the Ministerio Público or FUNAI have to first publicly announce what land is up for investigation, giving ample time for the landowner to prepare to dodge notification.

Even before this, the working group has to identify the landowner and has three attempts in which to hand deliver the notice to them. However, the working group cannot always identify the property owner, for multiple reasons. Much irregularity is in the land titling in many regions of Mato Grosso do Sul. Many holders of titles know that their papers are irregular (legally flawed) and are thus resistant to having the state investigate the legitimacy of their holdings. They may be irregular because the initial title holder (for example, the father of the property occupant) that held the land title has died, and the inheritors settled the division of the property informally, never bothering to have the titles transferred.

Or, as an example of another common occurrence, the property owner may have somehow gotten the land from a previous titleholder who did not get the title properly transferred, or some such other irregularity. Sometimes, however, the landowner does not produce a title because it is simply fraudulent; the owner could have first gained the land from a *grileiro* (informal, often dishonest, land dealer) or through illegal or extralegal, violent means (e.g., by aiming a gun at the previous land occupants). Moreover, the working groups confront the problem that the state does not have proper records or means of regularizing or tracking land titles and title transactions. There is no centralized system, with *cartorios*[15] most often maintaining land-title records.

Opposition to investigations of Indigenous land claims is in part driven by a desire to keep in place irregularity that is otherwise passing under the radar. The state does not act to regularize such titles because that would call into question private land holdings across the Brazilian countryside, the effect of which could have unimaginable, widespread consequences. Protest campers threaten to upset the apple cart, as it were. Thus, fazendeiros pursue a strategy of open violence against campers, perpetual delay through legal challenges, and evasion strategies that have succeeded for years in preventing land-demarcation studies.

The aforementioned development rhetoric on the "emptiness" of the countryside is part of knowledge-making discourses that create a reality of their own (Escobar 1995; Ferguson [1990] 1997) whose effects are lived as real regardless of the detachment of these discourses from longstanding land conflicts across the countryside. What can be known—and what is known as rendered by powerful institutions and actors—is part and parcel of space-making practices. These discourses produce what counts as the city and the country, what counts as the reservation, where the lines of the city are drawn, and subsequent ethnoracialized spaces of belonging. This understanding of the countryside as abstract, in addition to the more particular variation of it as also being empty, produces a notion of the countryside as a site of the past and future frontier of development. Land activists contest this vision.

There prevails an ironic juxtaposition of space as belonging to a group historically (e.g., the previously cited quote of the Ministerio Publico official that "all of Mato Grosso do Sul was once Guaraní territory") and the fact of impermanence and displacement as a rule. The camp, indeed, is an instance of the very contorted logics underlying these practices. They remain unmarked and unremarked upon except in reckoning with the spectacle of the protest camp, whose presence challenges that lived space is not the abstract domain of market logics. Spatial arrangements are not completely settled.

In Dourados the prevailing mode of production insists on an abstractness of space in which we should take for granted a country-city distinction as one of the idyllic versus the modern, and the natural versus the industrial. Despite a complex history of land law and development politics, though, such taken-for-granted binary categories are premised on a version of history both mythological (national heroic) and abstract (razed out of struggle or understood as natural and timeless). This version amounts to an assignment of the countryside as a progressive frontier of agro-industrial production and national ascent. These terms of city-country distinction are consistent with other histories of urbanization, the rise of market society, and forms of social authority accompanying bourgeoning nation-state bureaucracies in the nineteenth and twentieth centuries. However, the particularities of Brazil's history of agro-industrial production of space have produced the protest camp form as a by-product.

For Lefebvre, the point of this approach to thinking of space as produced is the necessity of reversing what he saw as the dominant trend toward social fragmentation, separation, and disintegration. He supports the concept of a *truth of space* rather than a true space. A so-called true space can be constituted or constructed as a thing in itself, without regard for how it comes to be or understood as such. By contrast, one generates a truth of space by analyzing discourses and practices of the representations of space and their material enactment through mechanisms of power in which state power is ultimately the final recourse.[16]

Lefebvre states that society is not a closed system that is cohesive. Instead, it is a totality that is decidedly open. He explains that it is "so open, indeed, that it must rely on violence to endure" (Lefebvre [1974] 1991, 11). In the context of Brazil, we should see this violence as anything but unique to this moment, but certainly contoured by the particular structuring of life entailed in the configuration of agribusiness space. Such are the terms for insurgency and mobilization for land taking place in protest camps in Dourados, in addition to the violent imposition of spatial delimitations on movement and mobility. I analyze these issues in greater detail in chapter 5.

In the case of the Dourados region, representations of space distinguish the city from the Indigenous reservation and distinguish the city from the countryside, which involves necessary contradictions. For example, the reservation is a site of accommodation and protection for Indigenous people. In the early twentieth century, Serviço de Proteção aos Índios (SPI)[17] increasingly restricted the Guaranís to "protected" areas (reservations). This occurred sometimes by force, due to settler violence, and sometimes by choice, due to the diminishment of resources, such as forests, or the encouragement of missionaries (Brand 1997, 123–33).

The SPI demarcated discontinuous areas for reservations in Mato Grosso do Sul, denominating what amounted to small islands of land for their administrative jurisdiction (Eremites de Oliveira and Marques Pereira 2009, 49). The SPI did not prioritize demarcating land already occupied by Indigenes. The legislation of the period primarily concerned establishing areas for Indigenes whose previously occupied areas had become choice spaces for plantations. They established these reservations near cities to facilitate administration and control.

By contrast, demarcation of terras indigenas, a legal category established in the 1988 constitution, indicates land traditionally occupied by Indigenous people. According to paragraph 1 of Article 231, the concept of Indigenous land is defined as "land occupied by them in a permanent character, utilized for their productive activities, and needed for the preservation of the natural resources necessary for their physical and cultural reproduction, in accordance with their uses, customs, and traditions." Paragraph two of the same article guarantees exclusive usufruct of riches of the soil, rivers, and lakes, as national patrimony of the federal state. The lands are inalienable and cannot be used by anyone except Indians.[18]

Moving away from the earlier acculturationist political model, the multiculturalist 1988 constitution sought to resolve questions regarding space and the Brazilian citizen-subject through an understood spatial accommodation of the cordoned reservation or Indigenous land. In their brazen presence on the roadside, hugging the border of the plantation, threatening to breach, Indigenous camps interrupt the internal coherence of space ordered by a nation-state bureaucratic structure as well as the sense of shared belonging as abstract national citizen-subjects that supposedly accommodates ethnoracially marked difference.[19] Like their non-Indian counterparts in the MST or FAF, Indigenous camps openly embrace vulnerability to state or third-party violence in their affront to the spatial order of city-reservation-countryside. Therefore, we can view them as a sort of civil disobedience.

At the same time, protest camps reinforce something already intrinsically understood: namely, that space is in flux. A central contradiction in the assertion of abstract space, in which a supposedly natural arrangement of land use serves as a basis for productive order and security enforced by the state, is that, the state simultaneously enforces a seemingly opposing tenet: space is not settled, and no settlement is permanent.

Land values, for example, supposedly naturally go up and down. There is a fragility and precariousness of holdings, eminent domain necessitated by state projects and modernization schemes, and so on. Protest camps, as a threat and affront to the waves of settler colonialism that dislocated prior rural dwellers, especially Indians, thus disrupt politics as usual. They therefore face resentment and violent lashing out from private security forces. In such confrontations we see a dialectic between the settled and unsettled, the taken for granted and violently insisted upon, which transpires in regard to state mediation as a contest for land.

Douradenses speak of the town and the reservation in relation to each other, whether explicitly or implicitly. One understands the reservation as Indian, for reasons that are self-evident. As such, the reservation is an exceptional space. The city is non-Indian–white, and the countryside is also. Regularly, I heard the refrain "O lugar do Índio é na reserve" (The place of the Indian is on the reservation). Such arrangements of space have been subject to rearrangement, as Indians were displaced onto reservations, violently emptying the countryside of Indians, in different waves of colonization in the twentieth century. The federal government established more than a dozen reservations in Mato Grosso do Sul over this period, with several more in various stages of demarcation and provisional study for possible later designation as such.

However, such arrangements carry scrutiny and tumultuous contestation, as exemplified by legal efforts to implement the *marco temporal* (temporal landmark). Proponents of Indigenous land rights, however, point out that those rights are originary. As anthropologist Carneiro da Cunha (2017, 409) writes, "They are deemed to exist, like the Swiss 'cantons,' prior to the state itself. The role of the state is not to grant Indigenous peoples land rights but to recognize and demarcate them." This means those rights are not conferred by the constitution, but merely affirmed. Anthropologist Rubem Caixeta (2017, 410) notes that the marco temporal argument that Indigenous people only have the right to land that was already in their possession when the federal constitution was promulgated, on October 5, 1988, is a "not-so-veiled way of dismantling and preening the enactment of Indigenous land rights, for we know that several of these peoples were simply decimated, others violently expelled from their lands, or confined to tiny reserves, as well as subjected to forced removals on a large scale. Many others were only able to reclaim their lands after 1988!" The push to pass the marco temporal change to Indigenous law demonstrates the magnitude of the ruralist efforts to more deeply entrench agribusiness space.

In this chapter I described the social production of space giving rise to camping as a political strategy and tactic. Land is ever more expensive due to agricultural policies that favor large-scale landowners, agribusiness complexes, and agricultural real estate speculation. In the city of Dourados, urban real estate speculation factors no less in the incitement to displace and confine. Most of the protest campers with whom I conducted fieldwork held multiple jobs in addition to working as manual agricultural laborers. Most maintained small gardens at the camps to supplement the state welfare cestas basicas (food baskets) and wage earnings.

Yet, the configuration of real estate markets, insufficient wages, and expensive housing rents do not fully account for why the practice of camping would be compelling at that moment. Although by the time these protesters joined their camps-tekohas, camping had long been a well-established and well-known tactic in Brazil (thanks to the MST movement), we may usefully question why these Indigenous protestors in Dourados took up camping at that moment and since the 1980s. Likewise, we may ask why seeking a land title through this practice in Brazil made sense. Having discussed the structural transformations giving rise to the type of permanent transience demonstrated in camps and concomitant with the production of space as empty and abstract, in the following chapter I examine the particular protest-camp histories and biographies of camp leaders.

# Mobilizing against Forced Transience     **5**

Dolores asked me to start recording video as we stood talking in the camp-tekoha. She pointed to the front of her brother Diego's tentlike shelter and described how they cannot live in the way the Indians used to, as she put it. Rather, she said that in the camp they have to live like "pigs." She pulled back the flap of thick black plastic that served as the entrance to the shelter. The plastic used for the side panels of his tent had holes, a misfortune that allowed in wind and rain. Diego's shelter was about four feet wide and a little over five-and-a-half feet high. His bed consisted of long branches tied together with ropes into a flat plank. Shorter sticks elevated the bed a foot and a half above the ground. A pink blanket lay strewn about the bed. Dolores described how she had gone to the FUNAI office in Dourados several times to ask for more *lona* (thick black plastic), only to hear that they did not have any more in stock. She said that she explicitly told them that the lona was not for her, it was for the *communidade* (community).

We then walked the twenty meters across the camp-tekoha to the tent of Carmen, Dolores's sister. The tent had completely collapsed. Carmen stood before me and looked into my camera, describing what she called the "sacrifices" that she and her family were making by staying in the camp. I had heard that word often from the campers. One of her older sons talked about the sacrifice of having his toddler son experience severe diarrhea from the polluted water of a nearby creek. He walked me across the highway to the small stream of water, not more than a foot wide, which flowed through dirt and rocks. I later learned that the campers washed clothes, bathed, and gathered drinking water from a much wider and boisterous point on the creek set back in the relatively small preserve of forest in the interior of the plantation. (See figure 7.)

The difficult material conditions in the camp were evident to me from first glance. The camps-tekohas overall were far worse off because they lacked potable water. The members repeatedly stressed the sparse material conditions to me. In formal-sounding speeches, the default mode of communication in my first weeks in the camp, they acutely noted to me their sacrifices. They wanted me to present their testimonies in a way that detailed their hardships and their defiant survival. Although the material conditions of the camp were really terrible, the campers were not merely complaining as a means of catharsis, stating facts as small talk, or opening up to better inform me as a researcher. That the protesters have experienced deprivation was a major emphasis in claiming the land where they were camping. They sought to highlight the question of why they would live this way. They push us to ponder what specifically brought them to the camps at that moment and under such harsh conditions.

In this chapter I discuss the process of piecing together the histories of the protest camps and protesters based on my conversations and observations during ethnographic fieldwork. This process, in hindsight, illuminated the constraints of the terms for Indigenous land protests imposed by these histories. That Guaraní need land not just to reproduce life as Guaraní but also to imagine and establish a whole set of social relations whose ideals and contentions with neocolonial violence they are working to forge. This is the case regardless of non-Indians' perceptions of the attainability or credibility of their efforts.

To be clear, the histories of the core members of the camps-tekohas indeed stemmed centrally from prior forced displacements from the lands that they were revindicating. However, the particular histories of the camp mobilizations and specific circumstances that brought the protesters to a given parcel of land imposed considerable obstacles to formulating a singular narrative to the cohesion of a group claiming a given parcel of land on a particular plantation. Though the protesters whom I worked with indeed were displaced from their territories and

Fig 7. A creek on a camp-tekoha. Photograph by LaShandra Sullivan.

indeed still engage in intimate cosmogonic relations of belonging to and through those landscapes (as I discuss in more detail in chapter 6), their claims nevertheless also spring from the particularities of further dislocations wrought with the rearrangements of agribusiness space, social upheavals, and politics in the region. Thus, the biographical narratives relayed to claim a given parcel of land worked rhetorically in ways neither straightforward nor lacking in veracity. Such rhetorical operations point to the need to apprehend the broader basis of their claims to land restitution, historical dislocation, and the resulting importance and justice of land restitution in Mato Grosso do Sul.

Activists faced great difficulties to adequately make use of Indigenous land law given the terms for land politics at the time of my fieldwork—that is, the double bind of cultural essentialism that I describe in more detail in chapter 6. Nevertheless, we should see their land claims as valid, therefore rejecting the double bind of essentialized cultural difference required by land law and persistently yoked to Guaraní people and their advocates. I am making a case in favor of the protesters that neither completely plays into the liberal model of an individual propertied self as a basis for citizenship and inclusion (see Holston 2008, Locke [1690] 1980, Hegel [1807] 1991), nor relies on purported ancestral or cultural connections to land for an essential Indian subject. The latter presumes a primordial emplacement counter to the larger history of migration and displacement in the region. The land protesters and the histories of their mobilizations draw our attention to the waves of settler colonial displacements and the ever-shifting machinations of ruralists to undo constitutionally Indigenous land rights—for example, with their push for the so-called marco temporal.

Brazilian anthropologist and longtime advocate for Indigenous rights in Brazil Manuela Carneiro da Cunha (2017, 409) summed up the ongoing efforts by ruralists to pull the rug out from under Indigenous land claimants with the marco temporal mandate. She describes the imbroglio as follows:

The 1988 Constitution defined what counts as Indigenous land: it is the territory necessary for the physical and cultural reproduction of the society in question. It is hardly surprising that the report of the Parliamentary Commission of Inquiry on FUNAI and INCRA would take up again a theory supported by one part of Brazil's Supreme Court, known by the name *marco temporal*, which might be translated as "temporal landmark."

The rights of Indigenous peoples to their lands have been enshrined in every Brazilian constitutional text since 1934; they were declared even in colonial times. The 1988 Constitution asserts that Indigenous rights are "originary"—i.e., they are deemed to exist, like the different Swiss "cantons," prior to the state itself. The role of the state is not to grant Indigenous peoples land rights but to recognize and demarcate them. Yet this new doctrine, the temporal landmark interpretation, holds that the only Indigenous peoples who can benefit from the recognition of their right to land are those who were occupying their territory on the day when the 1988 Constitution was promulgated.

There were immediate objections to this temporal landmark interpretation. For one, it could not hold for Indigenous peoples that had forcibly been expelled from their land. The theory's advocates responded by posing a condition: these peoples would need to prove that they had not ceased to resist, either by arms or by legal means. Given the reality of the facts, this condition is absurd. The targets of this aberrant interpretation of the 1988 Constitution prominently are the Guaraní of the Center-West of Brazil, expelled from their lands since the 1940s. They were crammed into small reservations and were not, at the time, legally entitled to launch a lawsuit. Their capacity to do so was not recognized until the 1988 Constitution.

Crowded onto reservations, starting in the 1980s, land activists in Mato Grosso do Sul took to the surrounding countryside to insist that those areas come under scrutiny and seizure as Indigenous land. They fashion the camps into overtly political spectacles, highlighting and calling attention to the unforgotten violent, ethnoracial takeover of land by non-Indian settler colonists. In their testimonies to me, protesters consistently called my attention to spatial reconfiguration of the landscape into city-countryside-reservation that came into being through histories of movement, dislocations, deforestations, and built transformations of areas into agribusiness installations and an agribusiness boom-driven city. The protest camps raise the prospect that the matter is not settled, that it is unfinished business, so to speak.

Piecing together those histories through ethnographic fieldwork illuminated for me the danger to the established order of agribusiness rule in the region presented by the protests, particularly in that their histories were often obscured. The unofficial histories of the protest mobilizations alert us to the need to amend the required terms for state land demarcation— that is, establishing proof of cultural ties to, and displacement from, the particular parcel land claimed. Such terms constrain activists' efforts by requiring provenance from specific plots of land. Though often such ties exist in their biographies (Eremites de Oliveira and Marques Pereira 2009), as I discuss in the chapter, such demonstrable ties may be difficult to lay out in a straight line because of the histories of series of disruptions and displacements suffered by the land claimants. In this chapter, I challenge that such a narrow requirement for land restitution present an impossible trap for land activists in that it obscures the larger history of displacement in which their belonging to land and conditions of displacement unfolded.

In what follows, I demonstrate the perversity of the proposed marco temporal law, given the forced displacements, structurally imposed by the circumstances and nested within larger political and economic processes in the region. These processes land on each of the activists in ways distinct to their biographies, though continuous with larger networks of relations in which they are enmeshed.

## Layered Histories: Complex Stories of Protest Camps

There are multiple layers to the histories of Indigenous protest camps in the Dourados region of Mato Grosso do Sul; no two camps are the same. On one level, we should understand the camps as arising due to a larger predicament of dislocations inscribed by the state-mediated and imposed political and economic organization that I have outlined in the previous chapters. In Chapter 4 I described how the rearrangements imposed by agribusiness space gave rise to protest camping out of its imposed conditions of permanent transience, to which protest camps were a response. The mediation of the state and substate levels in this shifting relation to land, and the concomitant production of the city-country-reservation distinction, is part of the insidious history of creating a market for land in the region. The shift from conceiving of areas as sites of dwelling to mere abstract real estate has taken place through the imposition of a view of land as vacant and empty for economic development. Urban and rural development required just that normative understanding and its violent expression by which it was taken for granted that formerly rural people were moveable and mobile. Violence and mobility are a hallmark of the history of the region. Whereas these processes are not new, their manifestation in land conflict and the camp occupations is distinct. The processes relate to a different level of history imbued throughout the biographies of both the camps-tekohas themselves and the particular life histories of their organizers and members.

We can see that one of the primary questions threading through this book, then, is how to analyze Indigenous protest camping as a practice in Dourados, its historical emergence at these different levels, and its subsequent presentation of certain paradoxes. By the latter, I refer to how the protesters presumably invoke a shared history of belonging to a particular parcel of land as part of their life histories. And yet, I learned that their stories, as they recall them, are divergent. Moreover, the protesters sometimes call upon different terms, or personal rationales, for their land claims and to make sense of their tactics. For example, regarding claims as Indigenous land, the protesters reference the disputed parcel of land as a site of primordial belonging. But they do so, however, through what amounts to practices of transience for all but the camp-tekoha leaders and a core group of members. This point is of crucial significance: some members of camps may sometimes come and go. The people in the camps may live in them only part time; they may move on to something else or live elsewhere as life demands. Non-core members may come and go, leave and then later come back or not. Members may live and work elsewhere while maintaining residence in the camps.

In the case of the members of the Guaraní-led camps-tekohas with whom I worked, we may consider their land claims valid in that they arise from their consciousness and their families' violent removals from the lands, which has transpired over multiple generations. This is evidenced also in multigenerational living in the camps-tekohas, which leaders reference in their testimonies regarding assassinations of their affines, for example. The biographies they shared with me, including via maps, photos, and oral testimonies, attested to this. The Guaraní protesters were displaced—this they know—and they demand restitution under the law despite the fact that that law will not grant them the land unless they successfully perform a version of Indigeneity in which the state may deem them deserving of land.

Accounts of the disjuncture between the ways the campers live day-to-day, the ways they talk about their histories toward making official claims on land, and the specific camp histories exemplify the inanity of the marco temporal as it applies on the ground, to the comings of goings of land rendered into real estate by colonial histories of movement of people and capital. The stories coalesced for me through semistruc-tured interviews, casual conversations, and observations as I was able to piece them together after multiple years of fieldwork. In this chapter, I describe how the broader history of the rise of the agribusiness sector in Dourados and transformation of land into a commodity in the second part of the twentieth century played out in the lives of these particular camps. I show how these forces have created the slipstream (Appadurai 2004) of material precariousness in which campers are scrambling in the day-to-day to merely survive.

At the same time, the campers are using camping as a form of polit-ical practice. The tensions between these two things—the camps as an outcome of and a response to increasingly uncertain conditions of life—transpire along different time horizons. People operate in at least three sets of time horizons. There is both a short time horizon, in which individuals scramble to reproduce life in a day-to-day way, and a longer time horizon, in which people reach for a way out as offered in land restitution. Finally, there is the time horizon given by and debated over in traditional Guaraní cosmologies regarding space and time, which I discuss separately in chapter 6. In contrasting the official and unofficial narratives of origin stories and life histories of the protest camps, we can see the ways in which the constant scrambling necessitated by daily life fails to have any traction on a longer arc of time or on that ideal contained within.

## Dourados and Urbanization:
## Rise of an Agribusiness City and Region

The history of the city of Dourados and its relationship to its environs help contextualize demands for land restitution in the region. Over decades of displacement, many brancos moved to the city from rural areas elsewhere in Brazil. Likewise, Indigenous people in the region moved onto reservations, some to those closest to cities, in search of greatest access to government services. Proximities to cities also provided the possibility of remunerated work. In this regard, Dourados by far outpaced other cities in the region.

From 1940 to 2010, spanning the first government-conducted population census in Dourados to the time of my research, the population grew from roughly 15,000 to 225,000 people (see table 1). With the rise of agribusiness, however, the dramatic push of people out of the countryside into the city took place more recently. In turn, the 1970s brought with it a structural transformation of space in line with these interests.

**Table 1. Population of Dourados**

POPULATION CENSUS (1940–2010)

| Census Year | Total | Urban | Rural |
|---|---|---|---|
| 1940 | 14,985 | 1,821 | 13,164 |
| 1950 | 22,834 | 4,730 | 18,104 |
| 1960 | 84,955 | 16,468 | 68,483 |
| 1970 | 79,186 | 31,599 | 47,587 |
| 1980 | 106,493 | 84,849 | 21,644 |
| 1991 | 135,984 | 122,856 | 13,128 |
| 1996 | 153,191 | 139,695 | 13,496 |
| 2000 | 164,674 | 149,679 | 14,995 |
| 2010 | 196,068 | 181,086 | 14,982 |

Source: (Instituto Brasileira de Geografia e Estatística 2012a).

From the beginning, Dourados was a city born in conflict. With the completion of the War of the Triple Alliance against Paraguay, Brazilians began to migrate to the southern part of Mato Grosso do Sul around 1870. In 1884, near the Dourados River, in-migrants founded the village of São João Batista de Dourados. The municipality of Dourados was officially created in 1935. Through the early decades of the twentieth century, a few dozen families inhabited the area. During these early years, the area was virtually isolated from all but Indigenous populations due to the lack of roads connecting to the railroad network, which had also hindered the flow of production in the region. This changed in 1943 when the Vargas government launched the Colônia Agrícola Nacional de Dourados (National Agricultural Colony of Dourados). The colony attracted waves of Brazilians to the region, many of whom had not been successful in other such colonies. The decreed area of the colony was 300,000 hectares and held approximately ten thousand families. With the creation of the National Colony also came private colonization companies that eventually acquired large areas of forests.

Simultaneous to the initiation of the agricultural colony, the government played a pivotal role in urban expansion in the 1940s, marked by the launch of the first urban settlements in Dourados. On March 12, 1946, legal degree number 9055 created the county and municipality of Dourados. Accompanying this change came a new land-tenure policy of selling lots in a market. This was a shift from a previous land-tenure policy of concessions (*aforamento*), which had been the sole form of land distribution. The opening of a market, especially in the city of Campo Grande (the capital of Mato Grosso do Sul since 1979), precipitated land speculation, leading to the rapid rise in prices of lots in Dourados. This dynamic eventually encouraged owners of small farms located near the Dourados (acquired mostly through the new tenure policy) to become *loteadores* (real estate owners of the newly created lots). From the early 1950s, the owners of farms, especially those located near the urban core, dismembered their property into lots and inserted themselves in the business of real estate transaction.

In 1960, greater Dourados still had 84,955 inhabitants, with only 16,468 in urban areas and 68,483 in rural areas. The 1960s saw the greatest explosion in population for Dourados due to in-migration, mostly from rural Rio Grande do Sul, the Northeast, São Paulo, Santa Catarina, and Paraná, as well as from Japan and Paraguay.

The great shift in the 1970s from rural to urban inhabitants took place as the price of land decreased and as a result of the perception that land was more abundant in Dourados than in neighboring regions along Brazil's eastern littoral. In the agricultural colony of Dourados, the struggle for possession of lots intensified with the formation of new planting areas and farms. The introduction of more capital-intensive farming techniques redefined the region's inclusion in national agriculture, transforming it into a space specializing in capitalist production of agropastoral products like beef and grains. These transformations, driven by the need to meet the demand of the international market (as described in chapter 4), attracted a skilled, technoscientific and information-oriented workforce (e.g., agricultural engineers, surveyors, veterinarians, accountants, doctors, and university professors). Beyond those changes in the agricultural economy, federal interventions greatly impacted Dourados during this period as well, including changes in public administration and housing loans.

In 1976 INCRA implemented in the city of Dourados the Projeto Fundiário do Sul de Mato Grosso (Land Project of Mato Grosso). The initiative contributed to the development of Dourados as a major agricultural center of the state and the country by paving more than 1,200 km of roads and extending the electricity network from Campo Grande to Dourados. In the same period, the development policies triggered the expansion of an agricultural system for agribusiness interests. In the southern portion of Mato Grosso do Sul, the expansion of the system was the result of the convergence of three simultaneous processes begun in the late 1960s: (1) the depletion of the agricultural frontier in the state of Rio Grande do Sul; (2) the vigorous expansion of the international market of soybeans; and (3) policies of a state development initiative to encourage expansion of agriculture for capitalized exports, with a strong focus in the central-west region. In this context, Dourados then began to assume the role of regional hub. The population growth spurred the creation of a consumer market and subsequently enabled the expansion of commercial activity. The city began to concentrate traders and owners of agricultural machinery capable of cultivating large areas.

In the 1970s the entrance of construction firms brought higher private investment in housing production. Their larger-scale production streamlined sector activities that had been previously restricted to transactions based on the purchase and sale of unbuilt lots. However, housing development intervened in this framework. The use of buildings as residential units became a significant object of business transactions (purchase, sale, and rental). Such changes also boosted institutions involved in the field of real estate marketing, such as brokerage firms, construction companies, developers, investors, landlords, and owners of large areas in the city, among others, which featured a complex network of relations between the different actors involved in the production, consumption, and appropriation of urban space.

Amid all of this, people streaming into the city faced a market for land and rents for housing that favored private developers, with scant attention to public housing or accommodation of lower-wage settlers. In 1980 the city of Dourados reached 106,493 inhabitants. Although this figure is miniscule compared with that of cities like São Paulo and Belo Horizonte, which experienced similar trajectories and forces driving urbanization, in the central-west region this growth (particularly its basis in agribusiness expansion) was remarkable. In the following twenty years, the city doubled in size. Since the late 1990s, Dourados has undergone a new phase of industrialization and growth, mainly in processing sugarcane to produce sugar and sugarcane-based ethanol fuel.

Many people crowding into the city peripheries and reservations through this period of economic growth circulated back to rural areas to work as manual laborers (particularly cane cutters) for agribusiness firms. Some came to interject themselves into this history by calling for an interruption, and thereby a protest camp for land reform emerged, which was unique for the Indigenous people.

The circumstances surrounding the initiation of some of the earlier Guaraní protest camps were the subject of diverse renderings shared with me by activists and academics. They described the period as one of intense persecution carried out by one of the political factions on the Dourados reservation, which included events that led up to launch of some of the camps. I emphasize that I only heard rumors regarding this history of such happenings on the reservation during that period. These stories were neither substantiated nor documented. Yet, to the degree that these histories were relayed to me orally, they provided a context and periodization for some of that era's movements and mobilizations. The larger context of agribusiness displacements over many decades further beset these circumstances.

These events took place in the 1990s and led to the launching of all of the camps in which I studied. These camps, as a small subset of those in the region, hardly exemplify a shared origin story of Indigenous protest camps. Yet, the significant conflict on the reservation helped to catalyze the flight of multiple eventual camp leaders, including Rubem and Carmen. The minimal mention of the story of the intrareservation conflicts in the official rhetoric of campers and camp leaders is important for reasons that I will explore in detail subsequently. Still, despite its importance, we may also consider such conflicts as somewhat perfunctory, if punctuated in the testimonies regarding the history of the protest camp mobilizations and history of the Dourados reservation. As described by those with whom I talked in the region, anthropologists and activists alike, the conflicts were merely a few of the encounters among many like them involving violent political disputes over land, delimited space, and power struggles mediated by the state. In other words, events on the reservation, conflicts resulting from overcrowding, and internal politics were all factors mediated by state administration of the reservation and broader region (see, for example, my discussion of the spatializing in chapter 5).

In sum, various caciques who went on to become leaders of camps-tekohas left the reservation to retake their ancestral lands, catalyzed (in part and in that particular moment) by conflicts taking place under conditions on the reservation. They set out to revindicate an area that I am calling Prima Estampa as a conjoined force. These endeavors included caciques who were indeed originally from Prima Estampa before having been displaced onto the reservation of Dourados many years before. Additionally, this group included José, Rubem, Carmen, and her now-deceased husband, who had formerly led Aldeia A and went on to lead camps-tekohas in areas from which they had been previously displaced.

These events were part of the larger advent of the Guaraní protest camp tactics in the Dourados region in that era. They are continuous, if notably distinct, with the larger history of violent colonial settler and agribusiness expansion that had led to the predicament of displacement of Guaraní onto the Dourados reservation in the first place. State attempts to both impose and manage the resultant social organization produced unintended consequences that it nevertheless continues to attempt to control. Unsurprisingly, land is the object of dispute and desire, given the extent of crowding on the reservation and conflicts over production and circulation of goods like food and rents. Housing on the reservation is also a source of power and conflict. Anyone who migrates to the reservation without kin ties has to live on someone else's land in exchange for rent. One of Carmen's sons, for example, formerly lived on the Dourados reservation, though she and most of her family have closer family ties to reservations elsewhere in the region. However, such impetuses to launch protest camps merely contextualize and instantiate a larger predicament of longstanding displacement and land loss in the region.

In 2011 I talked with members of the Prima Estampa aldeia (which by then was in the process of being recognized as a new Indigenous reservation) who had been involved with Prima Estampa since its start. While drinking tereré together, a few of the leaders of Prima Estampa described to me the period in which they retook the land in 1998. The conversation stretched over hours, similar to many such conversations that I had during fieldwork. We sat in a circle of chairs on the red-hued ground outside a house. Residents swept and beat the radius of earth surrounding houses to keep the area free of any grass, as snakes would then be visible against the dark red dirt.

Participants in that day's discussion included Thais, a woman in her fifties who had been described to me as the most powerful person at Prima Estampa; her daughter; and her mother. Several men of multiple generations participated as well. A twentysomething who had trained as a teacher took much of the lead in the conversation. Indeed, both he and Thais's daughter were quite vocal, although they must have been children at the time of the retaking of Prima Estampa. In her leadership, Thais exuded almost subdued calm, being measured and deliberate in her speaking. I noted that this was a sharp contrast to Rubem, José, and Carmen. Like the other leaders, though, she was extremely friendly and extended her time and community to me. Because I had been introduced to Thais by a member of a federal agency who has a long history of advocating for Indigenous people in the region, her community recognized me as someone friendly to their struggle.

The leaders of Prima Estampa described how they had arrived there with Rubem, José, Carmen, and Carmen's now-deceased husband. They all set up the camp together, living there to reclaim the land from the fazendeiros who were using the area as a cattle ranch. A fencing structure for cattle still stood in the distance, visible from where we were sitting. Confronting the fazendeiro by setting up camps-tekohas right in front of them was harrowing, they shared. The fazendeiro and his security guards shot at them and threatened other forms of violence.

At the same time, the leaders' shared efforts were not without conflicts. According to one of the grandmothers in the aldeia, one day there was a fight over cestas basicas. When Rubem angrily left, he made quite a ruckus, taking with him the *banheiro* (toilet) and other things from the house that the group had constructed. He threw furniture in the *poço* (water well) as well. "Things got very ugly," she recalled. Carmen and her husband left with Rubem to set up Aldeia D around 2003 or 2004. From there, Carmen left Aldeia D after assisting him to get settled, and she and her husband established their own camp, Aldeia A.

### Histories in the Day-to-Day

Working on the side of the highway in the camps, conducting interviews, chatting, and observing, I experienced vulnerability that I suppose anyone would while sitting in a protest camp. Participating in a political protest requires submitting yourself to a certain degree of willful vulnerability and putting yourself in a crossfire. I recorded testimonies of violent encounters—security forces running over campers with trucks, hacking them with machetes, and threats of worse. Several of these encounters involved ongoing police investigations of murder and assault. All of this gave me the paranoid sense that anything could happen at any moment.

Similarly, the campers maintained a steady awareness of what was happening around them, even at relaxed moments. Seemingly out of fear of surveillance and more threats and attacks, they commented cautiously on the occasional truck that would linger for too long by the side of the road. The camps hugged the edges of highways, sites not intended for lingering passers-by. After all, highways are meant for hurrying along, for transport, for movement. The camps' interruption of that understanding of the road therefore presented an abasement of the very concept of highway, which made anyone else's presence and lurking on the roadside already highly suspect.

In addition to the lack of central organization to the Guaraní land protests, there was sometimes also a lack of perceived shared interest both on the reservation and across camps. The leaders of the camps in which I conducted research were skeptical of each other's claims, at times even antagonistic. Carmen said outright that José's claims were not substantial and that he already had land on the reservation. Additionally, local anthropologists working on the Dourados reservation made it clear to me that some of the Guaraní on the reservation are not in favor of state demarcations of land for some of the protest campers. Such is the heterogeneity and complexity among Guaraní, who of course hold diverse viewpoints. For example, in my conversations, some people shared their worry about what would happen to the availability of work on the agribusiness plantations depending on how demarcations play out.

Over time, protest campers described most misfortunes that befell them as the results of the malice and misdeeds of fazendeiros. For example, on one of my first trips to Aldeia A, the campers took me to the sugarcane fazenda to show me where they had buried their aunt. They accused the fazendeiro of having disinterred the aunt's body. In contrast, though, an official investigation by the Ministerio Publico Federal treated the story skeptically, noting that the aunt had probably not died from foul play.

As another example, one day at Aldeia B, the camp leader José asked me to assist in tracking down his daughter-in-law. He explained that she had disappeared after a violent confrontation with fazenda security forces. He stated that the daughter-in-law had been living in the camp with one of his sons and the couple's baby. Security forces had arrived and, after many threats and insults to the campers, kidnapped her. José wanted my help to drive him and his wife into Dourados to track down the daughter-in-law. After many stops along the way, for example at Fundação Nacional de Saúde (the national health agency FUNASA) and FUNAI, I learned that the most credible explanation for the daughter-in-law's disappearance was that she had run away from the son after he had beaten her. She was probably in hiding with relatives or friends on the Dourados reservation, where she was born and had lived her whole life.

Yet José and his family maintained that the reports of the Women's Hospital (Hôspital de Mulher) administrators, which confirmed that the daughter-in-law had indeed gone there days before for treatment for injuries, did not undercut their accusations against the fazendeiro. The daughter-in-law, however, had described to the administrators how her injuries resulted from domestic violence at the hands of her drunken husband. José denied the daughter-in-law's testimony, stating that her story was in fact a part of the fazendeiro's conspiracy against the camp. According to José, the daughter-in-law had lied to officials at both the state agencies and hospital due to the bribery and coercion of the fazendeiro's security. At that point, José declared that he simply wanted to track down the daughter-in-law for her own safety and that my help was especially urgent given the depth of the fazendeiro conspiracy.

Each aldeia relayed particular histories, which I describe in greater detail in the sections that follow.

*Aldeia A*

The campers' official narratives of their ties to the land emphasized the organization of dwelling structures in relation to rivers, forests, and animals in the region. The official historian of Aldeia A, who was the designated vice-captain of the camp, showed me a hand-drawn map of the camp's aldeia; he explained that the map was designed to show the aldeia before invasion by fazendeiros.

Importantly, the map did not represent any particular time. The proportions of distances between places were irregular, and different times when people lived in different places overlay one another. He repeated a refrain throughout the explanation: *"A gente sabe onde morreu"* (We know where a given person or thing died).

Another recurrent idea concerned the preoccupation with documentation itself. In a 2011 interview, the same interlocutor pointed out that with and for the non-Indians–whites, *"Pela palavra ninguem resolve. Tem que por no papel, bem direitinho. É a nossa história"* (No one resolves anything with words. You have to put it on paper, just so. This is our history.) He showed me handwritten notes in Portuguese, testimonies of different campers living in the aldeia regarding the violence suffered at the hands of fazendeiros. I asked questions about the topic, such as the following:

PROTEST CAMPER: The father and ex-leader (cacique/capitão) was run over by a car. He left for the city, then a car came and ran him over. He died and everyone became deflated. We had no one to take care of our people. The next day a *karai* (spiritual leader) prayed and also became cacique. The new leader did not speak Portuguese, only Guaraní. Then, there arrived a Brazilian saying he'd bought the land.

SULLIVAN: All of this after the death of [the former camp leader].

CAMPER: The karai brought the people together. When we lost the leader, a Brazilian bought the land and the Guaranís were not united (*ficou cada Guaraní a seu lado*). The Brazilian said that he had already registered the land under his name, but the Indians only left at gunpoint (*á tira*). The first that he killed was the captain. Before, the land was all forests. There were no cane fields (*lavoura*). All of the map was all forest. The first thing the fazendeiro did was start to knock down the trees (*derrubar a mata*). He also burned the prayer house (*casa de reza*).

SULLIVAN: Who constructed the road that bifurcates the aldeia?

CAMPER: Before this was the road that cut through the forest. *Y'pi-aru* [sp.?], that's what everyone called it. *This* is the river that runs across the northern border, constitutes the northern border of the aldeia. This other river is the eastern border of the aldeia. The southern border is the road that goes to [a nearby town]. The fazendeiro killed [another leader] at the southeastern corner. [The leader] got up early and went down to the river at the southeast corner to get water to drink and a *jagunça* [fazendeiro security] shot him in the back of the head. There are cemeteries where he is buried. Before he died he told the story of the aldeia written here. I made these paper documents here.

An example of such a document was a letter addressed to FUNAI that included the lines "We are going to wait a little bit more. We have to go with a little more patience. We will wait for the results of the studies that the authorities request. The Ministerio Publico asked this of us."

Descriptions of violence dominated my first weeks in Aldeia A. I recorded video of passionate shouting by the campers. For example, in one video Oswaldo (a son of the camp leader) spoke to the camera:

> When the fazendeiros kill me, I want to be buried on the other side of that fence. I am going to enter [the plantation]. I'm going back there. I was born there. I'm going back there. And when they kill me, I will stay there.

Oswaldo was a man in his twenties who lived in the camp with his wife, a woman whom he had met at another camp not far from Dourados. He was one of the four sons of Carmen and the former camp leader.

Over the course of the seven months that I spent conducting fieldwork in the camp, Oswaldo mysteriously disappeared. I later discovered that he and an associate of his (a non-Indian who lived in Dourados) had been arrested and jailed in the city on charges of drug trafficking. There is no shortage of media coverage of drug use, drug trafficking, street violence, underaged sex workers, and descriptions of myriad delinquency on the Dourados reservation. Documentaries on national TV news shows broadcast Mato Grosso do Sul's "troubled Indians," as they described them. These descriptors could apply no less to the region's non-Indian population; troubled youth narratives cut across both Indian reservations and city peripheries.

By the time I finished my fieldwork in the camp, another of Carmen's brothers, his wife, and her close kin had also joined the camp from another nearby disbanded camp. Their old camp was unraveling for multiple reasons, including in-fighting and pressure from the manager of the small-scale factory that was located on the property, in which some of the protest-campers also worked. Their former manager ran a company that grew grass sod and managed a brick-making factory. Many of the land protestors at that site worked in those enterprises in exchange for the manager looking the other way about their camp. However, toward the end of my fieldwork stint in 2011 that manager began evicting most of them, for reasons that they were not telling me. Their relocation to join Aldeia A was a boon for Carmen. Numbers are a must in roadside camps; roughly two dozen people at any given time were living in Aldeia

A. The more people they have, the more support exists to maintain life in the camp and stand up against attacks. Higher numbers also bolster the camps' visibility on the roadside.

In addition to state welfare cestas basicas delivered by INCRA and FUNAI, the camps maintained small crops for subsistence. Carmen took on the extra task of raising chickens, and she sold eggs and chickens to nearby non-Indian land-protest camps. However, this activity presented the challenge of acquiring sufficient cash from the remunerated labor of her sons and a daughter to buy the necessary dried corn to feed the chickens. This combination of reliance on the remunerated labor of her children, her small trade in chickens, and state welfare benefits meant that even the bare maintenance of the camp required quite a bit of circulating to different sites in the region for additional resources. These challenges included reviving the camp-tekoha with every attack by fazendeiros' hired security. I spent many days in the camps providing transport between Carmen's camp-tekoha (Aldeia A), Aldeia C, and the FUNAI office in Dourados. Carmen needed to go to FUNAI regularly to plea for more lona (plastic covering for the shacks) and cestas basicas. The latter often did not arrive with sufficient frequency to meet her camp's needs.

The women in Carmen's camp mostly stayed in the camp, unless they visited their family in nearby reservations. Oswaldo's wife told me that she considered leaving, to ensure that she would have enough for her and her children to survive. I asked several activists and an anthropologist why the division of labor along gender lines occurred in this way. They pointed out safety as a major consideration, particularly cases of gang rape of women at the plantations where workers sometimes lived part time in dormitories during cane-cutting season. It was unusual that Carmen's daughter worked for a firm in the countryside. Carmen's daughter and son-in-law remained in Aldeia C even after its disbanding, because they were both brick makers for the firm. Although all of the branco women in the Federation of Family Agriculture (FAF) camp worked for agribusiness firms, Carmen's daughter was the only female Guaraní protest camper that I encountered who did such work. Furthermore, she did so despite having small children.

Carmen's preoccupation with maintaining a substantial population in the camp sometimes clashed with her concern over gendered violence and the ethnic divisions that splintered Aldeia A. For example, while Carmen was away attending a land-reform rally in Brasilia, a Terena man in the camp-tekoha allegedly attempted to rape her sister's older daughter. I say allegedly only because the Terena campers disputed the allegation. The Terena in the camp were led by Maria, a woman in her forties, who had lived in the camp for months with her daughter, three sons, and an unidentified white woman. It was never clear to me how many people were affiliated with Aldeia A at a given moment; the number fluctuated regularly. Maria had lived there for three months at the time of the alleged attack.

The tensions between the Terena and Guaraní in the camp eventually reached a point at which Carmen wanted to evict them. I arrived at the camp one morning to a rather heated meeting in which the campers were airing their grievances. Allegations of theft and attempted rape flew back and forth in a mixture of Portuguese and Guaraní languages. Earlier that day, Carmen had already gone to the FUNAI offices in Dourados to request help with the eviction, walking many miles from the camp to the bus into town. Her handwritten note to FUNAI (presumably written by another camper since Carmen did not know how to write) stated that the Terenas living in the camp should be removed because one of them had twice attempted to rape her niece. Carmen stated in the letter that the camp is for Índios only. Terena and brancos should not be there, she said, specifically complaining of the presence of the white woman. In the camp meeting, Diego chimed in as well, as upset as Carmen. She later told me that FUNAI replied to her that they would send someone there to investigate. She also told me that if the white person had not left voluntarily by the next day, the police would arrive and force them to leave. I asked Carmen how the branca had come to live there in the first place. I got no response. In that same conversation Diego volunteered that he had been to the Dourados reservation earlier to talk to the reservation *capitão* (captain) about moving the Terenas back to the reservation. Apparently, they did not have anywhere to move back to. According to Diego, the Terenas living in the camp were not wanted on the reservation either.

The situation eventually culminated in Carmen bringing in reinforcement allies from Aldeia C to forcibly remove the Terenas. I had driven the

**Fig 8.** Plantation field in countryside of Dourados. Photograph by LaShandra Sullivan.

route many times before, shuttling Carmen and other campers between the sites. One day she asked me to help transport her brother and three other men from Aldeia c to Aldeia a. They carried nightsticks and wore navy blue smocks. The back of the smocks read "Segurança Tekoha" (Tekoha security) in gold lettering, with a gold silhouette of an Indian headdress blazoned in its center. I was curious about the smocks and

wondered if they had any official designations or commissions from
FUNAI or another other state agency. Despite this show of force, the
Terena did not move until FUNAI sent a truck to help them move their
things several days later.

Guaraní and FAF campers welcomed my documentation of their claims
in my fieldwork. Carmen and her sons stated that my work could pos-
sibly contribute to their getting state attention and a procedural path
to legal demarcation of land. Over the course of months of fieldwork, I
pieced together that Carmen had initially voluntarily participated in the
Aldeia A mobilization after leaving the reservation on the outskirts of
Caraapó. Her mother and most of her family still live there. She met her
husband, former camp leader Luis, some time ago. They had embarked
upon their lives as land protestors under the circumstances described.

Over the course of different stints of fieldwork between 2007 and 2011,
it became clear that the camp leaders' official biographies and camp
histories, like many biographies, are carefully crafted. However, the
campers' life stories of perpetual movement are not unique. They are, in
fact, commonplace among formerly rural people in the region. Campers
hoped that their struggles, suffering, and sacrifices would bring favorable
results. They held hope in part because similar violence and hardships
suffered by other camps-tekohas had borne fruit, including such examples as Prima Estampa and Rubem's settlement. Both of those former
camps-tekohas had gained some degree of state recognition of their land
claims and enjoyed state services like water sanitation.

## Aldeia B

As touched upon earlier, neither Carmen, Rubem, José, nor any of the
campers mentioned the 1990s intrareservation conflicts in their official
testimonies to me of their histories in the camps. Instead, they emphasized how they were too long kept away from the land they were claiming,
expressing a belonging to those places—physically and spiritually, as I
will describe in more detail in chapter 6. They relayed details of their
expulsions from those lands, happenings that preceded their time on
reservations.

The cacique leaders' strategies for maintaining their camps and seeking
demarcation differed. Carmen led her camp while living there full time

and circulating to meetings, travelling to the FUNAI office in the city of Dourados, and maintaining and cultivating allies at other camps. In contrast, the Aldeia B leader, José, fought a war (so to speak) on two fronts. In addition to confronting fazendeiros that held the land that his camp-tekoha revindicated, he was engaged in a struggle to maintain family land holdings on the Dourados reservation.

### Aldeia D

Since his participation in protest camping, Rubem has been a notable cacique in the Guaraní social movements in the region. I had previously seen Rubem in a documentary film from anthropologists and activists specializing on the region's land conflict. Years ago, when Rubem lived on the Dourados reservation, he had risen to become a captain (capitão). He lost his position of leadership due to a decline in support among residents on the reservation. As a camp leader, Rubem later became famous for a clash with police officers in his camp, in which he mistook the police for fazendeiros' private security forces.

The camp had long been subject to surveillance, harassment, and threats. Rubem and the other campers thus armed themselves with knives and machetes in the event of an attack. One day, plainclothes police officers arrived in unmarked cars. The officers fired a shot into the air while calling for one of the campers to come out. The police were reportedly there to investigate a crime that had taken place in Dourados. They suspected that the accused, an Indigenous Guaraní who was rumored to be affiliated with the camp, had taken refuge there. But due to the lack of uniforms and unmarked car, the campers did not know that the men were police officers. They therefore attacked the men, stabbing them repeatedly. The resultant publicity from the stabbings, subsequent imprisonment of the campers involved, and later Rubem's house arrest made the news far and wide throughout the state and the region.

After this incident, the state finally authorized and designated anthropological studies on the camp's land claims, with the camp gaining provisory degrees of recognition. Camp members were afterward able to occupy a broader swath of the plantation's land. I was there in 2010 as FUNASA installed a water system to provide clean water for the camp.

And when I returned in 2011, the camp-turned-demarcated-Indigenous-area was thriving. The aldeia included multiple extended family groups, consisting of dozens of people. I share an excerpt from a conversation with Rubem during one of my visits to the aldeia:

SULLIVAN: So this is your garden and is just your family's?

RUBEM (pointing to the areas around him): Just of me and my family. This is squash. Here is manioc. [He pulls out a manioc plant from the ground to show that it is soft.] This is young still. If it wasn't you wouldn't be able to uproot it like this.

He later explains:

RUBEM: Therefore, this is what I am saying to you and to everybody, to give us back our land just so that we can plant. We need manioc. And here there's no more room without encroaching up on another family. Over there where you see corn, already that's another family's land.

SULLIVAN: Another family on the aldeia?

RUBEM: Family from the aldeia, yes—of our brothers. So, it's like this, young lady.

Then he later elaborated:

SULLIVAN (remarking on the relatively good material well-being of the aldeia, compared to some of the other camps): You guys have everything here, eh?

RUBEM: Thanks to god. But this here is not our land—not yet. We want more land, more in order to plant. If we had forty or fifty acres . . . right now is enough for us to eat. But if we could have enough to send a box of bananas to the city— We have very little money, young lady. How are we going to be able to buy what we need? Of course, the white people (os brancos) would make money for us if we sold these bananas. Look how they are ripe, beautiful. Our children here get sick sometimes. And we don't have money. How are we going to buy for the children? So, this is all. I am not complaining, but we want more already. If we had a surplus— We have enough for the children to eat, but we have to sell for us to buy. Here no one has money to buy sugar. We no longer have forests to be able to forage honey. We no longer have so many kinds of honey.

SULLIVAN: So you have to be able to buy?

RUBEM: You have to buy. And with money from producing we have to buy sugar, no?

SULLIVAN: So, you are wanting to produce enough to be able to sell and make enough money to buy necessities?

RUBEM: Of course, of course. We have to buy sugar, we have to buy soap, we have to buy all that we have to buy. And how will we buy it? That's why we work today. I just got done saying that we work in the sugarcane fields. Today we have to train to study. If you are going to cut cane, you have to know how to cut cane. If we are going to be tour guides for tourists, we have to take classes for training.

Later, he continued:

RUBEM: We need a teacher on the aldeia and the school to be fixed. The municipal government built us a school, but then they abandoned it. Our children take a bus to school in the city and come back starving from the trip. How are they going to learn? How are they going to become good citizens?

In stark contrast to other camps, with these expanded holdings, they produced enough food to live. Rubem nonetheless complained that they needed more land in order to produce a surplus to sell. Likewise, many of the adult male campers still commute to work as remunerated labor for agribusiness firms. Rubem's son worked for a bridge-construction company and travelled to Paraná (the neighboring eastern state) to construct a bridge. The booming agro-industrial economy and influx of nationally and internationally financed infrastructure projects in the region had been good for his son's line of work, Rubem said.

As the transcription attests, the need to expand holdings followed the ongoing insistence on not moving again, even after having attained some success. Furthermore, Rubem's testimony sometimes included a commonly expressed sentiment among the campers: a possibility for things like school education for children. Such rhetoric is both politically savvy and an insight into internal debates among Guaraní leaders about inclusion in Brazil as Guaraní and as Brazilians.

Guaraní land activists and anthropologists corroborated that Rubem led a group of people who were indeed most likely displaced from precisely the very area that they were reclaiming. As an experienced political leader and former reservation captain, Rubem had the skills to lead such a mobilization and successfully guide it toward state attention and demarcation studies, no matter how tenuously and at times tragically. To establish evidence in the demarcation studies, he drew upon the experiences and stories of the people who had been displaced from the area over the course of generations.

The efforts of José, Carmen, and Rubem demonstrate that the camp leaders' success and skill in maintaining the camps require deploying strategies and tactics to (1) maintain the security of the camp; (2) manage internal conflicts and challenges; (3) procure basic resources like cestas basicas and lona from state agencies; and (4) seek out the assistance of anthropologists, NGOs, and other activists to put in motion legal studies and other processes to gain state recognition. To verify histories of ties to a given parcel of land is difficult if the family has faced multiple moments of displacement. For example, colleagues relayed to me that Carmen's family currently resides in Lima Campo, an area hundreds of kilometers from the plantation where Aldeia A is located but, due to multiple displacements, the area where they currently find themselves. An anthropologist advised me that the Guaraní concept of tekoha guasu (extended home region) nevertheless captures their ties to the area. Vietta (2007) argues that although a disputed area is not the exact place of an inhabitance, it may be part of the larger tekoha guasu of the protest campers. This approach helpfully situates the Guaraní land claimants' testimonies, since often in the camps-tekohas—despite the tenuous ties the the leader is able to provide evidence for—some of the members of the camps, previous generations, or both have lived in a specific area they are claiming. Sometimes—seemingly most likely for Aldeias A and B—some of the members of the camps-tekohas had also lived in areas adjacent or nearby the land lot that they are occupying. The mobility alerts us to the historicized arbitrariness of state cadastral lines derived from previous colonial settlement.

As an anthropologist working in the region explained to me one day, as well as corroborated in my conversations with my activist colleagues in the camp, some Indians also moved around on the reservation. They frequently deconstructed houses and moved to another place. This presented complications with the government programs for the provision of immobile construction materials for houses carried out a few years before my fieldwork. When construction materials for homes were lent only to fixed structures, some families moved by simply exchanging one house for another. Unlike real estate transactions, or the type of forced transience imposed by labor conditions, however, these relocations often arose from ways of dwelling having to do with cosmogonic relations to the landscape (discussed in more detail in chapter 6).

### Violence, Mobility and Time Horizons

The ethnographic details presented in this chapter illuminate the dilemma of the campers' slipstream of material precariousness and deprivations imposed by the prevailing political and economic structures of land and labor. The claim to land is a claim to a cessation of displacement and forced transience, vividly demonstrated by Diego's case in chapter 2. Moreover, the vignettes of this chapter point to a slipstream of powerlessness that land activists seek to counter.

We see something similar (and yet different) to Holston's (2008) observations about land protests in the peripheries of São Paulo. Holston describes how Paulistanos weave together claims of long-term generational belonging to place; in so doing, they really do construct such belonging through building houses. This building process may occur over multiple generations. Yet those practices of belonging can be undone in a moment's notice because, for example, those living in such housing do not have proper state documentation (e.g., building permits or a land title). Holston describes how building houses is, in this way, a sort of construction of a self. The building of a house is never completed. There is always the coming project of a new roof, a side panel, or flooring, for example, that requires quotidian tasks of construction, accumulation of materials and means, and so on. Holston nicely captures a set of conditions not unlike those of the land protesters that I describe in this ethnography. Due to their impermanence, camps are also a practice of unending construction and reconstruction. The parallel unending construction of a self-narrative, of an abideable and recognizable legitimacy, is an effort at fixedness and permanence. Though, importantly, the Guaraní protesters go about this in distinct ways and terms.

The history of the Guaraní camps and the protesters' ongoing day-to-day practices and strategies to maintain themselves make clear that their claims-making both instantiates and falls somewhat short of the sort of autoconstruction of self as citizen purportedly conferred by land title (whether individual or communal, as in the case of Indigenous lands). Instead, what I show in this chapter is that their existence had become transitory in a very literal sense. The logic of the solution—protest camping—is specific to the problem. Like the work documents that I describe in chapter 2, what is supposed to facilitate upward mobility actually creates a condition of constraints and binding, which protest camps seek to elude. I will more elaborately argue in the following chapter that they insist on relations to and through landscapes that are not amenable to real estate logics. Protest campers seek to both materially survive current circumstances and to establish a toehold for attaining something beyond mere survival. Attention to the political, economic, and social structures determining movement, dislocations, and relocations undercuts ruralist attempts to delegitimize Indigenous rights to land in Dourados.

Many members of the camps-tekohas testify to histories of dwelling on parcels of land as constrained by the exigencies of land law, yet they hold on to hope that those stories will allow them to overcome their dilemma of perpetual material insecurity. It is worth querying why the state agents that arbitrate land demarcation cannot accept a plea to demarcate land by Indigenous activists such as "we just need enough land"; they can only hear, for example, "we need this space for our cultural integrity." We can ask and challenge the delimitation by law of what kinds of claims can be viewed as authentic based on individual biographies of the members of the camps-tekohas. Perceptions of discrepancies and veracity matter because the state cannot consider certain kinds of claims politically viable. And as the marco temporal efforts underway show, the anti-Indigenous political pressure is ever unrelenting.

**Fig 9.** Sign at an Indigenous protest camp that reads, "Murderous State." Photograph by LaShandra Sullivan.

The Guaraní activists push back against such pressure and criticize state complicities in their oppression. For example, see figure 9.

Given the position of material deprivation in which the protest campers wage their battle for land, we should view their strategic testimonies as an attempt to establish some traction in their slipstream of precariousness from which to make a case against further displacement. Along these lines, making sense of the invocations of Guaraní culture as a basis for a way of life and ties to land requires interrogating the campers' preoccupations beyond the short time horizons in which they are required to act for daily survival. Although they necessarily have to operate within short turnover cycles in their struggle to materially reproduce life, their land claims point to longer time horizons of both displacement and regaining of place in a *longue durée*.

In light of the ethnographic analysis of this chapter, we should view the protesters' claims as in part directed toward increasing their capacity to achieve movements through life cycles beyond the short turnover time of survival required in organizing day-to-day life in the camps-tekohas. Toward different ends and in different ways, not always synchronously nor harmoniously, they balance this longer view amid and despite the hustle and bustle of maintaining the camps, not to mention the challenges of attacks from security forces and the disdain of mainstream non-Indian society in Dourados. The struggle for land is a struggle for the means to aspire, to be able to take a longer view and time horizon in concrete detail. This time horizon does not contradict the alternate conceptions of time (and space) referenced in Guaraní cosmologies (see chapter 6), which likewise do not conform to temporal logics of non-Indians.

# The Space to Be                                          6

In this chapter I describe how the constraints of the culture concept present a double bind that restricts how protesters can frame both the problem of historical displacements and the solution of land titling. The ways that the concept of culture operates in Brazil may unduly and inadvertently constrain Indigenous land protesters in Mato Grosso do Sul. As mentioned in previous chapters, demonstration of cultural ties to the landscape are requisites of Indigenous land law. The constraints of the culture concept overarch, underlie, and interlace activists' efforts.

The juridico-political determinations for how activists present their relations to land do not fully encompass their day-to-day experiences or conceptualization of such relations. Such relations can be difficult to disentangle, though, especially when such parsing presents perils for how state agencies and courts assess the veracity and legitimacy of those claims. Thus, I do not attempt such parsing here. Rather, in this chapter, I discuss how activists presented said relations to me and how myriad outsiders, including anthropologists and government officials, take them up. I go about this grounded in analysis of both the anthropological literature on Guaraní relations to and through land, ethnographic work with Guaraní land activists, and attention to the juridico-political situatedness in which the contests for land play out.

I do not pretend to present the truth of said Guaraní relations to and through land nor speak for the Guaraní activists with whom I worked. Collaboratively engaged work toward those ends are valuable, but by now it should be clear that such an attempt on my part would be farcical and contrary to my project. Rather, I seek to get at how the entanglements of protest campers' ongoing and complex relations to and through landscapes, in practice, entail grappling with the presence of, and constraints imposed by, anthropologists, governmental officials, agribusiness-related antagonists, and land laws.

Guaraní protestors invoke a prior and ongoing way of life, an alternative cosmology, and ethnoancestral ties to land to contest the agribusiness hegemony. Insofar as the Guaraní camps-tekohas encompass relations between people and spirit owners (donos or *jary* in the Guarani language) that dwell in the landscape, for example, the land conflict is a contest over ways of life that pits a cultural regime (based on cosmogonic relations) against one grounded in a disenchanted capitalism. By contrast, agribusiness space refers to both the discursive and material production of the countryside as devoid of such dwelling, what Lefebvre ([1974] 1991) would call abstract space or absolute space.

The importance of always situating discussion of Guaraní culture in the land conflict echoes sentiments expressed by both the people with whom I worked in the camps-tekohas and Guaraní anthropologists in the region. For example, Guaraní anthropologist Tonico Benites wrote the following about how to treat Guarani concepts in this regard: "The re-signification of these concepts took place, above all, from the context of the struggle for the reoccupation of their tekoha, including being associated with other socio-cultural practices. This is the case, for example, of some religious rituals that can only be understood in terms of the delicate situations that the reoccupation process triggers, raising the possibility of a conflict that obliges indigenous families to defend themselves effectively" (Benites 2014, 30).

In this chapter I discuss a *festa de milho* (corn festival), as well as other invocations of cosmogonic relations to spirits and deities that I witnessed during fieldwork, as moments that help us understand the double bind faced by Guaraní land activists and the anthropologists who work with them. I was invited to attend that *festa de milho*, called *avati kyry* (new corn) in the Guaraní language, in December 2011. It took place at Panambizinho, one of the few areas in southern Mato Grosso do Sul where the ritual reportedly still occurs.

Thinking through treatments of such testimonies in the anthropological literature, I foreground attention to my role as an anthropologist, particularly to the fact that I am a non-Indian (and an American one at that). Throughout fieldwork and writing this book I felt constantly aware of the ethical responsibility of mediating my ethnographic interlocutors' self-representations to wider publics. The Guaraní protesters are well aware of this situatedness of my work, as Diego's appeal that I pretend to be his American lawyer (described in chapter 2) exemplifies. I emphasize, though, that my grappling with the protesters' awareness of our mutual situatedness does not mean that we should simply reduce their testimonies and what I observed in our work to their merely instrumental character. Calling attention to my place as an outsider and non-Indian, with the attending limits to understanding what I witnessed, in addition to the limits to what the people I worked with shared with me, allows us to see the particular perspective that I bring to this analysis. Mine is a position of limited knowledge. Many things I simply did not know and should not know regarding the folks with whom I worked. At these interstices, we can nevertheless gain insights on the land struggle between the activists and agribusiness interests.

In this foregrounding, I am reminded of anthropologist Alcida Ramos's (2012, 485) call for humility as it concerns non-Indian anthropologists' pretenses to fully understand Indian cultures.[1] I have no such pretense. Instead, in this chapter I attempt to make sense of my moments of witnessing and documenting the Guaraní activists' self-conscious enactments of cosmogonic relations to landscapes, an element of the cultural ties to land demonstrated in the activists' claims for land.

The primary point of this chapter is to present protesters' testimonies regarding relations to and through spirits and rituals like the corn festival. I'm interested in the ways that both anthropologists and Guaraní utilize the culture concept toward self-consciously political debates and ends. Activists do so in ways that dialogically emerge from relations with each other (human and nonhuman actors) as those relations transpire and transform on the ground. Regarding self-consciousness, I am further reminded of a moment during fieldwork when one of the activists that I worked with described anthropologists as "living off of Indians." Such a characterization deliberately foregrounded the instrumentalist aspects of anthropological knowledge production and occurred in the context of a conversation about solidarities and mutual collaboration. It was not lost on me that my fieldwork with her camp-tekoha fit such a characterization, no matter how collaborative and grounded in intentions for long-term and mutually beneficial relationships. The self-consciousness that we both participated in at that moment and throughout fieldwork frames my treatment of culture in this chapter.

In "Adieu, Culture: A New Duty Arises" Trouillot (2003, 115) writes, "Quite often the word culture blurs rather than elucidates the facts to be explained. . . . Words such as style, taste, cosmology, ethos, sensibility, desire, ideology, aspirations, or predispositions often better describe the facts that need to be studied because they tend to better limit the range of traits and patterns covered and are . . . more grounded in the details that describe living, historically situated, localized people." Along these lines, my concern in this chapter is to home in on what the deployment of the culture concept contains in the specific context of the land conflict. Namely, the entanglement of questions of culture with the Indian question in Brazil animates the ongoing colonial displacements contended with by Indigenous land-protest camps.

The double bind of the culture concept both helped and hindered Guaraní activists' efforts for land restitution. They nevertheless navigated those binds both strategically and sincerely. I relate culture as an intrinsic system of signs, bodily practices, and habitus, which is distinguished from culture as an extrinsic system. The latter is similar to what Carneiro da Cunha (2009) calls a reflexive awareness of one's own culture, which I view as an effect of institutionalized knowledge-production processes, externally imposed for different purposes by state and nonstate actors.

In what follows, I first explain what I mean by the double bind of culture in that latter sense, as it occurs in Indigenous land titling processes. I then provide context for how I am presenting the festa de milho ritual and relations with spirits with which I began this chapter. I do so via a discussion of how such cosmogonic relations have been taken up in the anthropological literature on the Guaraní toward cultural-preservationist arguments for land restitution, reviewing the treatment of the interconnections of Guaraní rituals, land-use practices, and social organization. Importantly, such interconnections sometimes featured prominently in land activists' own uses of cultural-preservationist rhetoric and mentioning of a primordial culture.

In what follows, after explaining the double bind of culture, I describe my encounters with land protesters' attested understandings of the colonial histories affecting them in their decolonial wrangling for land, livelihoods, and ways of living. The positioning of anthropologists in Brazil and anthropological approaches to culture, difference, and cosmology permeate the politics and positions of stakeholders on all sides of the land conflict.

### The Double Bind of the Culture

As it concerns defining and shaping approaches to culture, the role of anthropologists and Guaraní land activists in Brazil requires some sorting out. Land activists sometimes strategically deploy the term *culture* to disrupt their historical and ongoing colonial subjugation. Ironically, opponents of Indigenous land-reform activists also utilize the concept of culture to counter those activists. This antagonism creates a tricky terrain across which Guaraní activists and their advocates must maneuver regarding the culture concept. More than merely an abstract debate concerning lifeways, cosmology, and ontological differences, questions of culture matter for who gets what on the ground, literally.

Cultural-preservationist arguments foreground Indigenous cultures as both uniquely distinct as forerunners to Brazilian national culture, being the first occupants of Brazil, and integral to the uniqueness of Brazil and its national patrimony. This, the argument goes, explains the urgency of designating and protecting Indian occupation of traditional land in order to safeguard their culture. That land activists consciously engage in such rhetoric and terms for land restitution and may sometimes carry out such cosmogonic relations is hardly contradictory. The terms *consciously* and *may sometimes* in the last sentence are key, though. That such a statement can be disqualifying for Indigenous claims-making for land in Brazil reveals much about the double bind that Indians navigate. It also points to the salience and rub of the cultural requirements in criteria for land restitution.

Although Indigenous people ignominiously endure material deprivations due to ethnoracial marking—racism and prejudice—they rely on ethnocultural distinction (and concomitant aforementioned rights) for access to the material means to counter that denigration. This conundrum occurs in the terms for rights and rights discourses forged over the history of anthropology in Brazil. I am not saying they occur because of those terms. I am saying that the context elides a facile cause-effect relation. Indeed, since Cândido Mariano da Silva Rondon spearheaded the creation of the SPI in 1910, some anthropologists have sought to resist and overturn the injustices caused by the violence suffered due to anti-Indigenous actions and policies of the larger society. However, as Teresa Guzmàn (2013) notes, at different moments such interventions sometimes have occurred through the presentation of Indians as in need of tutelage, irreducibly different, and in need of mediators for their own protection. This perpetual reproduction of the image of a "hyperreal" Indian (Ramos 1994) engenders the multiple forms of violence against real Indians. As explained in the previous chapters, on the ground, settlers have brutally sought to integrate real Indians into both national imaginaries and transnational economies of such goods as yerba mate, rubber, gold, soy, and sugarcane.

In their long history of solidarity with Indians, advocates (including some anthropologists) have carved out a protective role as mediators with the state. Of course, Indigenous people themselves lead some such efforts, including joining the state as congressmen and city councilmen, for example. Some vociferously and passionately defend the rights of Indians as culturally (even ontologically) distinct, set apart from the national society. These differences have been the fodder for anthropological theory and earnest political battles. This has been a far from easy task amid the aforementioned, ever-expanding territorial frontier of national integration vis-à-vis national-development policies and often violent integration of farther flung territories since the late nineteenth century.

For Brazil's Indians and ethnologists alike, the distinction between culture as a way of life and culture as a premise for an ethnically differentiated citizenship that can be studied, recognized, and deployed sits uneasily at the heart of this dilemma. Amid this, Brazil's Indians have also been savvy political actors and bravely defiant against violence. For example, in Mato Grosso do Sul, Marçal de Souza was an Indigenous activist who was assassinated in 1983 for his outspoken pushback against this violence. He was one of the creators of the Brazilian Indigenous movement and was one of the principle leaders of the União das Nações Indígenas (Union of Indigenous Nations, or UNI), which was founded in 1980. Indian activists may take up claims to land by utilizing cultural-preservationist arguments, in large part in line with those utilized by anthropologists across myriad contexts.

Opponents of Indigenous land rights assert a collapse of cultural distinctions between Indians and non-Indians in their opposition to Indigenous land demarcation. Arguing that Indians in Dourados are not real Indians, they both denigrate Indigenous activists and deny them redress for their historical denigration in one swoop. That is to say, such assertions claim that Indigenous people in Dourados are not true primitives who lived as they did in the past. According to this logic, those Indians thus do not deserve land demarcation designed for cultural preservation because they have been effectively urbanized in their proximity to the city of Dourados. Such demarcation, opponents argue, would be tantamount to granting special rights to people who are not distinctly Indian and who therefore do not qualify for nor deserve such distinction.

The contradictions of racial ideology in Brazil, which is central to the construction of a universal Brazilian citizen-subject, are on full display here. Famously, Brazilian national mythology champions ethnoracial miscegenation. The aforementioned opponents of land demarcation may deny cultural difference with Índios as a legitimate basis for their land claims by taking recourse to a historical narrative of nation-making through mixture and acculturation. This narrative particularly exoticizes Indian women, especially those mixed with white (e.g., Portuguese) settlers in the colonial history of the region and the making of the Brazilian nation (Ramos 1998). According to this disturbing narrative, brancos pacified wild Indians and incorporated them into the nation as modern laborers. Indigenous consumption of commodities and adaptation to the way of life of the brancos, wearing branco clothes for example, count as evidence in this regard. For example, in public forums against Indigenous land demarcation in towns across southern Mato Grosso do Sul, I observed townspeople and ruralistas pointing out that Indian protesters use cell phones and their children wear disposable diapers. The latter were particularly damning evidence, they argued, against Indigenous activists' claims that they are truly or fully Indians.

On one hand, we should view such arguments as brazenly prejudiced attempts to justify ongoing Indian dispossession and material deprivation, which I have detailed in the preceding chapters. On the other hand, we see in operation the constraints of the double bind facing activists. Solidarity demands adherence to the need to maintain an impassioned defense of the distinctiveness of Indian experiences of dislocation. I also must speak to their experiences in terms considered cultural (qua cosmological).[2] As I've pointed out, though, in this book I am doing so without sole recourse to cultural-preservationist arguments. I am charting a course that also incorporates the political and economic machinations, strategies, and tactical deployments self-consciously undertaken by my interlocutors. During and after finishing my fieldwork, consciously and carefully I pondered how to account for the transformative effects of colonialism, Brazilian nationalism, and the overlapping histories shared by Indian and non-Indian formerly rural people. Therefore, in this chapter, I keep in mind the historical changes that have occurred with respect to both the constructedness of ethnoracial categories and distinctiveness described in anthropological studies. Moreover, in doing this work I continue to grapple with the particularities of the context of Dourados as it concerns ethnoracial land politics described over the course of this book. The differences in how Indians and non-Indians in the region experience agribusiness relations of land and labor exemplify such politics.

An example of the differential treatment of Indians and non-Indians by the state is the treatment of an informal settlement, or houseless encampment, of non-Indians in the early 2000s. The municipality of Dourados generously relocated those in the camp, located at the five-hundred-mile marker of the federal highway referred to as Brazil 500, to publicly financed (municipal-government led) housing. (See figure 10.) Newspaper articles titled "Favelados começam a deixar assentamento Brasil 500" (Favela dwellers begin to clear out of Brazil 500) (*Dourados News* 2001) and "Famílias vivem em situação sub-humana" (Families live in subhuman conditions) (*Progresso* 2011) sympathetically described the

**Fig 10.** Federally subsidized housing construction, circa 2007. Photograph by LaShandra Sullivan.

informal settlement of non-Indians and subsequent relocation to state-sponsored housing, including photographs of *buracos* identical to those that I saw on the Dourados reservation and in the protest camps-tekohas.

During my time in Dourados, I noted the lack of extreme poverty besetting non-Indians relative to Indians. Indeed, townspeople routinely commented that no such extreme poverty in Dourados exists. I found this striking compared to the dire houselessness that I had witnessed in Rio de Janeiro and São Paulo, for example. Douradenses explained that this was a result of directives from the reigning political class in the municipality. I also found it notable juxtaposed to the prior circumstances of starvation on the Dourados reservation, which had reached dire proportions prior to interventions like the cestas basicas of the PT era. The history of local politics in Dourados also features PT victories in recent decades, which are important to consider in the policies of the more conservative political elites in the region. Given the government interventions to lift non-Indians from conditions of houselessness or shanty dwellings, the deplorable material conditions prevailing in some of the Dourados reservations are especially despicable.

The designation of Indian as distinct from nationally integrated society takes the form of ethnoracial exclusion, segregation, subordination through prejudiced forms of violence and stigma, and historical dispossession and dislocation. Survival hinges, in part, on rights afforded to them on the basis of ethnoracial differences described as cultural, and even sometimes as ontological; that indeed exemplifies the terms in which Indigenous politics constitutes a double bind, for both Indians and anthropologists. In this sense, this case presents the classic conundrum of the politics of recognition of liberal multiculturalism (Povinelli 2016).

As I will explain, those ethnoracially marked as Indians in Dourados face structurally induced difficulties in accessing the material means to perform a prescribed, if contested, notion of Indigeneity and, more specifically, Guaraní-ness. I support this line of argument insofar as it underscores practices of being in relation to land that reject the disenchanted environmental destruction of capitalist and settler colonial ways of living, of which agribusiness is the latest iteration. Indeed, as I will ethnographically describe, the land activists with whom I worked engaged in cosmogonic relations to and through land that were neither reducible nor amenable to such strictures. This shapes their capacity to enact their conceptions of the right way to live, the right way to be Guaraní. The latter varies and is subject to debate. As a non-Indigenous person new to the community who did not speak the Guaraní language, I was not fully privy to such debate nor positioned to fully understand the nuances. This was true while I was charged by my collaborators to convey what was shared with me and the evident differences in their relations to the land they were revendicating, relations that evidenced what I call the fact of alterity. Preoccupations with Indian cosmologies have featured prominently, especially in anthropological discussions on the so-called ontological turn.[3] The debates in that literature are interesting for my purposes in that they relate to some of the particularities of the role of anthropology as a discipline in Brazil in its mediations of Indigenous land claims.

My sense is that the very real inability to live a certain way, as lamented by some Guaranís and their advocates, involves the dilemma of deciphering, debating, settling on, and working out what exactly is the right way to live. Such a dilemma arguably besets anyone unmoored by the displacements and upheavals described over the course of this book. My concern here is to present how histories of land loss and anthropological accounts of such changes confront activists with the double bind of culture, while being mindful that my role is not to interpret the Guaraní mind or convey the intricacies of internal debates among the Guaraní regarding the right way to live. I don't pretend to have the means or the moral standing to do such work or share this work as it is being done by the people with whom I conducted fieldwork. Instead, in what follows, I share some of the ways the anthropological literature utilizes culture in order to spell out what activists have to dialogue with and to navigate toward reclaiming land. What I share concerns the realities of material loss incurred with dispossession, the terms for overcoming that loss spelled out in the literature—that is, cultural preservation—and ongoing dialogue with anthropologists.

## Material and Spiritual Relations

It is no coincidence that the festa de milho endures at Panambizinho. Located about a half-hour drive from the city of Dourados, Panambizinho sits several miles away from the highway. According to some, Panambizinho is a more ideal community of contemporary Guaranís in Mato Grosso do Sul because it is far less crowded and more distanced from the city than the Dourados reservation (i.e., Jaguarpirú and Bororó aldeias). One must drive along dirt roads to reach the people living there, which become almost impassable after heavy rain, as the thick red mud of the region (terra vermelha, or red earth) is notoriously slick when wet. It quickly cakes to the bottom of the shoes, sticky and heavy, of anyone who attempts to walk across it. I heard quite a few stories over the years of cars becoming trapped in the red mud, leaving distressed the motorists who unwisely attempt to navigate through it. The evening of the festival, having gotten a ride with a colleague from FUNAI who had some experience successfully avoiding such distresses, we managed to get to the event safely.

The *festa* (festival) took place in a *casa de reza* (prayer house), a large structure made of straw and other organic materials that could house more than a hundred people. The interior consisted of one large room with a thatched roof, in the center of which large wooden pillars held the structure upright. The casa de reza was located behind a house made with conventional manufactured building material, the kind that you would see in any city in Brazil. Few lights were aglow in the vicinity; the dim lights in sight cast long shadows. In the near darkness I chatted with the many other people (both Indian and non-Indian guests alike) who were circulating in the area as I made my way across the reservation toward the *festa*. I then entered the well-lit party taking place in the casa de reza. The beating of drums and chanting intermingled with the chatter and laughter of the many dozens of people in attendance.

The festa de milho took place once per year at Panambizinho, starting Friday afternoon and lasting until Sunday evening. The festival gathered people and spirits for food, dance, and drink. In the festa, Guaraní shamans lead chants while circling around barrels of *chicha*, a beverage of fermented corn. The batch that night, a member of the community told me, included some fermented potatoes as well due to the shortage of corn. The shamans marched in the formation of a large circle around the barrels of chicha, spiraling around and around for hours, keeping in motion with their feet. They maintained their rhythm by pounding tall and relatively wide sticks into the ground, in rhythm with the singing and chanting.

The people gathered were of all generations, women and men. Attendees had travelled from far around in the region. Some of them were kin of people living on Panambizinho. Non-Guaraní attendees, like myself and those who invited me, mingled among the Guaranís while chatting about random subjects, mostly about the festa. Attendees came and went from the casa de reza at will. People lounged about, oftentimes not particularly paying attention. No one was in any particular hurry to do anything beyond the lounging, marching in a circle or dancing, chanting, and chatting. Most circulated back and forth, through the groups, joining and then leaving the spiraling chanters, checking their phones for the latest emails or social-media postings. There was a relaxed mood of the ordinary and the extraordinary that parties bring. The festa went on until the following morning. Children ran around playing happily and were sometimes unruly. A historian and anthropologist from a local university noted to me the contrast to the Guaraní children he had observed in the region's Pentecostal churches, who sat dutifully, rigidly, and silently still during the church services.

Dozens intermittently joined the circle of chanting and rhythmic marching. A group of girls linked arms while smiling, giggling, and talking among themselves. They moved along with the spiral wave of steppers. I also joined in for fifteen minutes. I had to move to the outer part of the circle to avoid becoming dizzy. By contrast, the continual circling and chanting induced a trancelike state in the participants, some of whom with many years of experience told me that, because of this trance, they do not get tired. By the next morning, they feel mentally and physically vibrant. Their legs are fresh.

The festa de milho had changed in prior decades, as the ceremony became more difficult to put on. One needs corn to have a festa de milho. To plant corn, one needs sufficient land to carry out the practices of division of labor, and for the festa one needs the concomitant social organization to produce it. A reason that Panambizinho is one of the few reservations in the region in which the festa de milho goes on is that its smaller size and location have insulated it from the deterioration of social conditions (e.g., starvation, crowding, and crime) infamously besetting the reservation on the outskirts of Dourados. More Indigenes lived in the Dourados reservation than in any of the thirty-two other counties of the state. These material conditions rendered it difficult to move through life cycles. The role of corn in practices around male initiation rituals is an example of how making kin through objects had been transformed as a result of the larger political and economic transformations facing the Kaiowá-Guaranís.

It is worth reviewing how anthropologists note such changes in the literature. For example, conducting her fieldwork in 1943, Virginia Watson (1944, 37) described social practices around and through land on the Taquapirí reservation in Mato Grosso do Sul. She observed that boys between the ages of eight and ten received a small parcel of land from their father to cultivate and consider their own property. In addition, most sons worked on their father's land until they were older, where they learned to hunt, fish, collect wild honey, and make baskets, bows, and arrows. Sons were usually initiated into the community at between eight and thirteen years of age. The initiates stayed in the longhouse during the day and learned songs at night. After several months of this routine, the final initiation ceremony took place. Only men of the village attended this ceremony. In the ceremony, the men pierced the lower lips of the boys in order to insert a *tembetá* (a long, thin stick). Before the lip-piercing, the boys received chicha to drink. Fathers of the initiates were not allowed to take part in drinking the beverage. However, the father needed to have produced a certain quantity of corn for this ceremony to contribute to the chicha. If he had had a bad harvest or for any other reason could not provide the corn, he turned to his brother or his wife's brother for help. Watson (1944, 38) recalled that this initiation ceremony had already disappeared on a number of Kaiowá reservations at the time of her research.

Anthropologist Antonio Brand (1997, 12) relates that the disappearance of the male initiation ceremony (*kunumi pepy*) was a subject of frequent complaint from his informants. He explains that the ceremony was preceded by rigorous preparation, including assuring that there was enough food, proper costumes, and an ogajekutu (longhouse). All of the community engaged in these activities, although only the men of the village and initiates participated in the actual ceremony. Brand's informants lamented the abandonment of the ceremony (46).

Having land for corn harvest is vital in this case, as it was regarding the earlier discussion about access to objects for kin-making practices. Guaranís need land to enact the traditional way of life. Land restitution would also provide the means to create the objects through which one crafts those so-called traditions and pursues movements through life cycles so critical to concepts of living well (*bom modo de viver*), which is to say tekoha.

Mura (2004) writes that Guaraní-Kaiowá rituals, such as the ritual for corn harvest, avati kyry, are important elements of group cohesion. The rituals contribute to the maintenance of a cosmological equilibrium. To maintain equilibrium in the world means to subscribe to ethics and positive morals (*teko porã*) that facilitate the maintenance of sacred conduct (*teko marangatu*) in human actions and activities. Such conduct ensures that the earth (*yvy*) does not suffer evil that may ultimately bring the end of the world and men. According to these accounts, the Kaiowá believe the land was created as part of the cosmos under the care of Ñande Ru

Guasu, the supreme entity of the Indigenous pantheon. He also created the Guaranís (*ava*), who emerged from the seeds that Ñande Ru Guasu planted in that land. This was the origin of the telluric relation between the Indians and the soil, the basis for the understanding of autochthony.

Shamanic communication with mythical-historical realms often aims to overcome the impasses of daily life. In the case of the Kaiowá-Guaraní, there is a continuity between the world as it is inhabited and that world where supernatural phenomena take place. The maintenance of the proper relations of reciprocity between macrofamilial groups and of ritual practices contributes to well-being in the world. The possibility exists, however, for the imminent destruction of the world by gods (through meteoric phenomena, fire, or water). This exercises strong pressures to conserve the proper conduct within the family, in addition to community and ritual practices. For example, in ritual, this may take place through the constant and extenuating repetition of sacred songs (ñembo'e).

The anthropological literature has paid much attention to this notion of family and its enmeshment in cosmogonic practices. For example, Fabio Mura (2004) explains in his work with Kaoiwá communities that a cosmological balance presides between the supernatural entities, the land, and men that is maintained through rituals. This type of relation with the land is established through *jeroky* (dances) in front of *mba'e maran-gatu*, a type of altar where Kaoiwá people place ceremonial ornaments and other symbols like crosses (*Kurusu ñe'engatu*) and other insignias (*yvyra'i*) made of wood. According to Mura, the primary function of these dances and objects is to mediate between the relations of men and the earth and, in so doing, with supernatural entities (Mura 2004). He argues that such objects represent a primordial link between the supernatural and families that conserve and provide continuity to the mythical foundation of their cosmos. This balance prevents the end of the earth as described. Positive efforts are thwarted by incorrect use of sacred objects or conduct of ritual or violation of the correct mode of being of the tekoha. However, enactment of these prescriptions on fixed plots of land was sometimes put aside in favor of migration, particularly migrations to the land without evil.

Movement and mobility under colonial conditions figure prominently in Hélène Clastres's ([1975] 1995) work. She additionally notes that movement and perpetual displacement constitute a recurrent element of the history of Guaraní-speaking people in Brazil, one that predates the era of Iberian conquest of the Americas. According to Clastres, this aspect arises from the tensions between the political and religious elements endemic to Guaraní social organization. She analyzes missionary accounts and literature from colonial-era Brazil and Paraguay. Clastres describes day-to-day life in the longhouse structure as highly hierarchical under the authority of household heads. Spiritual leaders (shamans) lived among the group or family, sometimes also serving as the household heads. Especially powerful shamans, however, lived apart from family settlements. Called karai, they were thought to be without paternal descent and without family.[4] This enabled them to pass through a variety of communities, some of which were warring or rivals, with impunity.

The visits of the karai to communities to perform rituals were met with fanfare. The karai were considered spiritually powerful. For this reason, Clastres ([1975] 1995, 35) argues, they threatened the household heads' authority over their communities, the territory belonging to men. Because Guaraní cosmology holds out the possibility for overcoming earthly obligations to join the gods in the "land without evil," the karai could help guide people from the land of mortals to the land of the gods. Clastres explains that the Guaranís idealize the land without evil as the inverse of the day-to-day realm of social obligation and hierarchy. There, one can join the gods as equals. It is a place copresent with the earthly realm, often said to be located at the end of the horizon. Migrations were a voyage to find that land without evil. They were undertaken, according to Clastres, when a karai gained the influence and reputation to garner a following.

The important point for my purposes here is that Clastres denies a primacy of the proper *modo de ser* will (way of life) as valued in itself. Although others (e.g., Meliá 1981) argue that the proclivity for migrations arose due to the social strife that came with colonization, Clastres holds that such possibilities and desires were built into the Guaraní value system and social organization independent of such factors. Migrations were frequent for two main reasons: (1) the disdain for the constraints imposed in the land of men and (2) the quotidian village life that spurred longing for the mythical land without evil. Indeed, such voyages were undertaken prior to Iberian contact. The tensions between political and religious authority encapsulated the idealization of the land without evil as an escape from the less-desired strife of daily life on earthly, mortal terrain. The migrations were foremost, according to Clastres ([1975] 1995, 35), a counter to the political-kinship hierarchy predominant in village life. Political authorities (i.e., household heads) attempted to counter the power and influence of karai. Although migrations for the land without evil were not a constant agenda of karai, their influence nevertheless made them a rival. In the mythical land without evil, men live as gods among the gods without the social order dictating village life. In travelling to the land without evil, the proper modo de ser to maintain a delicate balance with the earth through proper conduct are left behind.

In my work with Guaraní protesters, references to land restitution, spiritual relations, and moral conduct related to notions of family are inextricably entwined, though in ways that foregrounded the self-conscious political nature of such interlinkages. Notions of family did not conform to a patriarchal family structure prominent among non-Indians. Note, for example, my discussion of the history of the social organization in the Brazilian countryside in chapter 3. As anthropologist Diógenes Cariaga (2015) notes in his fieldwork with Guaraní on reservations in Mato Grosso do Sul, Kaiowá kinship can been described as a broad network of relationships that combine modalities of consanguinity, descent, and affinity strongly marked by residence and commensality, which produce broad forms of relationality. Among the Kaiowá-Guaraní, family relations, particularly having children, is a main means of achieving and disputing prestigious positions, as the condition of the ego is always a mediator between different ways of being, marked by generational positions within the kin. Women can and do head households. Cariaga writes that "the importance of understanding the notion of the Kaiowá person [emerges] from the relations produced between the broader categories of sociality—*ñande reko*—through native ways of enunciating the differences in the ways of meaning the world between the Kaiowá and other humans and non-humans—*ore reko*" (Cariaga 2015, 443). Positioned in a web of social relations in this way allows one to assume the management of kinship practices and to learn teko marangatu (Kaiowá concept of shamanism). This also plays out in assumption of leadership positions in the land protest camps-tekohas.

## The Space to Be

The chanting in the festa de milho ceremony, the sounds and words uttered, as well as the embodied turning about the casa de reza, are entwined with the materiality of the corn and the bodies of those who dwell in that place. For example, my work with activists almost always began with a prayer, ñembo'e. Anthropologist Graciela Chamorro (2002) explains that among the Kaiowá-Guaraní, the terms ñe'e, ayvu, and ã, translated as "word," also signify "voice, speech, tongue, language, soul, name, life, origin, personality" and, above all, possess a spiritual essence. God is Word, and is, by excellence, a being of speech. Importantly, this range of significations underscores the material *and* semantic oneness to which the concept of word (*palabra*) refers. Guaraní regard each person as an incarnation of the divine word. At birth, the word sits and provides a place for itself in the child's body. As a child is about to be born, words are spoken to the soul-word that is going to incarnate: "Then go to earth, my son (my daughter); remember me in your erect being, and I will make my word circulate through your bones to remember me" (Chamorro 2002, 330). When circulating through the human skeleton, the divine word is the one that keeps it in a vertical position, the one that humanizes. This in contradistinction to animals, who do not stand upright.

Regarding prayers, Chamorro describes the redemption of speaking, of activating the divine presence in the human constitution, that would recur in prayers or in councils. Through such speaking, the Guaraní claim divinities that restore their words and allow them to reach good and beautiful words. Through the word, the human being overcomes animal horizontality and acquires the characteristic verticality of divinities. "Rising up" also appears in the context of healing. People gather innumerable restorers of the word and so make their voices heard, make their cries heard. "To stand up," "to restore what is said" is, as a rule among the Guaraní, the culmination of a series of improvements that took place in the community (Chamorro 2002).

Also prevalent in testimonies to anthropologists is the oneness of the material and the semantic, an important element of Guaraní senses of place, in which relations to and through material objects, including bodies, landscapes, spirits, and divinity, occur. In my work with land activists, I noted that this conception also contains the ways that the performance of Guaraní-ness entails cultural difference vis-à-vis the aforementioned Indian or non-Indian binary so central to the regional Douradense context of a racial ideology (described in more detail in chapter 1). This binary arises from historically specific conditions and, moreover, operates not as merely oppositional but also as a dialectical coconstitution of ethnoracial categories. Guaraní criticize the ethnic hierarchies put in place with their material dispossession, namely land loss.

Such centrality of material-spiritual self-making and place-making strikes me as particularly important as it regards the representations of cultural performance and its relevance to land protests. Here, material needs factor mightily, even as we should not and must not reduce cultural performance to material utility. For example, in the festa de milho that some consider so emblematic of a Guaraní way of life, one must acquire the corn through planting, harvesting, and transporting it. These all require arrangements of labor and land tenure that have changed over time. Whereas in previous eras Guaranís acquired such corn for festas de milho through a social organization of land occupation and land-use practices particular to those eras, the era of agribusiness forecloses such prior configurations of social relations to and through land.

Returning to the question of space and place treated in earlier chapters allows us to analyze the festa de milho for the possibilities of land politics in Brazil that do not rely on the double bind imposed by approaches to culture and ethnoracial categories as constructed at the time of my research. If we view the Guaraní land protesters as "testimonial people" (Nash 2001), we must factor how such testimonies arise in contexts that produce them as consciously deployed toward instrumental ends, in addition to being rooted in alternative ontologies regarding the semiotic-material world. I am pointing precisely to the Guaraní protest campers in Dourados's decided lack of rootedness imposed by agribusiness hegemony. The context of agribusiness space that I describe throughout the book has produced and continues to compel transience from which the camp protesters mobilize and strategically deploy conceptions of Indigeneity and Guaraní-ness to make land claims.

The Guaraní cosmologies invoked in land-use practices that facilitate the festa do milho reference ways of living only partially achievable under conditions of displacement. Given the context of agribusiness space, it is impossible for many Guaraní people to adequately perform Guaraní-ness, as enacted in rituals like the avati kyry, on crowded reservations. Their displacement onto such reservations has taken many Guaraní out of the ideals for living the word referenced in and through prayers.

The ideal represented by Panambizinho and the festa de milho has not been sustainable insofar as it is premised on land-use practices not replicable in the agribusiness spatial order: city-countryside-reservation. We must further factor exploitation of Guaraní labor, with its extraction of time and surplus value, implicated in land-use practices (described in chapter 2). Labor exploitation, particularly devaluation of rural labor, makes agribusiness production possible and profitable, a central structural pillar of land dispossession.

Indigenous labor has long provided a principal source of manual labor in the south of Mato Grosso do Sul. In the last few decades, Indigenous labor has largely been the principal source of cane-cutting labor. In 2011 a FUNAI official pointed out to me that there would most likely soon be little to no work cutting cane as firms switch to ever more mechanization of cane cutting, which will further devalue labor. Thus, policy makers are already attempting to factor in support for family agriculture in considerations that include, though extend beyond, Indigenous communities in the region. For example, the federal government already supports such family agriculture through the cestas basicas program, for which a percentage of the food comes from family farms. FUNAI officials explained that they confront the challenging obstacle of limited space (i.e., land).

The aspirations to a future that returns a "past" way of life seem unsustainable if one bears in mind that the history of social relations in those prior social configurations is more complicated than the idyllic scenes described in the anthropological literature, idealized undoubtedly both then and now by some anthropologists and Guaraní activists. Although informants describe the festa de milho as would-be normal life—in opposition to the crowded conditions on large reservations like the Dourados reservation—as I described in chapter 5, such places may actually be fraught with extreme political discord and material inequalities. So, the idyllic scene presented in the festa de milho exemplifies some of the Guaranís' creation of, and longing for, a future that can return an iteration of the past.

For the vast majority of Guaraní, which is to say Guaraní who are land-deficient, they are the historical inheritors of displacement from land. Consequently, the inaccessibility of rituals like the festa de milho point to the difficulty of carrying out such prior social practices of the right way to live. Even among Guaranís with sufficient land holdings on reservations such as Panambizinho, prescriptions for what is the right way to live may be contested across generations and between Guaranís of nontraditional faiths (e.g., Pentecostal or Guaraní-Kaiowá). The diversity of views on the land conflicts, along with differing opinions on leasing reservation lands to agribusiness firms, for example, complicates the view of the protesters or any of the Guaranís as necessarily embodying alternatives to capitalist and agribusiness logics. Such debates and contests regarding Guaraní-ness and the right way to live as it regards self-making across time and space are ever in formation and ongoing.

In the historically produced, political-economical, and cultural terms in which an appeal to a way out of dire material circumstances and alienation through land claims makes sense, I have not intended to downplay or discredit the importance of the alternative cosmologies presented by Guaranís. This is so regardless of how these ways of life are taken up, transformed, and challenged by those identifying as Guaraní. Such contests over Guaraní-ness draw our attention to the protesters' potential power to challenge hegemony in attempts to counter the radical dispossession and deracination wrought with national developmentalist projects and their settler colonialist forebears.

The festa de milho vignette I shared in this chapter makes a case for the importance of land that is not quite synonymous with the Indigenous connection to land via cosmology, shorn of political, economic, and historical context. And yet it is also not a replication of the non-Indian ideal of land as inert backdrop and resource for human productivity. The Indian land claimants whom I worked with are simply not just like the non-Indians (for example, protest campers in the FAF camp) in this regard. Against ruralist opposition to Indigenous land titling, we should not collapse ways of living on the basis of what are, nevertheless, very real shared practices of commodity consumption, labor regimes, styles of dress, and so forth that have unfolded over the history of the region of Dourados.

My point is that Guaraní land activists' efforts point to the need for land not just to reproduce living as Guaraní but also to establish a whole set of social relations whose continued recovery from colonial violence they are working to forge. This is the case regardless of their perceived cultural authenticity by non-Indians. The biographical histories of the camps-tekohas and what brought the protesters to a given parcel of land (described in chapter 4)—the oftentimes messy histories of dislocations—do not invalidate this broader basis of their claims of belonging to land and the need for land restitution. The ethnographic vignettes presented in this chapter regarding the reverence for the festa de milho are a case for the importance of land restitution irrespective of the given activists' unique ties to a particular parcel of land.

My characterization of cultural differences flags the rather fraught dilemma of the contradictions in Indigenous politics and ethnoracial ideology in Brazil. Sometimes, the material requirements for practicing Guaraní ways of life may not be accessible due to their displacement onto small land tracts of reservations in the region, as well as their incorporation into the rural economy of agribusiness production. Such Guaraní may not be able to afford to enact a prior way of life and relations to land as it is idealized by many land protesters. Activists, anthropologists, and their advocates may likewise valorize such ways of living in appeals to Indigenous land law—that is, by emphasizing cultural reproduction of their ways of living.

For example, consider the testimony in a speech given by a Kaiowá-Guaraní protest leader in 2011. Speaking at an aty guasu (formal political gathering of Kaiowá-Guaraní activists) about the importance of solidarity among villagers in his community, their fight for land, and resisting bribes from *fazendeiros*, he said,

> For that reason, we have this culture and there where I live in the village [redacted] every day. I have to shout every day because the children can no longer sleep right, because of the noises coming into their ears. They cry . . . but we are not for this continuing. We

want our land, our village, our era to be a place for our culture. Of song is what we had requested for our village. . . . We did not win this land for nothing. We won for our leaders, caciques, and all the people. It is for them that we won our land. So for that that we were there. And so I speak here.[5]

The protest leader speaks of culture as a condition of defiance. He describes it as a point of opposition and contrast. In its discursive operation, I found it impossible to distill his use of the culture concept from the multilayered political context of its deployment. The Brazilian state championed the advent of structural economic conditions (i.e., land loss) that have disallowed that cultural way of life by effectively attempting to render it inaccessible for Indigenes. Activists, anthropologists, and other advocates seek to counter the increased inaccessibility of rituals like the festa de milho, rightly attributed to ongoing settler colonial dislocation, by appealing to the state for more material resources, namely more land.

Opponents of land restitution espouse a view of culture that amounts to essentialized, intrinsic differences for Indians, exemplified by the testimonials in public forums (as analyzed in chapter 1) where proruralist sul-matogrossenses[6] complained that activists aren't really Indians since they have cell phones and use disposable diapers for their infants. The culture concept, popularly misconstrued in this way, engenders a context in which the very terms by which Indians have been historically denigrated and continue to be underserved by a national society operates to reproduce ethnoracial discrimination and nonfulfillment of Indigenous rights.

The culture concept as a tool for land restitution and as a hard fight for means to restore stolen land may persist alongside observation of its constraints and limitations. As evidenced in the data presented throughout this book, the land activists with whom I worked face great difficulties to adequately make use of Indigenous land law amid the politics as they existed at that time in Brazil. Those conditions grew exponentially worse after the time of my fieldwork with the ascent of rabidly anti-Indigenous-rights president Jair Bolsonaro. The imperative to recognize the double bind of culture as it imperils activists' pursuit of justice persists.

# Notes

## Introduction

1. Dourados, Mato Grosso do Sul, Brazil, lies in the southern cone of the state, which is in the central-west region of the country. Dourados is the name of the city and the greater municipality in which it is the seat of government.

2. Mato Grosso do Sul has the second largest Indigenous population of any state in Brazil. While Guaraní (Kaiowá and Ñandeva) and Terena make up the overwhelming majority of inhabitants of the Dourados reservation, Chamacoco, Guató, Kadiwéu, Ofaié-Xavante, are also sizably present. Among this population, the Guaraní account for 37,317 people. This is a significant portion of the more than 50,000 Guaraní living in Brazil (Aylwin 2009, 34).

3. In this book I primarily use the terms *Indian* (*Índio*) and *non-Indian* (*não-Índio*) because I most frequently heard these used while conducting fieldwork in Mato Grosso do Sul. The terms work by way of imposed binaries, as I discuss more in chapter 1.

4. Farms of more than 1,000 hectares (ha) occupy 77 percent of Mato Grosso do Sul's agricultural area. Farms of 10 to 100 ha and of less than 10 ha represent 2.9 percent and 0.2 percent of landholdings in the state, respectively (World Bank 2010, 77).

5. *Terra indígena* belongs to the state, which secures for the Indigenous community that lives on it the permanent usufruct of its resources, in conformity with prevailing law (Eremites de Oliveira and Marques Pereira 2009, 50).

6. For example, nineteen homicides of Indigenous protest leaders occurred in 2004, twenty-eight in 2005, twenty-seven in 2006, and fifty-three in 2007 (UN Human Rights Council 2009).

7. I use *Guaraní* to refer primarily to the Kaiowá and also to the Ñandeva, two subgroups of Guaraní-speaking people. These groups comprise the majority of Indigenous population in Mato Grosso do Sul. The Kaiowá are a self-identified Guaraní subgroup that numbers roughly eighty thousand people, of whom approximately thirty-seven thousand live in Mato Grosso do Sul. They make up the dominant Indigenous group in the southern region of the state. They are also the region's chief suppliers of cane-cutting labor. The Kaiowá live in a variety of settlement types, including twenty-four reservations (Ferreira Thomas de Almeida 2001, 19).

8. *Guanarílogos* is a term I heard while in Dourados that refers to academics who specialize in the study of Guaraní communities.

9. In the case of Indigenous land law, land rights of those peoples predate the 1988 constitution.

10. The proposed change would require that Indigenous land claimants have occupied the land that they seek to gain at the time of the adoption of the 1988 constitution, despite the histories of forced displacements besetting Indigenous activists like those protesting land in Dourados.

## 1. Ethnoracial Politics of Agribusiness

1. *Index* refers to *indexicality*, a term used in semiotics and linguistics that means "the phenomenon of serving as a sign of something else, of pointing to that which is indexed as a referent."

2. Although Mato Grosso do Sul has a largely agricultural economy, most of the population is urban. An estimated 86 percent of the population of 2.3 million people live in urban areas (World Bank 2010, 76).

3. Farms of more than 1,000 hectares occupy 77 percent of Mato Grosso do Sul's agricultural area. Farms of 10 to 100 hectares and of less than 10 hectares represent 2.9 percent and 0.2 per cent of landholdings in the state, respectively (World Bank 2010, 77).

4. A notable exception is João Pacheco de Oliveira's (1998) concept of *territorialização* (territorialization), the process by which an ethnic boundary is mapped onto a demarcated land area due to the imposition of a colonial state structure. Analyzing "mixed Indians" in Brazil's Northeast, he argued that the historical reorganization of social relations for the exercise of a political mandate—spatial regulation of a colonial state—provided the genesis for the coherence of Brazil's Indigenous ethnic groups.

5. Brazil's Indigenous land laws demand this to determine if land is *terra indígena*. Researchers must show that a particular group of people was expelled from the disputed land and say which people were responsible for the despoliation, in

addition to when and why it took place. Likewise, the researchers must show how the disputed area is vital for the physical and cultural reproduction of the Indigenous community involved in the judicial dispute.

6. Hunger and suicide rates, particularly among Guaraní youths, far exceed national averages (Hamlin and Brym 2006).

7. The context of Mato Grosso do Sul resonates with Jan Hoffman French's (2009) analysis of Brazil's Northeast and the process that she describes as "legalizing identities," which involves the interpretation and enactment of legislation related to ethnoracial rights. The approach views pertinent legislation as a part of a mutually constitutive relationship of identity formation. Indigenous identity is formed through a revision of self-identification that takes place as a result of the promulgation and taking up of the law as a meaningful way to access resources.

8. I observed regular displays of aesthetic idealization of cowboy culture that we might regard as a contemporary hangover from the settler agrarian past (Dent 2005). Examples include the widely successful *música sertaneja* (Brazilian country music) and popular bumper stickers featuring silhouettes of cowboys on horseback. As an example of their sometimes-gendered inflection, a memorable variation of the latter depicts a mounted cowboy roping a busty, big haired woman by her high heels. These expressions of rurality take place within cities broadly dependent on capital-intensive agro-industrial production, including derivative industries like frozen food (*frigorífico*).

9. According to Fabio Mura (2006), traditional Kaiowá believe the land was created as part of the cosmos under the care of Ñande Ru Guasu, the supreme entity of their pantheon of gods. He also created the Guaraní (*ava*), who emerged from the seeds that Ñande Ru Guasu planted in that land. This was the origin of the telluric relation between the Indians and the soil that serves as the basis for the construction of an understanding of autochthony. Accordingly, the Kaiowá feel that they belong to the land, as opposed to the land belonging to them.

10. *Tekoha* is the Guaraní term for "territory." It is the land necessary for survival of the Guaraní way of being, the good way to be, where and how one's ancestors lived and where future generations will live.

11. Opponents of land demarcation criticize anthropologists' advocacy for those who are among the weakest in Brazil. However, the centrality of a political project does not discount the scientific merit of their research, as argued by anti-Indigenous publications like *Veja* (Coutinho, Paulin, and de Medeiros 2010). The latter assume that by pointing out the political objectives of anthropologists, they discredit them. To the contrary, in the study of ethnic land claims, the political stakes are ever present for those on all sides of the issue, including those who claim to be unbiased.

12. Although landowners are required to preserve a part of their land area for forests, there is lax enforcement of this requirement by the authorities. Indigenous use of these areas provokes conflicts with *branco* landowners.

13. As I discuss in other work (Sullivan 2017), in Dourados the category of branco–non-Indian can be inclusive of negro.

14. Mato Grosso do Sul has the second-largest Indigenous population in Brazil (behind the state of Amazonas). The Indigenous population numbers 73,295 (Instituto Brasileira de Geografia e Estatística 2012b). Indigenous groups include the Guraraní, the Kadiwéu, the Kamba, the Kinikinawa, and the Terena (World Bank 2010, 76).

15. That's my translation. The original reads, "Os Índios não atrapalham o desenvolvimento do Estado. O Mato Grosso não está em dificuldade financeira."

16. Again, that is my translation. The original full quote reads as follows: "'A falta de demarcação é que gera insegurança jurídica sobre o direito das propriedades e inibe os investimentos. Neste caso, empresários de outros locais não vão adquirir novas terras porque temem a sua transformação em território indígena. Se não demarcar, a insegurança vai ficar para o resto da vida,' comentou, frisando que os Índios não vão passar fome sem protestar pela ampliação das reservas."

17. In this effort I am particularly speaking about some of the Indigenist Brazilian social science already cited.

### 2. Floating Labor in a Bind

1. As in other chapters, I use a pseudonym for the activist in order to protect confidentiality.

2. In MS, to best facilitate federal administration, reservations established by the federal government starting in the 1920s were strategically located in border cities.

3. An example of such a system elsewhere in Latin America is *concertaje* in the Andes.

4. These documents included the *registro nacional* (national registration), the *cartão do bolsa família* (which facilitates transferring monthly parcels of food to families), and the aforementioned *carteira de trabalho*.

5. Under the Human Rights programs of the National Justice Council (CNJ), the stated goal is to register Indians who live in urban centers. The program accounts for the work being done by FUNAI to update the national registration. As part of the program, FUNAI is investigating the number of Indigenous people without birth certificates in Brazilian cities. The CNJ states that civil registration of birth is the first step in obtaining citizenship rights, but it is a *facultativo* (optional) document for Indigenous people. After registration, the CNJ, in partnership with other state and federal organizations or with

representatives of those registered, seeks to give to Indigenous people identity documents (*documento de identitidade*) and work documents (*carteiras de trabalho*) and provide orientation about civil rights (Souza 2011).

6. *Gatos* (third party contractors of agrarian labor) are widespread in Brazil and commonplace among non-Indigenous and Indigenous labor alike.

7. Another example of this narrative is the federal sting resulting in the arrest of Dourados's ex-mayor, Ari Artuzi, which had just occurred as I returned for fieldwork in 2011. The Federal Police (Policia Federal) carried out an operation called Operação Uragano that investigated corruption in Mato Grosso do Sul, focusing principally on Dourados. The operation included wiretaps and secretly recorded video of bribery, fraud, and other schemes. In addition to the mayor, federal police arrested or detained dozens of others in state and local government (Globo.com 2010).

8. The original text of the headline reads, "Após morte de líder indígena, clima na cidade é como se nada tivesse acontecido."

9. Although Mato Grosso do Sul features a mostly agricultural economy, most of the population is urban. An estimated 86 percent of the population of 2.3 million people live in urban areas (World Bank 2010, 76). Farms of more than 1,000 hectares occupy 77 percent of Mato Grosso do Sul's agricultural area. Farms of 10 to 100 hectares and less than 10 hectares represent 2.9 percent and 0.2 percent of landholdings in the state, respectively (World Bank 2010, 77).

10. Consider an example of international capital investment: In 2007, AOL founder Steve Case, Sun Microsystems cofounder Vinod Khosla, supermarket giant Ron Burkle, film producer Steve Bing, and former World Bank president James Wolfensohn worked with Petrobras president Philippe Reichstul to create the Brazilian Renewable Energy Company, or Brenco. Americans invested $31 million in the company, whereas Brazilians contributed $20 million. In March 2007 the group raised an additional nearly $150 million from other Euro-American investors. Brenco planned to spend $2.2 billion to harvest 1.5 million acres of sugarcane, build ten ethanol mills, and produce 1 billion gallons a year by 2014, primarily for export (*Business Week* 2007). Wilkinson and Herrera (2011) stated that, in 2008, Brazil's public prosecutor charged Brenco with inhumane working conditions for migrant and Indigenous laborers. The Ministry of Justice blacklisted one of its top firms, COSAN, for illegal labor conditions.

11. Frank states that, during the period of political domination of the Mário Correia da Costa family from 1880s through 1930s in Mato Grosso do Sul, there were internal political rifts. One such dispute involved Pedro Celestino and Mário Corrêa da Costa over the relationship between the state and the Matte Larangeira Company. Mário backed the company through the 1920s. Pedro Celestino had openly criticized the company monopoly since his stint as state

president in the 1910s. Pedro Celestino accused Mário of favoring the monopoly over the best interests of the state. Mário, at the time president of the senate, accused his uncle of being "senile" and "the Rasputin of Cuiabá" (Frank 2001, 61). These exchanges took place in 1923 and 1928, respectively.

12. This region contained the most votes of any region in Mato Grosso during this period. Agostinho (2009b) talks about the alliance between Filinto Müller (and the Vargas Estado Novo government) and the local political bosses (coronéis). The União Democratica Nacional (UDN) and the Partido Social Democratico (PSD) were the main players. The latter is the party of the governistas, directly linked to Filinto Müller, thus controlling much of the patronage associated with the railroad (Estrada de Ferro Noroeste do Brasil). UDN's regional characteristics in Mato Grosso are different from the national profile. In southern Mato Grosso do Sul, the UDN consisted of large landholders in the south of the state. Nationally, the UDN was the party of the urban, petite bourgeois and industrialists. Agostinho is also keen to point out that the battle between the different political parties was not ideological, but merely along party lines and between different interests and factions.

13. The Rural Worker Statute, promulgated under Goulart on March 2, 1963, set up a system of 1 percent taxation on commercialized agricultural products to fund the nation's first social welfare programs for rural workers. Farmers would pay the tax themselves. The military regime set up an autonomous administrative organ to run the welfare programs through two complementary decree laws. The Decree Law 276 of February 28, 1967, on the purchase of agricultural farm produce made enforcement easier, as receipts track the transactions. The second decree, Decree Law 61.554 of October 17, 1967, created an autonomous administrative structure for rural medical and dental services that came to be known as FUNRURAL: Fund for the Assistance of the Rural Worker. FUNRURAL was subordinated to the National Institute of Social Welfare (INPS), which was obligated to generate FUNRURAL's funding from the 1 percent tax. FUNRURAL had a Commission of Directors that included leaders from the National Confederation of Agricultural Workers (Mayberry-Lewis 1994, 39).

14. The government created legislation designed to solve these problems by creating the Program for Assistance for the Rural Worker (PRORURAL) and by the decree law following shortly thereafter that established PRORURAL's regulations: Complementary Law Number 11 of May 25, 1971, and Decree Law Number 69.919 of January 11, 1972 (Mayberry-Lewis 1994, 40).

15. In Mato Grosso and later Mato Grosso do Sul, organizing among rural workers took the form of the Federation of Workers in Agriculture of the State of Mato Grosso (Federação dos Trabalhadores na Agricultura do Estado de Mato Grosso or FETAGRI-MT), which was founded on October 23, 1971, in Cuiabá.

The Ministry of Labor officially recognized it on May 18, 1972. It is affiliated at the national level with CONTAG and represented around 250,000 agricultural families, workers, and rural workers in Mato Grosso in 2011. In 1971 eight rural workers syndicates existed. After the creation of the separate state of Mato Grosso do Sul in 1979, workers in that new state founded a FETAGRI for Mato Grosso do Sul (FETAGRI-MT). FETAGRI (2011) states that the last dozen years have been important, as they have featured implementation of the Projeto Alternativo de Desenvolvimento Rural Sustentável e Solidário (PADRSS, or Alternative Project for Sustainable Rural Development and Solidarity) as part of the Programa Nacional de Fortalecimento da Agricultura Familiar (PRONAF, or National Program for the Reinforcement of Family Agriculture). This program proposed a transformed relation between the city and country whereby development would include "equality of opportunities, social justice, environmental conservation, sovereignty and food security, as well as economic growth" (FETAGRI 2011). The elaboration of PADRSS features the concept of sustainable rural development, with its fundamental axes being the struggle for land reform, reinforcement of family agriculture, the fight for workers' rights and better conditions for salaried and unsalaried workers, technical assistance, credit, market assistance, cooperation, and construction of new attitudes and values related to gender in the fight for social politics and democratization of public space. "Returning politics to the countryside," the FETAGRI site reads. This list, seemingly painstakingly constructed to check off the multiple issues at stake to the activists, points to the lack of tradeoffs, at least in rhetoric, in the struggle of rural workers. They are demanding it all, and seemingly all is accounted for and elaborated on in the PADRSS program.

16. Brazilian currency is the real. The plural form in Portuguese is reais.

17. Elsewhere (Sullivan 2013; Sullivan 2017), I provide a more detailed ethnographic analysis of these points.

18. I use this term both as a specific legal object and as the broader possible referents, including elements and relations in and with the landscape, such as with spirit owners of forests (Fausto 2008), earth beings (Cadena 2010), or *cuancuan* (Cepek 2016). As Cepek reminds us, there is no consensus among such groups regarding the ontological status of such entities and elements, though we must always note the situatedness of such elements and claims in political contestations regarding decision-making and Indigenous fight to maintain (or in the case of the Guaraní land activists in Dourados, to take back) control over lands and territories.

19. The underlying premise of my argument regarding the historical production of the seen and unseen is that knowledge based on perceiving is not lent purely by the senses, nor is it merely imbued by reason through the cognitive faculty

of appraising. That is, it is a capacity to reason beyond the vagaries of the particulars lent by the senses in a given instance. Instead of this Kantian (Kant [1783] 2004) distinction between the appearances of things (phenomena) and numena (i.e., things in themselves), Hegel, and later Marx, insisted that the faculty of appraising or understanding must yet account for how the faculty itself comes into being—thus, their recourse to dialectics (Hegel [1807] 1977; Marx [1844] 2000). What Cyril Lionel Robert (C. L. R.) James ([1969] 1980) calls the dialectal relation of substance (objective reality) and subject (mind) comes together not as givens but as processes of coming to be (i.e., becoming), ever-shifting and moving as moments ceaselessly in the process of accounting for themselves, making each other. These processes, in perpetual construction at each moment, must in turn account for their production through a history that is not just a prior moment but one inextricably bound up in a determination of being that is unfinished. Their determinateness is a past that has not passed and also has yet to come. That such processes are always unfinished relates to the possibilities of their rupture or cessation.

20. This line of argument is inspired by Moten (2008), who argues that hypervisibility and surveillance are intrinsic to racialized being. He calls for work on comparative racializations.

21. Such protests remained timely amid former president Jair Bolsonaro's proposed "reforms" to labor regulation in Brazil. His green and yellow card (*carteira verde e amarela*) would not require employers to pay into the social security system. Instead, the worker and the state would pay into a private investment retirement savings account, effectively privatizing social security (R. Rocha 2018).

### 3. The Protest Camp

1. The problem of displacement onto the Dourados reservation is especially acute. In Mato Grosso do Sul, the federal government demarcated discontinuous areas for reservations, denominating what amounted to islands of land for their administrative jurisdiction (Eremites de Oliveira and Marques Pereira 2009, 49). Unlike in the Amazon, for example, where wide swaths of land were designated to guard against settler encroachment, in Mato Grosso do Sul Indigenous people were often relocated to reservations near cities to facilitate administrative management of the areas.

2. *Conservative modernization* is a term frequently used to describe approaches to economic development, particularly rural development, enacted after the 1964 coup.

3. Guaraní anthropologist Tonico Benites utilizes Victor Turner's concept of "social drama" to capture how the land conflict does not occur primarily within Guaraní families and communities, but rather between those communities

and white farmers. He points out that the legal framings of the state impose the contoured stage for the events.

4. A *posseiro* is someone who occupies a parcel of land despite lacking official documentation of ownership. In other words, the person lacks a land title.

5. They were known as the Caaguá, and later the Kaiowá, a variation on "Cayua," *caa* meaning "forest" and *awa* meaning "man" in Guaraní (Koenigswald 1908, 1–3). Alternate spellings for Caaguá include Cayugá and Kainguá as well as alternate Kaiowá spellings like Cayuá, Kayová, and Kaiuá.

6. Presumably, they were hiding from capture into Jesuit missions prior to the Brazilian takeover of the region following the War of the Triple Alliance in 1870 or from slave raiding *bandeirantes* headed west from São Paulo in the nineteenth century. A Brazilian federal decree transferred the catechism and "civilizing" of Indians from the central to the state governments in 1889. The constitution of 1891 transferred dominion over the devolution of land to the states without regard to the rights of Indigenous people.

7. *Erva mate* (*yerba mate* in Spanish) is an herb mixed with water to make a beverage stimulant.

8. The SPI mission of "protecting" the Indians was implemented as a policy of accommodation and acculturation for the supposed well-being of Indigenous populations; the mission was a rationalization of confinement onto reservations. This state agency created to execute Indigenous policy was transformed into the Fundação Nacional do Índio (FUNAI) in 1967.

9. In Mato Grosso do Sul, all claimants take recourse to notions of earlier ways of life that they assume provide historical grounding of their land claims. The Federation for Family Agriculture (FAF or Federação de Agricultura Familiar) protestors may seek land redistribution by rhetorically invoking a model of family farming, or large holders may seek protection from land indemnification to maintain family legacies vis-à-vis progress (these include owners of large-scale agro-industrial installations). Indigenous movements, at least in rhetoric, seek to protect a mode of life that is both prior and ongoing. That way of living is indissociable from cosmological ties to landscapes. In both cases, invocations of earlier ways of life lend emotion and weight to the claims made. Historical narratives of land-use practices animate understandings of being Brazilian, whether non-Indian or Indian.

10. Mota (2015) uses the cognate *acampamento-tekoha* (camp-tekoha) to refer to the protest camps.

11. The original text from the website states, "Atraídos pela sustentabilidade, em 01/03/2007 o Grupo Bertin e o Grupo São Marcos Energia apostou na produção do Etanol, combustível verde, energia limpa e menos poluidora com a implantação da Unidade termoelétrica de Biomassa da São Fernando Açúcar e

Álcool Ltda, instalada na Zona rural do Município de Dourados/MS na rodo-via MS 379, sentido Laguna Caarapã, em área de 1,6ha. O empreendimento insere-se na bacia hidrográfica do Rio Paraná e sub-bacia do Rio Dourado. Distante aproximadamente 15km da sede do município e 240 km da Capital Campo Grande. Empreendimento que conta atualmente com a geração de aproximadamente 2.500 empregos diretos e 10.000 indiretos, com mais de 100 parcerias agrícolas, sua área plantada totaliza 34.500 hectare. Possui um projeto pautado no desenvolvimento sustentável e na governança corporativa, no qual se destaca o respeito às leis trabalhistas, a inovação tecnológica e a cogeração como características do novo modelo de gestão sucroalcooleira."

12. I emphasize that I am not describing a strictly binary gender opposition of men and women attributed to sex or nature. Instead, as Diógenes Cariaga (2015, 444) puts it, "Marital relations are seen as political forms of prestige production and affect the way people are qualified in relation to marriages that can be fruitful in terms of status. For both men and women, the status that being husband-and-father and wife-and-mother confers on people the politi-cal importance conferred through conjugality and the production of kinship among Guaraní-speaking collectives—express forms of political action that do not equate to relations between genders, such as the feminine reduced to the domestic/private/nature and the masculine to the social/public/cultural . . . on the contrary, it [gender] is a landscape densely populated by entities that give it a political economy of relations. . . . It is possible to verify the existence of households led only by women in which the condition of headship, for both men and women, does not require of conjugality."

13. The term *te'yi* specifically refers to the kin who compose the extended family group of the tekoha. It includes a couple, their single children, the married chil-dren and their spouses, the grandchildren and single and married descendants and their spouses, in addition to the previous and following generation to the original couple. Also included in the *te'yi* are uncles, nephews and aggregates. To each *te'yi* there corresponds a *tamõi* (grandfather) who heads and directs the family. The *tamõi* coordinates political, economic, and religious actions within the family.

14. My translation: "The category of space is fundamental for the Guaraní culture. It assures liberty and the possibility to maintain ethnic identity."

15. In the Guaraní cosmology, land is a part of a larger way of life, sets of rela-tions to spirits by which they, as people, belong to the land, not the other way around. Guaraní land protestors claim land that was previously their tekoha. A wider Guaraní tekoha guasu concept (Vietta 2007) is useful. The concept encapsulates the broader scale for Guaraní conceptions of landed territory beyond the immediate parameters of familial dwelling for the Guaraní. The

concept is long held by Guaraní within their cosmological frameworks of space and time.

16. At the same time, FUNAI also carries out agricultural support programs on reservations, providing tractors and other instruments and machinery for modern agriculture.

17. I return to this in far greater detail in chapter 6.

### 4. Agribusiness Rearrangements of Space

1. By *hegemony*, I mean "domination," similar to Gramsci's (1999) use of the term. *Domination* means something is unquestionable, but not in absolute terms. I do not mean to suggest that others cannot at all question a way of thinking. In the case analyzed here, there are those who contest agribusiness hegemony. However, during my fieldwork such questioning could result in murder with impunity. The first such cases made it to trial only in 2011. Moreover, and this is the argument about ideology that I make in the course of this book, the terms for contesting agribusiness hegemony (i.e., ethnoracial land demarcation) ultimately reinforce the very logic of agribusiness space that gave rise to them.

2. As explained in chapter 1, *branco* (white) in Dourados may refer to any non-Indigenous person regardless of ethnoracial identifications.

3. I discuss the entwinement of anti-Blackness and anti-Indigenous sentiments in Dourados more fully in my article "Black Invisibility on a Brazilian 'Frontier': Land and Identity in Mato Grosso do Sul, Brazil" (Sullivan 2017).

4. My observations in Dourados matched those documented by other researchers in Brazil, for example Twine (1998) and Telles (2004), regarding an absence of extreme residential racial segregation in Brazilian cities. Importantly, neither of those authors worked in the context of urban Indian reservations, where in Dourados the Indian and non-Indian distinction features so prominently. Moreover, as Borges (2008) notes, we must explain historically how even moderate (as compared with U.S. hypersegregation) levels of segregation have increased from prior periods of relatively less segregation, as in the case of São Paulo (Andrews 1991). Here, the degrees of historical changes in spatial stratification between the city and reservation remains a question for this project. Of note, though, the founding of the reservation predates that of the city.

5. Original text, "Em Mato Grosso do Sul, frequentemente se observa pessoas a dizer que deveríamos ter feito aqui o que teria sido feito nos Estados Unidos com os povos indígenas de lá: aniquilação total! Segundo alguns pensam, ou querem fazer crer, naquele país o General Custer [George Armstrong Custer] teria exterminado por completo a população indígena daquele país no século XIX, quando comandou o Sétimo Regimento de Cavalaria e fez guerra contra vários povos indígenas" (Eremites de Oliveira 2012).

6. Protest leaders in the region routinely refer to themselves, and are called, *caciques*.

7. Dourados is only sixty-two miles from the border with Paraguay, which partly contributes to the rate of drug trafficking.

8. Campers reporting of wages varied little. One camper oscillates from working for a tijolo (brickmaking) company on the fazenda at Aldeia c and cutting cane. He makes almost thirty reais (roughly fifteen dollars) a day at the tijolo company, working from 7:00 a.m. through 4:00 p.m. At the fazenda/usina (plantation/distillery) he makes 3.50 reais per ton of cane cut.

9. Such development projects have been attempted with Indians in the Dourados region as well. See Fabio Mura's (2005) article "Por que fracassam os projetos de desenvolvimento entre os Guaraní de Mato Grosso do Sul? Notas críticas para uma política de sustentabilidade" ("Why Do Development Projects Fail for the Guaraní of Mato Grosso do Sul? Critical Notes for a Sustainable Politics" along these lines).

10. The denomination *frontier* is both a colloquial and official term determined by the União (federal government). Land titles within 150 km of the country's borders must be emitted by the União (Burgos de Oliveira n.d.).

11. This program expanded specifically to Mato Grosso and Mato Grosso do Sul in 1987. The Japanese investments in infrastructure, technical training, and other inputs were especially significant for soy production. Brazil's central-west went on to become the leading soy producer in the world. "Not only is it the world's biggest soy exporter, a title it seized from the U.S. in 2006, but it has the world's biggest farm trade surplus, $27.5 billion last year. (The U.S. surplus was $4.6 billion.) The leading producer of beef, poultry, pork, ethanol, coffee, orange juice concentrate, sugar, and tobacco, Brazil has seen farm exports grow an average of 20% a year since 2000, according to the USDA" (Hecht and Mann 2008).

12. Mueller (2004, 8) defines *agribusiness complexes* as industries that "furnish agriculture with machinery and inputs and of those which process inputs originating from agriculture . . . they provide inputs and markets for the farmers but they also have a significant participation in the marketing of agricultural products and in the financing of agriculture. Moreover, their quality requirements have also induced technical change in agriculture." Agribusiness complexes benefit from both exports and expansion of the domestic market.

13. The opposition agro-ecology movement, consisting of those sympathetic to land reform like the MST, call for utilizing select native plants and mixed crops as opposed to pesticides, herbicides, and monocrop production. They challenge the sustainability of the prevailing model introduced for and through agribusiness.

This countermovement is also a response to crises in the availability of foreign reserves for financing of pesticides, GMO seeds, and agribusiness products and production techniques that triggered food crises in much of the global South in the 1990s and 2000s (McMichael 2009).

14. The Estatuto da Terra Indigena (Indigenous land law) had been in effect since the 1970s, although never fully enforced.

15. A cartorio is form of notary office, either of the government or a private agency, that has custody of documents.

16. Lefebvre ([1974] 1991, 9) writes of spatial practice, which "consists in a projection on a (spatial) field of all aspects, elements and moment of social practice." He writes, "In the process . . . society as a whole continues in subjection to political practice—that is, to state power."

17. Before the onset of the first phase, the Kaiowá-Guaraní eluded missionaries and slave raiders in the colonial era by hiding in the forests (Meliá, Grunberg, and Grunberg 1976, 175–177). Late-nineteenth century legal precedents and settler expansion altered these relations. The SPI mission of "protecting" the Indians implemented a policy of "accommodation" and acculturation for the supposed well-being of Indigenous people that rationalized confinement onto reservations. This state agency created to execute Indigenous policy was transformed into the Fundação Nacional do Índio (Funai) in 1967.

18. Original Portuguese: Parágrafo 1° do artigo 231 da Constituição Federal, o conceito de terras tradicionalmente ocupadas pelos Índios é definido como sendo: aquelas "por eles habitadas em caráter permanente, as utilizadas para suas atividades produtivas, as imprescindíveis à preservação dos recursos ambientais necessários a seu bem-estar e as necessárias a sua reprodução física e cultural, segundo seus usos, costumes e tradições." Embora os Índios detenham o "usufruto exclusivo das riquezas do solo, dos rios e dos lagos" existentes em suas terras, conforme o parágrafo 2° do Art. 231 da Constituição, elas constituem patrimônio da União. E, como bens públicos de uso especial, as terras indígenas, além de inalienáveis e indisponíveis, não podem ser objeto de utilização de qualquer espécie por outros que não os próprios Índios.

19. In chapter 1, I discuss the construction of the Brazilian national subject, abstract citizen-subjects, and national belonging. I describe how the ethnic category of Índio versus não-Índio operates in the normative configuration of the nation-state territory as particular to the regional constructions of Mato Grosso do Sul.

### 6. The Space to Be

1. Ramos calls for anthropologists to practice a "frugality of humbleness and self-criticism" (2012, 485).

2. Of course, culture and cosmology are not the same but get lumped together in much of the literature and ways of referring to Indigenous culture. I am speaking about this tendency by way of interrogating it.

3. This literature is vast and contentious, ranging across disciplines, including phenomenology, science and technology (particularly theories and ethnographies of interspecies relations), and politics. My approach both shares features with and differs from that found in some anthropological books on Indigenous populations generally and Brazilian land reformers specifically. Those treatments often view Indigenous relations to land as grounded in ontological alterity (Blaser 2010; Cadena 2010; Viveiros de Castro 1998). According to this view, for the cases that I study, Indigenous protestors' claims to ethnic land titling would require translating their concepts across onto-epistemological difference to equivocate their conceptions with liberal political-juridical-economic concept of property. By contrast, the work of Brazilianist anthropologists like Ramos (2012), Turner (2009), and Pacheco de Oliveira (1998), and of anthropologists elsewhere in Latin America, such as Bessire (2014) and Postero (2017), might focus on how invocations of culture arise with transformations in the organization of political economy.

4. Note in chapter 5 the mention of karai in the vice-captain's narratives of the campers' relations to the land they were claiming.

5. The full speech intermingled the Portuguese and Guaraní languages.

6. The term means "people from the state of Mato Grosso do Sul."

# Bibliography

Adecoagro. 2010. "Sugar, Ethanol and Energy." Accessed January 2, 2011. https://www
.adecoagro.com/index.php/en/our-businesses/sugar-etanol-energy.

Agence France Presse. 2012. "Brazil President Makes Final Changes to Forestry Law."
Phys.org, October 18. https://phys.org/news/2012-10-brazil-forestry-law.html.

Agostinho, Pedro. 2009a. "Os municípios e o poder político dos coronéis em Mato
Grosso" (Municipalities and political power of the *coronéis* in Mato Grosso).
*Gosto de Ler* (blog). Accessed December 28, 2011. http://www.gostodeler.com
.br/materia/9083/os_municipios_e_o_poder_politico_dos_coroneis_em_mato
_grosso-uno.html. (Page removed.)

———. 2009b. "Grupos associados e coronéis: Os interesses políticos em Mato
Grosso na década de 50" (Associated groups and *coronéis*: Political interests
in Mato Grosso in the 1950s). *Gosto de Ler* (blog). Accessed December 28, 2011.
http://www.gostodeler.com.br/materia/9066/grupos_associados_e_coroneis
_os_interesses_politicos_em_mato_grosso_na_decada_de_50.html. (Page
removed.)

Anaya, James. 2009. "Promotion and Protection of All Human Rights, Civil, Political, Economic, Social and Cultural Rights, Including the Right to Development:
Report of the Special Rapporteur on the Situation of Human Rights and Fundamental Freedoms of Indigenous People." *United Nations Addendum: Report
on the Situation of Human Rights of Indigenous Peoples in Brazil.* Human Rights
Council Twelfth Session, Agenda Item 3, August 26.

Anderson, Benjamin. 2006. *Imagined Communities: Reflections on the Origin and
Spread of Nationalism.* London: Verso.

Andrews, George Reid. 1991. *Blacks and Whites in São Paulo, 1888–1988.* Madison
WI: University of Wisconsin Press.

Aparecida de Moraes, Maria. 1999. *Errantes do fim do século* (Errors of the end of the century). São Paulo: Fundação Editora da UNESP.

Appadurai, Arjun. 2004. "The Capacity to Aspire: Culture and the Terms of Recognition." In *Culture and Public Action*, edited by Vijayendra Rao and Michael Walton, 59–84. Palo Alto CA: Stanford University Press.

Aylwin, José. 2009. *Os direitos dos povos Indígenas em Mato Grosso do Sul, Brasil: Confinamento e tutela no século XXI* (The rights of Indigenous people in Mato Grosso do Sul, Brazil: Confinement and tutelage in the twenty-first century). São Paulo: Grupo Internacional de Trabalho Sobre Assuntos Indígenas (IWGIA) e Faculdade de Medicina da USP (FMUSP).

Bandeira, Regina. 2011. "Indígenas recebem documentos em Mato Grosso do Sul" (Indigenous receive documents in Mato Grosso do Sul). *Agência CNJ de Notícias*, June 15. http://www.cnj.jus.br/noticias/cnj/14778:indigenas-recebem-documentos-em-mato-grosso-do-sul. (Page removed.)

Barth, Frederick. 1969. *Ethnic Groups and Boundaries*. Boston: Little, Brown.

Beldi de Alcantara, Maria Lourdes. 2010. *Reflections on the Complex Nature of Guarani-Kaiowá Suicide*. ResearchGate, July 10. https://www.researchgate.net/publication/236145778_Reflections_on_the_Complex_Nature_of_Guarani-Kaiowá_Suicide.

——. 2012. "The Dialogue Between Western Doctors and Young Indigenous Guaraní." Paper presented at British Sociological Association Annual Conference, April 11. Leeds, UK. http://content.yudu.com/library/A1w6ig/BSAAnnualConference2/resources/129.htm.

Benites, Tonico. 2009. "A escola na ótica dos Ava Kaiowá: impactos e interpretações indígenas" (*Schools from the Perspective of the Kaiowá: Impacts and indigenous interpretations*). Master's thesis, Museu Nacional, (Universidade Federal do Rio de Janeiro), Rio de Janeiro, Brazil.

——. 2014. "Rojerokyhina ha hoikejevy tekohape (rezando e lutando): O movimento histórico indígena dos Aty Guasu dos Ava Kaiowá e Ava Guarani pela recuperação dos seus tekoha" (Praying and fighting: The historic indigenous movement of the Aty Guasu of the Ava Kaiowá and Ava Guarani for the recovery of their tekoha). PhD thesis, Museu Nacional, Universidade Federal do Rio de Janeiro, Rio de Janeiro, Brazil.

Bessire, Lucas. 2014. *Behold the Black Caiman: A Chronicle of Ayoreo Life*. Chicago: University of Chicago Press.

Blaser, Mario. 2010. *Storytelling Globalization from the Chaco and Beyond*. Durham NC: Duke University Press.

Bloemer, Neusa Maria Sans. 2000. *Brava gente Brasileira: Migrantes Italianos e Caboclos no campo de Lages* (Great Brazilian people: Italian migration and Caboclos in the countryside of Lages). Florianópolis, Brazil: Cidade Futura.

Borges, Dain. 2008. "Residential Segregation by Race and Class in Brazilian Cities around 1872." Paper presented at the Latin American History Workshop, University of Chicago, January 31.

Brand, Antonio. 1997. "O impacto da perda da terra sobre a tradição Kaiowá/Guaraní: Os difíceis caminhos da palavra" (The impact of the loss of land on Kaiowá and Guaraní tradition: The difficult journeys of the word). PhD diss., Pontifícia Universidade Católica, Porto Alegre.

———. 2004. "Os complexos caminhos da luta pela terra entre os Kaiowá e Guaraní no MS" (The complex paths of the land struggle of the Guaraní-Kaiowá of Mato Grosso do Sul). *Tellus* 4, no. 5: 137–50. https://www.tellus.ucdb.br/tellus/article/view/82/88.

Brand, Antonio, and Rosa Sebastiana Colman. 2008. "Considerações sobre Território para os Kaiowá e Guarani" (Considerations on territory from the Kaiowá and Guarani standpoint). *Tellus* 8, no. 15 (July–December): 173–84. https://doi.org/10.20435/tellus.v0i15.166.

Brasil de Fato. 2011. "A crise internacional do capitalismo e o Brasil" (The international crisis of capitalism and Brazil). Brasil de Fato (website). August 11. http://brasildefato.com.br/node/7090. (Page discontinued.)

Bueno Mota, Juliana Grasiéle. 2015. "Territórios, multiterritorialidades e memórias dos povos Guarani e Kaiowá: Diferenças geográficas e as lutas pela descolonização na reserva indígena e nos acampamentos—Tekoha-Dourados/MS." (Territories, multiterritorialities, and memory of the Kaiowa-Guarani people: Geographical differences and the struggle for decolonization on the Indigenous reservation and in the camps). PhD thesis, State University of São Paulo-Presidente Prudente, São Paulo.

Burgos de Oliveira, Gustavo. N.d. *Faixa de fronteira—doutrina e jurisprudência* (The border region—doctrine and jurisprudence). Ministério Público do Rio Grande do Sul. https://www.mprs.mp.br/media/areas/urbanistico/arquivos/faixadefronteira.doc.

*Business Week.* 2007. "The Money Flying Down to Brazil." June 18. https://www.bloomberg.com/news/articles/2007-06-17/the-money-flying-down-to-brazil.

Cadena, Marisol de la. 2010. "Indigenous Cosmopolitics in the Andes: Conceptual Reflections beyond 'Politics.'" *Cultural Anthropology* 25, no. 2: 334–70.

Cariaga, Diógenes. 2015. "Gênero e sexualidades indígenas: Alguns aspectos das transformações nas relações a partir dos Kaiowá no Mato Grosso do Sul" (Indigenous gender and sexualities: Some aspects of transformations in these relations from the perspective of the Kaiowá of Mato Grosso do Sul). *Cadernos de Campo* 24: 441–64.

Carneiro da Cunha, Manuela. 1987. *Os direito do Índio: Ensaios e documentos* (Indian rights: Essays and documents). São Paulo: Editora Brasilense.

———. 2009. *"Culture" and Culture: Traditional Knowledge and Intellectual Rights.* Chicago: Prickly Paradigm Press.

———. 2017. Introduction to "Indigenous Peoples Boxed in by Brazil's Political Crisis," by Manuela Carneiro da Cunha et al., 404–10.

Carneiro da Cunha, Manuela, Ruben Caixeta, Jeremy M. Campbell, Carlos Fausto, José Antonio Kelly, Claudio Lomnitz, Carlos D. Londoño Sulkin, Caio Pompeia, and Aparecida Vilaça. 2017. "Indigenous Peoples Boxed in by Brazil's Political Crisis." *Hau: Journal of Ethnographic Theory* 7, no. 2: 403–26. https://doi.org/10 .14318/hau7.2.033.

Castilho Crespe Lutti, Aline. 2009. "Acampamentos indígenas e ocupações: Novas modalidades de organização e territorialização entre os Guarani e Kaiowá no município de Dourados—MS: (1990–2009)" (Indigenous camps and occupations: New modalities of territory and organization among the Kaiowá-Guarani in the municipality of Dourados, MS: (1990–2009)). Master's thesis, Universidade Federal de Grande Dourados, Dourados, Mato Grosso do Sul, Brazil.

Cepek, Michael. 2008. "Essential Commitments: Identity and the Politics of Cofán Conservation." *Journal of Latin American and Caribbean Anthropology* 13 (October 23): 196–222. https://doi.org/10.1111/j.1548-7180.2008.00009.x.

———. 2011. "Foucault in the Forest: Questioning Environmentality in Amazonia." *American Ethnologist* 38, no. 3: 501–15.

———. 2016. "There Might Be Blood: Oil, Humility, and the Cosmopolitics of a Cofán Petro-being." *American Ethnologist* 4, no. 4: 623–45.

Chamorro, Graciela. 1995. *Kurusu Ñe'ëngatu: Palabras que la historia no podría olvidar.* (Kurusu Ñe'ëngatu: Words that history would not be able to forget). Vol. 25 of *Biblioteca Paraguaya de antropología.* Asunción, Paraguay: Centro de Estudios Antropológicos.

———. 2002. "A redenção da palavra: Uma aproximação da soteriologia Guaraní" (The redemption of the word: An approximation of Guaraní soteriology). *Presbíteros e Cargos Políticos* 62, no. 246: 329–46.

Chileno, Victor. 2009. "Demarcação de terras domina debates na Assembleia de MS" (Land demarcation dominates debates in the Mato Grosso do Sul assembly). *Diario MS*, April 15. http://www.diarioms.com.br/leitura.php?can_id=16&id= 94096. (Site discontinued.)

Clifford, James. 1988. "Identity in Mashpee." In *The Predicament of Culture*, 277–346. Cambridge MA: Harvard University Press.

Clastres, Hélène. (1975) 1995. *The Land-without-Evil: Tupi-Guaraní Prophetism.* Chicago: University of Illinois Press.

Conceição d'Incão, Maria da. 1984. *A questão do Bóia-Fria: Acumulação e miseria* (The question of the Bóia-Fria: Accumulation and misery). São Paulo: Brasiliense.

Conklin, Beth A. 1997. "Body Paint, Feathers, and VCRs: Aesthetics and Authenticity in Amazonian Activism." *American Ethnologist* 24, no. 4: 711–37.

Coronil, Fernando. 1997. *The Magical State: Nature, Money, and Modernity in Venezuela*. Chicago: University of Chicago Press.

Costa Vargas, João. 2004. "Hyperconsciousness of Race and Its Negation: The Dialectic of White Supremacy in Brazil." *Identities: Global Studies in Culture and Power* 11, no. 4: 443–70.

———. 2012. "Gendered Anti-Blackness and the Impossible Brazilian Project: Emerging Critical Black Brazilian Studies." *Cultural Dynamics* 24, no. 1: 3–11.

Coutinho, Leonardo, Igor Paulin, and Júlia de Medeiros. 2010. "A farra de antropologia oportunista" (The spree of opportunist anthropology). *Veja*. Accessed August 5, 2011. http://veja.abril.com.br/050510/farra-antropologia-oportunista-p-154.shtml. (Page removed.)

Dean, Warren. 1995. *With Broadax and Firebrand: The Destruction of the Brazilian Atlantic Forest*. Berkeley: University of California Press.

Dent, Alexander Sebastian. 2005. "'Cross-Cultural 'Countries' Covers, Conjuncture, and the Whiff of Nashville in *Música Sertaneja* (Brazilian commercial country music)." *Popular Music and Society* 28, no. 2: 207–27.

Descola, Philippe. 1996. *In the Society of Nature: A Native Ecology in Amazonia*. Cambridge: Cambridge University Press.

*Dourados News*. 2001. "Favelados começam a deixar assentamento Brasil 500." July 31. https://www.douradosnews.com.br/noticias/brasil/favelados-comecam-a-deixar-assentamento-brasil-500-bdd2399710bb17841ce/100180/.

Durham, Eunice. 1973. *A caminho da cidade: A vida rural e a migração para São Paulo* (The path to the city: Rural life and migration to São Paulo). São Paulo: Perspectiva.

Encarnação Beltrão Sposito, Maria. 1999. "Espaços urbanos: territorialidades e representações" (Urban spaces: Territoriality and respresentation). In *Dinâmica econômica, poder e novas territorialidades*, edited by Eliseu S. Sposito, 3–29. Presidente Prudente, Brazil: UNESP/GASPERR.

Eremites de Oliveira, Jorge. 2012. "Sobre a presença Indigena nos Estados Unidos" (On the presence of Indigenes in the United States). *Turismo Rural Mato Grosso* (blog), March 3. http://www.turismoruralmt.com/2018/08/.

Eremites de Oliveira, Jorge, and Levi Marques Pereira. 2009. *Ñande Ru Marangatu: Laudo percial sobre uma terra Kaiowá na fronteira do Brasil com o Paraguai, em Mato Grosso do Sul* (Ñande Ru Marangatu: Study of Kaiowá land on the border between Brazil and Paraguay, in Mato Grosso do Sul). Dourados, Brazil: Universidade Federal de Grande Dourados.

Ernandes, Mercolis Alexandre. 2009. "A construção da identidade Douradense (1920 a 1990)" (The construction of Douradense identity (1920–1990)). Master's thesis, Federal University of Greater Dourados, Brazil.

Escobar, Arturo. 1995. *Encountering Development: Making and Unmaking of the Third World*. Princeton NJ: Princeton University Press.

Fabricant, Nicole, and Nancy Postero. 2015. "Sacrificing Indigenous Bodies and Lands: The Political-Economic History of Lowland Bolivia in Light of the Recent TIPNIS Debate." *Journal of Latin American and Caribbean Anthropology* 20, no. 3: 452–74.

Falconi da Hora Bernadelli, Mara Lúcia. 2006. "O caráter urbano das pequenas cidades da região canavieira de Cantanduva-SP" (The urban character of small cities of the sugarcane region of Cantanduva, São Paulo). In *Cidade e campo: Relações e contradições entre urbano e rural*, edited by Maria Encarnação Beltrão and Arthur Whitacker, 217–47. São Paulo: Editora Expressão Popular.

Fausto, Carlos. 2008. "Donos demais: Maestria e domínio na amazônia" (Other owners: Mastery and dominion in the Amazon). *Mana* 14, no. 2: 329–66.

———. 2017. "Anthropology in the Face of Brazil's Political Crisis." In Carneiro da Cunha et al., "Indigenous Peoples Boxed in by Brazil's Political Crisis," 413–15.

Ferguson, James. (1990) 1997. *The Anti-Politics Machine*. Minneapolis: The University of Minnesota Press.

———. 2005. "Seeing Like an Oil Company: Space, Security, and Global Capital in Neoliberal Africa." *American Anthropologist* 107, no. 3: 377–82.

———. 2006. *Global Shadows: Africa in the Neoliberal World Order*. Durham NC: Duke University Press.

Ferguson, James, and Akhil Gupta. 2002. "Spatializing States: Toward an Ethnography of Neoliberal Governmentality." *American Ethnologist* 29, no. 4: 981–1002.

Ferreira Thomas de Almeida, Rubem. 2001. *Do desenvolvimento comunitário e mobilização política: O projeto Kaiowá-Ñandeva como experiéncia antropológica* (From community development to political mobilization: The Kaiowá-Ñandeva as an anthropological experience). Rio de Janeiro: Contra Capa Livraria.

FETAGRI. 2011. "Quem somos" (About us). *Federação dos Trabalhadores na Agricultura do Estado de Mato Grosso do Sul*. Accessed November 17, 2011. http://www.fetagrims.org.br. (Site discontinued.)

Florêncio de Almeida, Luciana, Decio Zylbersztajn, and Peter G. Klein. 2010. "Determinants of Contractual Arrangements in Agricultural Credit Transactions." *Revista de Administração* 45, no. 3 (June): 209–20. https://www.academia.edu/81823345/Determinants_of_contractual_arrangements_in_agricultural_credit_transactions.

Foresta, Ronald. 1992. "Amazônia and the Politics of Geopolitics." *Geographical Review* 82, no. 2 (April): 128–42.

Forman, Shepard. 1975. *The Brazilian Peasantry.* New York: Columbia University Press.

Foucault, Michel. 1991. "Governmentality." In *The Foucault Effect: Studies in Governmentality,* edited by G. Burchell, C. Gordon, and P. Miller, 87–104. Chicago: University of Chicago Press.

———. 2003."Society Must Be Defended": Lectures at the Collège de France, 1975–1976. New York: Picador Reading Group Guides.

Frank, Zephyr Lake. 2001. "Elite Families and Oligarchic Politics on the Brazilian Frontier: Mato Grosso, 1889–1937." *Latin American Research Review* 36, no. 1: 49–74. https://www.jstor.org/stable/2692074.

French, Jan Hoffman. 2009. *Legalizing Identities: Becoming Black or Indian in Brazil's Northeast.* Chapel Hill NC: University of North Carolina Press.

Gadelha, Regina. 1980. *As missões jesuíticas do Itatim: Um estudo das estruturas socioeconômicas coloniais do Paraguai (sec. xvi e xviii)* (Historical aspects of the populating and colonization of the state of Mato Grosso do Sul, with a focus on the municipality of Dourados). Rio de Janeiro: Paz e Terra.

Garfield, Seth. 2001. *Indigenous Struggle at the Heart of Brazil: State Policy, Frontier Expansion, and the Xavante Indians, 1937–1988.* Durham NC: Duke University Press.

———. 2004. "A Nationalist Environment: Indians, Nature, and the Construction of the Xingu National Park in Brazil." *Luso-Brazilian Review,* 41 no. 1: 139–67.

Gartlan, Kieran. 2010. *The Global Power of Brazilian Agribusiness.* Edited by Katherine Dorr Abreu. London: Economist Intelligence Unit, November. https://impact.economist.com/perspectives/perspectives/sites/default/files/Accenture_Agribusiness_ENGLISH.pdf.

Gilroy, Paul. 2000. *Against Race: Imagining Political Culture beyond the Color Line.* Cambridge MA: Harvard University Press.

Glass, Verena. 2009. "MPF quer co-responsabilizar usina do Grupo Bertin em denúncia de tentativa de genocídio" (MPF blames Usina Grup Bertim for attempted genocide). *Reporter Brasil.* September 29. http://www.mst.org.br/node/8238. (Page discontinued.)

Globo.com. 2010. "PF prende politicos de Dourados suspeitos de fraude e corrupção" (Federal police arrest politicians in Dourados for suspicion of fraud and corruption). September 1. http://g1.globo.com/politica/noticia/2010/09/pf-prende-politicos-de-dourados-suspeito-de-fraude-e-corrupcao.html.

Graham, Laura. 2002. "How Should an Indian Speak? Amazonian Indians and the Symbolic Politics of Language in the Global Public Sphere." In *Indigenous Movements, Self-Representation and the State in Latin America,* edited by Kay B. Warren and Jean E. Jackson, 181–215. Austin: University of Texas Press.

Gramsci, Antonio. 1999. "Notes on Italian History." In *Selections from the Prison Notebooks.* Translated by Quintin Hoare and Geoffrey Smith, 52–120. New York: International Publishers.

Graziano da Silva, José, Mauro Del Grossi, and Clayton Campanhola. 2002. "O que há de realmente novo no rural Brasileiro" (What's really new in rural Brazil). *Cadernos de ciência e tecnologia* 19 (January-April): 37–67.

Gressler, Lori Alice, and Lauro Joppert Swensson. 1988. *Aspectos históricos do povoamento e da colonização do estado de Mato Grosso do Sul: Destaque especial ao Município de Dourados* (Historical aspects of the populating and colonization of the state of Mato Grosso do Sul, with a focus on the municipality of Dourados). São Paulo: Gressler & Swensson.

Guillen, Isabel. 1999. "A luta pela terra nos sertões de Mato Grosso" (The struggle for the land in the Mato Grosso backlands). *Estudos Sociedade e Agricultura* 12: 148–68.

Guzmàn, Tracy Devine. 2013. *Native and National in Brazil: Indigeneity after Independence*. Chapel Hill: University of North Carolina Press.

Hale, Charles. 2005. "Neoliberal Multiculturalism: The Remaking of Cultural Rights and Racial Dominance in Central America." *Political and Legal Anthropology Review* 28, no. 1: 10–28.

Hamlin, Cynthia Lins, and Robert J. Brym. 2006. "The Return of the Native: A Cultural and Social-Psychological Critique of Durkheim's 'Suicide' Based on the Guaraní-Kaiowá of Southwestern Brazil." *Sociological Theory* 24, no. 1: 42–57.

Harrison, Faye V. 1991. "Ethnography as Politics." In *Decolonizing Anthropology: Moving Further toward an Anthropology for Liberation*, edited by Faye V. Harrison, 89–110. 3rd ed. Ann Arbor: University of Michigan.

Hecht, Susanna B., and Alexander Cockburn. 1989. *The Fate of the Forest: Developers, Destroyers, and Defenders of the Amazon*. London: Verso.

Hecht, Susanna B., and Charles C. Mann. 2008. "How Brazil Outfarmed the American Farmer." *Fortune*, January 19. https://archive.fortune.com/2008/01/16/news/international/brazil_soy.fortune/index.htm.

Heck, Egon. 2011. "Em busca da verdade e da justiça" (In search of truth and justice). *Brasil de Fato*. Accessed March 5, 2011. http://www.brasildefato.com.br/node/5759. (Page discontinued.)

Hegel, Georg Wilhelm Fredrich. (1807) 1991. *Elements of the Philosophy of Right*. Cambridge: University of Cambridge Press.

Holloway, Thomas H. 1980. *Immigrants on the Land: Coffee and Society in São Paulo, 1886–1934*. Chapel Hill: University of North Carolina Press.

Holston, James. 2008. *Insurgent Citizenship: Disjunctions of Democracy and Modernity in Brazil*. Princeton NJ: Princeton University Press.

Inocêncio, Maria. 2010. "o PROCEDER e as tramas do poder na territorialização do capital no Cerrado" (PROCEDER and the wefts of power in the territorial capital in the Cerrado). PhD thesis, Universidade Federal de Goiás, Goiânia, Brazil.

Instituto Brasileira de Geografia e Estatística. 2012a. *Censos Demográficos de Mato Grosso e Mato Grosso do Sul* (Demographic Census of Mato Grosso and Mato Grosso do Sul). Brasilia, Brazil: Federal Government of Brazil.

———. 2012b. *Os Indigenas no Censo Demográfico 2010: Primeiras considerações com base no quesito cor ou raça* (Indigenous people in the Demographic Census of 2010: First considerations on questions of color or race). Rio de Janeiro: Brazilian Institute of Geography and Statistics.

Jackson, Jean, and Kay Warren. 2005. "Indigenous Movements in Latin America, 1992–2004: Controversies, Ironies, New Directions." *Annual Review of Anthropology* 34: 549–73.

James, C. L. R. (1969) 1980. *Notes on Dialectics: Left Hegelianism or Marxism-Leninism?* London: Allison and Busby.

Kant, Immanuel. (1783) 2004. *Prolegomena to Any Future Metaphysics.* Cambridge: Cambridge University Press.

Kelly, José Antonio. 2017. "Ordinary Rights, Ending Rights, and the Right to Be Ends." In Carneiro da Cunha et al., "Indigenous Peoples Boxed in by Brazil's Political Crisis," 415–17.

Koenigswald, Gustav. 1908. *Die Cayuas.* Braunsweig, Germany: Globus.

Leal, Victor. 1977. *Coronelismo: The Municipality and Representative Government in Brazil.* Cambridge: Cambridge University Press.

Lefebvre, Henri. (1974) 1991. *The Production of Space.* Translated by Donald Nicholson-Smith. Oxford: Blackwell Publishers.

Lobo Digital. 2008. "Vídeo Índio Brasil acontece em três cidades de MS." Dourados Agora (website). June 18. https://www.douradosagora.com.br/noticias/dourados/video-indio-brasil-acontece-em-tres-cidades-de-ms.

Locke, John. (1690) 1980. *Second Treatise on Government.* Indianapolis IN: Hackett.

Lyons, John. 2011. "The Dark Side of Brazil's Rise." *Wall Street Journal.* Last updated September 13. http://online.wsj.com/article/SB10001424053111904716604576544722103262938.html.

Maciulevicius, Paula. 2011. "Após morte de líder indígena, clima na cidade é como se nada tivesse acontecido" (After the killing of Indigenous leader, climate in the town is as if nothing had happened). *Campo Grande News,* November 20. http://www.campograndenews.com.br/cidades/interior/na-cidade-onde-acampamento-indigena-foi-atacado-e-como-se-nada-tivesse-ocorrido.

Mançano Fernandes, Bernardo. 2008. "O MST e as reformas agrárias do Brasil" (The MST and agrarian reform in Brazil). *Observatorio Social de América Latina* 9, no. 24 (October): 73–85. http://biblioteca.clacso.edu.ar/gsdl/collect/clacso/index/assoc/D4116.dir/04mancano.pdf.

Marques Pereira, Levi. 2002. *Relatório circunstanciado de identificação e delimitação da terra Guaraní-Kaiowá Guyraroká* (Report on the land identification

and delimitation of the Guyraroká Kaiowá-Guaraní). March 13. https://www
.socioambiental.org/sites/blog.socioambiental.org/files/nsa/arquivos/rel.ver_
.final_.1.pdf.

———. 2003. "O movimento étnico-social pela demarcação das terras Guaraní em
MS" (The ethnic social movement for the demarcation of Guaraní land in Mato
Grosso do Sul). *Tellus* no. 3: 4.

———. 2004a. "Imagens Kaiowá do sistema social e seu entorno" (Images of the
the Kaiowá system and its surroundings). PhD diss., University of São Paulo.

———. 2004b. "O Penticostalismo Kaiowá: Uma aproximação dos aspectos socio-
cosmológicos e históricos" (Kaiowá Pentecostalism: An approximation of the
historical and sociocosmological aspects). In *Igrejas evangélicas, pentecostais e
neopentocotais entre os povos indígenas no Brasil*, edited by Robin Wright, 267–
302. Vol. 2 of *Transformando os Deuses*. Campinas, Brazil: Editora de Unicamp.

———. 2010. "Demarcacao de terras Kaiowá e Guaraní em MS: Ocupacao tradi-
cional, reordenamentos organizacionais e gestao territorial" (Demarcation of
Guaraní-Kaiowá lands: Traditional occupation, organizational reorderings, and
territorial management). *Tellus* 10, no. 18: 115–37.

Marx, Karl. (1844) 2000. "Economic and Philosophical Manuscripts of 1844." In
*Karl Marx: Selected Writings*, edited and translated by David McClellan, 85–104.
Oxford: Oxford University Press.

Matos, Henrique de. 2011. "Exportações em Mato Grosso do Sul crescem 60.5%"
(Exports from Mato Grosso do Sul grow 60.5%). Diario MS (website). Accessed
April 14, 2011. http://www.diarioms.com.br/leitura.php?can_id=44&id=125050.
(Site discontinued.)

Maybury-Lewis, Biorn. 1994. *The Politics of the Possible: The Brazilian Rural Worker's Trade Union Movement, 1964–1985*. Philadelphia: Temple University Press.

McMichael, Phillip. 2009. "A Food Regime Analysis of the 'World Food Crisis.'"
*Agriculture and Human Values* 26, no. 4: 281–95. https://doi.org/10.1007/s10460
-009-9218-5.

Meliá, Bartomeu. 1981. "El 'modo de ser' Guaraní en la primera documentación
Jesuítica (1594–1639)" (The Guaraní "way of being" in the first Jesuit documentation (1594–1639)). *Revista de Antropologia* 24: 1–24.

Meliá, Bartomeu, Georg Grünberg, Fridl Grünberg. 1976. *Los Pai-Tavyterã: Etnografâ
del Paraguay contemporáneo* (The Pai-Tavyterã: Ethnography of contemporary
Paraguay). Asunción, Paraguay: Centro Estudios Antropologicos Universidad
Catôlica Nuestra Señora de la Asunción.

Mitchell, Sean. 2017. *Constellations of Inequality: Space, Race, and Utopia in Brazil*.
Chicago: University of Chicago Press.

Moten, Fred. 2008. "Black Op." *PMLA* 123, no. 5: 1743–47. https://doi.org/10.1632
/pmla.2008.123.5.1743.

*MS Noticias*. 2011. "OAB/MS pretende levar caso de Nísio Gomes à OEA" (OAB-Mato Grosso do Sul seeks to bring case of Nísio Gomes to the Organization of Americas). *MS Noticias*. Accessed November 24, 2011. http://www.msnoticias .com.br/?p=ler&id=76148. (Page removed.)

Mueller, Bernardo, and Charles Mueller. 2006. "The Evolution of Agriculture and Land Reform in Brazil, 1960–2006." Paper presented at Economic Development in Latin America: A Conference in Honor of Werner Baer, University of Illinois at Urbana-Champaign, December 1–2.

Mueller, Charles. 2004. "Brazil: Agriculture and Agrarian Development and the Lula Government." Paper presented at Meeting of the Latin American Studies Association, Las Vegas, Nevada, October 7–9.

Munn, Nancy. 1996. "Excluded Spaces: The Figure in the Australian Aboriginal Landscape." *Critical Inquiry* 22 (Spring): 446–65.

Mura, Fabio. 2004. "O tekoha como categoria histórica: Elaborações e estratégias Guaraní na construção do território" (The tekoha as a historical category: Guaraní elaborations and strategies in the construction of territory). *Fronteiras* 8, no. 15: 109–43.

———. 2005. "Por que fracassam os projetos de desenvolvimento entre os Guaraní de Mato Grosso do Sul? Notas críticas para uma política de sustentabilidade" (Why do development projects fail for the Guaraní of Mato Grosso do Sul? Critical notes for a sustainable politics). *Tellus* 5, no. 8/9 (April/October): 53–72.

———. 2006. "À procura do 'bom viver': Território, tradição de conhecimento e ecologia doméstica entre os Kaiowá" (In search of the "good life": Territory, tradition of knowledge and domestic ecology among the Kaiowá). PhD thesis, PPGAS-Museu Nacional, UFRJ, Rio de Janeiro.

Nash, June. (1979) 1993. *We Eat the Mines and the Mines Eat Us: Dependency and Exploitation in Bolivian Tin Mines*. New York: Columbia University Press.

———. 2001. "Globalization and the Cultivation of Peripheral Vision." *Anthropology Today* 17, no. 4: 15–22.

Obama, Barack. 2011. "Remarks by President Obama at Teatro Municipal, Rio de Janeiro." The White House Office of the Press Secretary. Speech presented at Rio de Janeiro Brazil, March 20. http://www.blogdowelbi.com/2011/03/remarks -by-president-obama-at-teatro.html.

Pacheco de Oliveira, João. 1998. "Uma etnologia dos 'Índios misturados'? Situação colonial, territorialização e fluxos culturais" (An ethnology of "mixed Indians"? Colonial context, territoriality and cultural flows). *Mana* 4, no. 1: 47–77.

———. 2018. "Interethnic Friction." In *The International Encyclopedia of Anthropology*, edited by Hilary Callan and Simon Coleman. Hoboken NJ: John Wiley & Sons. https://doi.org/10.1002/9781118924396.wbiea1825.

Parker, Ian. 2011. "The ID Man: Can a Software Mogul's Epic Project Help India's Poor?" *New Yorker*, October 3. https://www.newyorker.com/magazine/2011/10/03/the-i-d-man.

Pereira, Anthony. 1997. *The End of the Peasantry: The Rural Labor Movement in Northeast Brazil, 1961–1988*. Pittsburgh PA: University of Pittsburgh.

Perry, Keisha-Khan. 2013. *Black Women against the Land Grab: The Fight for Racial Justice in Brazil*. Minneapolis: University of Minnesota Press.

Pimentel, Spency. 2006. "Sansões e Guaxos: Suicídio Guaraní e Kaiowá—uma proposta de síntese" (Sansões e Guaxos: Suicide of Guaraní-Kaiowá—a proposal of synthesis). Master's thesis, Universidade de São Paulo, São Paulo.

Pompeia, Caio. 2020. "'Agro é tudo': Simulações no aparato de legitimação do agronegócio" ("Agribusiness is everything": Simulations in the agribusiness legitimating apparatus). *Horizontes Antropologicos* 26, no. 56 (January–April): https://doi.org/10.1590/s0104-71832020000100009.

Postero, Nancy. 2017. *The Indigenous State: Race, Politics and Performance in Plurinational Bolivia*. Los Angeles: University of California Press.

Povinelli, Elizabeth. 2002. *The Cunning of Recognition: Indigenous Alterities and the Making of Australian Multiculturalism*. Durham NC: Duke University Press.

———. 2016. *Geontologies: A Requiem on Late Liberalism*. Durham NC: Duke University Press.

*Progresso*. 2011. "Famílias vivem em situação sub-humana" (Families live in a sub-human situation). March 28. https://www.progresso.com.br/noticias/familias-vivem-em-situacao-subumana/18257/.

Queiroz, Renato S. 2006. *Caipiras Negros no Vale do Ribeira: Um estudo de antropologia econômica* (Black Caipiras in the Ribeira Valley: An economic anthropological study). São Paulo: EDUSP.

Ramos, Alcida. 1994. "The Hyperreal Indian." *Critical Anthropology* 14, no. 2: 153–71.

———. 1998. *Indigenism: Ethnic Politics in Brazil*. Madison: University of Wisconsin Press.

———. 2001. *Pulp Fictions of Indigenism*. Brasília, Brazil: Departamento de Antropologia, Universidade de Brasília.

———. 2012. "The Politics of Perspectivism." *Annual Review of Anthropology* 41, no. 1 (October): 481–94. https://doi.org/10.1146/annurev-anthro-092611-145950.

Reuters. 2013. "Reforma agrária não pode ser sinônimo de agricultura de subsistência, diz Dilma" (Agrarian reform cannot be synomous with subsistence agriculture, says Dilma). *Folha de S. Paulo*, February 4, 2013. http://www1.folha.uol.com.br/mercado/1225817-reforma-agraria-nao-pode-ser-sinonimo-de-agricultura-de-subsistencia-diz-dilma.shtml.

Rocha, João. 2010. "Triplicam Preços de Terrenos em Dourados" (Land prices triple in Dourados). *Dourados Agora*. June 23. http://www.douradosagora.com.br/noticias/economia/triplicam-precos-de-terrenos-em-dourados.

Rocha, Rosaly. 2018. "Bolsonaro propõe carteira de trabalho verde amarela 'sem direitos'" (Bolsonaro proposes green and yellow work documents "without rights"). Portal Central Única dos Trabalhadores (website), October 26. https://www.cut.org.br/noticias/bolsonaro-cria-carteira-de-trabalho-verde-amarela-para-os-sem-direitos-96d0.

Rodrigues Pacheco, Carlos. 2009. "A dinâmica territorial e os processos de (re) construção da terra Indígena Jaguapiré Memby em Tacuru/MS: A ação do estado e os conflitos de interesses entre indígenas e trabalhadores rurais sem terra (1954–2009)" (The dynamics of territory and processess of reconstruction of Indigenous lands at Jaguapiré Memby in Tacuru, Mato Grosso do Sul: A state action and the conflicts of interest between Indigenous and landless rural workers (1954–2009)). Master's thesis, Universidade Federal de Grande Dourados, Dourados, Mato Grosso do Sul, Brazil.

Sauer, Sergio, and Sergio Pereira Leite. 2011. "Agrarian Structure, Foreign Land Ownership, and Land Value in Brazil." Paper presented at the International Conference on Global Land Grabbing, Sussex, UK, April 6–8.

Sawyer, Suzanna. 2005. *Crude Chronicles: Indigenous Politics, Multinational Oil, and Neoliberalism in Ecuador*. Durham NC: Duke University Press.

Schaden, Egon. 1962. *Aspectos fundamentais da cultura Guaraní* (Fundamental aspects of Guaraní culture). São Paulo: Difusão Europeia do Livro.

Scott, James C. 1998. *Seeing Like a State: How Certain Schemes to Improve the Human Condition Have Failed*. New Haven CT: Yale University Press.

Seraguza, Lauriene. 2013. "Cosmos, corpos e mulheres Kaiowá e guarani: De Aña à Kuña" (Cosmos, bodies, and Kaiowá-Guaraní women: From Aña to Kuña). Master's thesis, Universidade Federal de Grande Dourados. Dourados, Mato Grosso do Sul, Brazil. https://repositorio.ufgd.edu.br/jspui/bitstream/prefix/116/1/LaurieneSeraguzaOlegarioeSouza.pdf.

———. 2017. "De fúrias, jaguares, e brancos: Notas sobre gênero, sexualidade e política entre os Kaiowá e Guaraní em Mato Grosso do Sul" (Of fúrias, jaguars, and whites: Notes on gender, sexuality, and politics between the Kaiowá-Guaraní in Mato Grosso do Sul). Paper presented at Seminário Internacional Fazendo Gênero 11 & 13th Women's World's Congress (Anais Eletrônicos), Florianópolis, July 30–August 4, ISSN 2179–510X.

Simpson, Audra. 2014. *Mohawk Interruptus: Political Life across the Borders of Settler States*. Durham NC: Duke University Press.

Skidmore, Thomas E. 1993. *Black into White: Race and Nationality in Brazilian Thought*. Durham NC: Duke University Press.

Souza, Gisella. 2011. "Cidadania, direito de todos chega a Manaus" (Citizenship, everyone's right arrives in Manaus). May 3. Conselho Nacional de Justiça. http://www.cnj.jus.br/programas-de-a-a-z/cidadania-direito-de-todos.

Stolcke, Verena. 1988. *Coffee Planters, Workers and Wives: Class Conflict and Gender Relations on São Paulo Plantations, 1850–1980*. New York: St. Martin's Press.

Sullivan, LaShandra. 2013. "Identity, Territory and Land Conflict in Brazil," *Development and Change* 44, no. 2: 452–71.

———. 2017. "Black Invisibility on a Brazilian 'Frontier': Land and Identity in Mato Grosso do Sul, Brazil." *African and Black Diaspora: An International Journal* 10, no. 2: 131–42.

———. 2019. "Spiritual Warfare and Ethno-Racial Land Conflict in Brazil." Paper presented at the Forced Displacements in the Americas Workshop, Brown University, April 4–7.

Taussig, Michael. (1980) 2010. *The Devil and Commodity Fetishism in South America*. Chapel Hill: University of North Carolina Press.

Telles, Edward. 2004. *Race in Another America: The Significance of Skin Color in Brazil*. Chicago: University of Chicago Press.

Trouillot, Michel-Rolph. 2003. "Adieu, Culture: A New Duty Arises." In *Global Transformations: Anthropology and the Modern World*, 97–116. New York: Palgrave Macmillan.

Turner, Terence. 1995. "An Indigenous People's Struggle for Socially Equitable and Ecologically Sustainable Production: The Kayapo Revolt against Extractivism." *Journal of Latin American Anthropology* 1, no. 1: 98–121.

———. 2002. "Representation, Polyphony, and the Construction of Power in a Kayapó Video." In *Indigenous Movements, Self-Representation and the State in Latin America*, edited by Kay B. Warren and Jean E. Jackson, 229–50. Austin: University of Texas Press.

———. 2009. "The Crisis of Late Structuralism. Perspectivism and Animism: Rethinking Culture, Nature, Spirit, and Bodiliness." *Tipití: Journal of the Society for the Anthropology of Lowland South America* 7, no. 1: 3–42.

Twine, Frances Winddance. 1998. *Racism in a Racial Democracy: The Maintenance of White Supremacy in Brazil*. New Brunswick NJ: Rutgers University Press.

UN Human Rights Council. 2009. *Promotion and Protection of All Human Rights, Civil, Political, Economic, Social and Cultural Rights, Including the Right to Development: Report of the Special Rapporteur on the Situation of Human Rights and Fundamental Freedoms of Indigenous People. Addendum: Report on the Situation of Human Rights of Indigenous Peoples in Brazil*. UN doc. A/HRC/12/1 3 (August 26, 2009) (by James Anaya). https://digitallibrary.un.org/record/663918?ln=en.

Valor. 2013. "Após anunciar R$ 133 bi a agricultores, Dilma diz que 'O que gasterem, nós cobrimos'" (After announcing R$ 133 billion to agricultural sector, Dilma says that "what we spent, we will get back"). *Folha de S. Paulo*, February 4, 2013. http://www1.folha.uol.com.br/mercado/1225592-apos-anunciar-r-133-bi-a -agricultores-dilma-diz-que-o-que-gastarem-nos-cobrimos.shtml.

Vietta, Katya. 2007. "História sobre terras e xamãs kaiowá: Territorialidade e organização social na perspectiva dos Kaiowá de Panambizinho (Dourados—ms) após 170 anos de exploração e povoamento não indígena na faixa de fronteira entre o Brasil e Paraguai" (History of Kaiowá lands and shamans: Territoriality and social organization in the perspective of Kaiowá of Panambizinho (Dourados, Mato Grosso do Sul) after 170 years of exploitation and non-Indigenous population on the border of Brazil and Paraguay). PhD diss., University of São Paulo.

Viveiros de Castro, Eduardo. 1992. *From the Enemy's Point of View: Humanity and Divinity in an Amazonian Society*. Chicago: University of Chicago Press.

——. 1998. "Cosmological Deixis and Amerindian Perspectivism." *Journal of the Royal Anthropological Institute* 4, no. 3 (September): 469–88.

Watson, Virginia Drew. 1944. "Notas sobre o parentesco dos Índios Cayuá" (Notes on the kinship of the Cayuá Indians). *Sociologia* 6, no. 4: 31–38.

Wilkinson, John, and Selena Herrera. 2010. "Biofuels in Brazil: Debates and Impacts." *Journal of Peasant Studies* 37, no. 4: 749–68.

Williams, Raymond. 1975. *The Country and City*. Oxford: Oxford University Press.

Wolford, Wendy. 2010. *The Land Is Ours Now: Social Mobilization and the Meanings of Land in Brazil*. Durham NC: Duke University Press.

World Bank. 2010. *Project Appraisal Document on a Proposed Loan in the Amount of US $300 Million to the State of Mato Grosso do Sul with the Guarantee of the Federative Republic of Brazil for the Mato Grosso do Sul State Road Transport Project*. Report No: 522 18-BR. N.p.: World Bank.

# Index

*Page numbers in italics indicate illustrations.*